Pastoral Prayers for
the People of God

Pastoral Prayers for the People of God

An Anthology of Classic Pulpit Prayers by
the Reverend Dr. David B. Watermulder

Paul Watermulder
Martha Watermulder

NRSV

Scripture quotations marked NRSV are taken from the New Revised Standard Version of the Bible, Copyright © 1989, by the Division of Christian Education of the National Council of the Churches of Christ in the United States of America. Used by permission. All rights reserved.

RSV

Scripture quotations marked RSV are taken from the Revised Standard Version of the Bible, copyright © 1946, 1952, 1971 by the Division of Christian Education of the National Council of the Churches of Christ in the USA. Used by permission.

KJV

Scripture quotations marked KJV are from the Holy Bible, King James Version (Authorized Version). First published in 1611. Quoted from the KJV Classic Reference Bible, Copyright © 1983 by The Zondervan Corporation.

Print information available on the last page.

Rev. date: 02/10/2017

To order additional copies of this book, contact:
Xlibris
1-888-795-4274
www.Xlibris.com
Orders@Xlibris.com
754345

Foreword

Dr. Watermulder was Senior Pastor at four Presbyterian churches in his service to the Church from World War II through the end of the twentieth century. His prayers have been requested by those hearing them both in Sunday worship services and at the numerous seminary, university and community functions at which he was asked to pray.

These prayers were delivered at the Presbyterian churches in Hightstown (New Jersey), Watertown (New York), Oak Park (Illinois), and Bryn Mawr (Pennsylvania). Using references to Bible stories and phrases from the scriptures, as well as hints of his favorite theologians, such a Bonhoeffer, Kierkegaard and Karl Barth, these prayers lift up a compelling vision of a caring and present God, an understanding God, and an unflinchingly just and merciful God—the One sought by those who come to Christ for faith and hope and love.

The prayers included in this collection reflect intentional wrestling with large issues of the day such as race relations, war, protest, governmental crises, and poverty. They also honestly treat the ongoing personal issues of every parish including birth and death, greed and lust, complacency and depression, marriage and divorce.

If the prayers on these pages bring comfort, guidance, and strength to those who seek the Lord even in these years after Dr. Watermulder's death, then its purpose has been served.

Faithfully,
The Watermulder family—Ruth, Paul, Peter, Martha

Notation

Reading these prayers is a reminder that they are pulpit prayers, meant to be heard rather than read silently. Perhaps reading them aloud will still enhance their power and beauty! Our father used cadence, inflection, volume, tone and speed to bring both the gravitas of the moment and the liveliness of a spirited faith to his leadership of prayers in worship, and so these are presented that the reader may "listen" for such a voice to speak to their soul as they read.

It will become readily apparent that these are not meant to be read like a book (page by page) so much as prayer by prayer. To read one prayer and let it abide may well produce a richer harvest of the Spirit than to read several in a row at the same time.

These prayers were written in the tongue of past decades, before gender-neutral language became the lingua franca of most Protestant worship. We have tried, in our editing of the prayers, to change all pronouns referencing people into non-gender specific words. In general, we have left those words which reference God in their original form, which often was the masculine. Our father did not believe God to be gender specific but, in keeping with classic English literature, used the masculine as also implying the feminine, but, above all, to keep it personal rather than neutered. Our intention is to honor God as revealed in these past decades by David Watermulder. Our intention, of course, is never to diminish anyone by use of such words.

Many prayers include poems which are words to hymns. These hymns are under copyright and found in either of two volumes, both commonly used in Presbyterian (PCUSA) churches:

- The Hymnbook (David Hugh Jones, ed. [the Presbyterian Church in the United States, Richmond, VA, 1955])
- The Hymnal (Clarence Dickinson & Calvin Weiss Laufer, eds. [The Presbyterian Board of Education, Philadelphia, 1933]).

The scripture references in these prayers are from either RSV or KJV, as below:

- The Holy Bible (the Authorized King James Version, the World Publishing Company, Cleveland, 1913).
- The Holy Bible (the Revised Standard Version, Thomas Nelson, Inc., Nashville, 1971, second ed.)

The prayers in this volume are copyright pending.

The Lord's Prayer

Our Father who art in heaven,
hallowed be Thy name.
Thy Kingdom come,
Thy will be done,
on earth as it is in heaven.
Give us this day our daily bread
and forgive us our trespasses,
as we forgive those who trespass against us.
And lead us not into temptation
but deliver us from evil.
For Thine is the Kingdom, the power
and the glory
forever and ever.

Amen.

SECTION 1

Advent and Christmas

December 8, 1974

O Lord our Father, whose love for us we celebrate in moments of joy and fulfillment, but whose concern and care for us are likely to become most real in our times of trouble and despair: like our fathers before us and their fathers before them, we bow before You now, admitting that we cheat ourselves out of life's goodness when we do not make room enough for Your spirit in our lives. For Your presence which sets our feet on a new path, we give thanks. For the expectancy of this advent season; for the sheer meaning of being alive to one another, to ourselves, to the causes which release us from our many forms of slavery, we give thanks.

Be attentive to our needs, O Lord. As You came among humble shepherds and wise folk long ago, so come among us now. Open our eyes and unstop our ears that life may become colorful and expressive once more. Especially today we commend to Your loving care and comfort those of our number who suffer, those who find life closing in on them, those who feel the pang of separation. Having done their best, may they be content to leave with You the rest! Even in our difficulties, O God, may we know that nothing can ever separate us from Your love in Christ. In our personal problems may we experience the meaning of Christian grace so that we may cast our guilt and our burden on You because You have come to our rescue, again and again. As the old hymn says, "Nothing in my hand I bring; simply to Thy cross I cling," and so may we with new freedom and abandon leave ourselves and our loved ones with You.

We pray for our nation, that we may seek Your Spirit and Your way. We pray for the nations of the world, that in the midst of hunger and greed, we may be instruments of nourishment and sharing. In these troubled times, baptize Your Church afresh with the power of the risen Christ, that Your Spirit and grace may move among us again.

May we move through Advent to the simple glory of Christmas with a greater grasp of our world, and deeper compassion for the needy and suffering, and a stronger commitment to Christ who is our Way, our Truth and our Life. As he taught us to pray (The Lord's Prayer)

December 8, 1985

Eternal God our Father: on this second Sunday in Advent, our anticipation arises as we ponder anew the birth of Christ our Lord. As we gather with Your children in Your house, mindful of all Your other children gathered across the world in Your church and assembled in light eternal as the Church triumphant, we offer our thanks to You for life; for this quiet time to collect our lives and put them back in Your hands; for this assurance of Your pardon for us and Your presence with us.

In the midst of the clatter and clamor of the season, may we have time for contemplation and renewed commitment, O God. In our hurry and worry, enable us to be still and know that You are God. In our frustrations and our failures—both small and large—may we gain the stability of knowing that underneath are the everlasting arms.

We pray for ourselves, but we also pray for others. Especially, we bring before You our loved ones, near at home and far away, those who are sick and need health; those who are seeking and need direction; those who are strong and need humility; those who are weak and need strength. May the miracle of Christmas be a miracle for them. We think, too, of our larger family, the Church. May those who are eager and glad and those who are weary and sad, both be heartened and inspired by Your powerful presence among them. We pray also for the even larger family of Your people across the world: for those who suffer today from human failure; for those who, having almost everything, have nothing; and for those who have nothing, that they may be given a share of this world's bounty and a fullness of Your Spirit. Hear our prayer for Your church as it confesses Your name to peoples in all kinds of places: be with those who hold high the torch of faith in a darkened world. Be with our president and our leaders, that we may be the instruments of justice, peace and mercy for peoples everywhere.

We hear the Christmas angels, the great glad tidings tell;
O come to us, abide with us,
Our Lord, Immanuel.

And now, as our Savior Christ has taught us we humbly pray (The Lord's Prayer)

December 9, 1979

Great is Your goodness, O God of love.
You have reached down to us in our need,
and lifted us up to higher ground.

May we, the people who walk in darkness, see a great light. On us may the light shine so that we may know what is the way, the truth and the life.

You have given us hands to know you
hearts to love you
and wills to serve you.

Yet, in Advent of 1979, we confess our confusion and our concern. O God, with the power of the universe at our fingertips, we seem powerless to bring peace or joy on this earth.

Hear our prayers, and the prayers of this nation, for the American hostages in Iran.[1] Hear our prayers for the families of the hostages. Hear our prayers, O Lord, that in calmness and coolness we may move through this crisis and arrive at a place of peace. Give us cool heads, strong hearts and steady hands. Spare us and our world from the kind of destruction we are capable of instigating.

May the power of peace, the Lord of justice and mercy, be enthroned among us, and in our might may we perceive our helplessness without Your Spirit pervading our lives.

As we pray for our nation and our world, we pray for our immediate loved ones and those of our church family. Bring comfort to the bereaved, strength to the weak, clarity to the confused, hope to the despairing.

So,
O Lord support us all the day long,
Till the shadows lengthen
And the evening comes
And the busy world is hushed,
And the fever of life is over,
And our work is done.
Then in thy great mercy,
Grant us a safe lodging,
and a holy rest and peace at the last.
Amen.

---

[1]   Dr. Watermulder references the Iran Hostage Crisis.

December 13, 1981

O God of Hope, who waits through the centuries for a people prepared to receive the gifts of Your Spirit, and who is willing to speak to us in ways we can understand, we offer our thanks for Your goodness. Your word has directed us; Your truth has been our standard; Your discipline has corrected us; Your Spirit has been our strength and shield.

In this holy season when hearts grow warm to human kindness, may we be attentive to the blessings and friendships which abound all about us, seeking to understand, rather than to be understood,

> to forgive, rather than to be forgiven,
> to serve, rather than to be served,
> to love, rather than to wait for love.

Grant that Your Spirit may open our eyes to see those things we have refused to see before, and to admit our need of You, which we have sought to escape before. May the Christmas carols once more speak to our souls of Your nearness, rather than serve as decoration for holiday festivities. In the clamor of this season, may we find Your calm. As we hurry about, may we not forget the simple quiet of the real Christmas. Through our attitude and our words, through our prayers and our participation, proclaim to us and our families what matters. Relate us to the larger family of all Your children around the earth, and in heaven, and make us channels for your compassion and care.

Eternal Power, in whose appointment all life stands, we pray for our nation in this day. In our weakness make us strong; in our wisdom make us humble. In our power give us the desire for peace. May Your guiding Spirit rest upon all who lead. We also direct our prayers homeward for loved ones, those who are sick, those carrying on the battle for life, those who are troubled and disturbed, those who have met with tragedy and sorrow. Give them Your Spirit. Bless those who mourn and support us all with the assurance of Your peace.

> We hear the Christmas angels
> The great glad tidings tell.
> O come to us, abide with us,
> O Lord, Emanuel.

And now, as our Saviour Christ has taught us, we humbly pray (The Lord's Prayer)

December 15, 1974

Eternal Father of matchless power: we give thanks for this Advent season when we reflect the ways You have come to save us. We thank You for the vigor and vision of Your Son Jesus Christ, and for His sacrificial death on the cross and the fresh, clean beginning He gives to each of us. As we prepare to enact the story in pageant or to sing it in song, we give thanks for the simplicities within this season and the many moments when mystery breaks through and becomes personal experience.

We bring before you the perplexities of these days: our abundant blessings, and yet our poverty; our immense opportunities, and yet our squalor and unrest; our inventiveness and progress, and yet our destructiveness and our regression. We pray that here in Your church we may find our notions swept aside and the visions of the Christ and the prophets sweeping over us. Here may we gain our spiritual perception and power because of Your presence.

O Father who exalts all human life by Your identity with us in Christ: enter into the human suffering and sorrow which we and our loved ones may experience at this time. Grant us the comfort of Your presence and the courage of Your Spirit. Bless our land with new resolve and clear purpose until we may learn Your way of understanding and justice of mercy and greatness. Bless our president and all our leaders that they may be controlled, directed and guided by the overarching awareness of Your presence. Bless Your Church in all lands and places, that She may show forth the glory of Your reality, and the compassion of Your Son our Lord, in whose name we pray, even as He taught us (The Lord's Prayer)

December 17, 1972

Almighty God, whose Spirit hovered over the universe even before the morning stars sang together, You are beyond our greatest thoughts or deepest dreams. Yet in this holy season, we are mindful that you took on our form and flesh to live among us. For this revelation of Yourself; for this sacrificial love poured out; for all the blessings of Advent and Christmas, as we recall again the multitude of Your mercies, we give thanks and praise.

Eternal and Almighty God, who speaks in the humble and simple events of life: grant us grace in this Advent season to hear Your voice. Amid the promoted babel of our high-paced lives, give us the integrity to be still and to wait. In the events which surround our lives and determine our days, speak to us. In this Advent season, may we prepare to receive anew the gift of Your Son, and as we rejoice in the joys of little children, may we marvel even more at the coming of the Christ child. Withhold not Your Spirit from us before this season departs, and unite us as one flock, strong in Your protection and compassionate in our dealings with all men.

Our God, our help in ages past, our hope for years to come: bless those in need, loved ones who are ill and facing crucial days. We pray for our president, his cabinet, and all the leaders of government. May we discern Your judgment upon us as a nation, O God. Purify our motives by Your Spirit. Give us direction toward peace and determination to achieve it. Grant the United Nations the blessing of our common purpose and good, so that all nations, so rich in different backgrounds, may live together as brothers.

O Lord of all worlds, before whom stand the spirits of the living and the dead: we bless Your name for all who have fought a good fight, finished their course, and are at rest. Help us to abide in their fellowship, and at the last be made partakers with them of the heavenly kingdom. And now as our Saviour Christ hath taught us (The Lord's Prayer)

December 17, 1978

Eternal and everlasting Father: before the morning stars sang together at the dawn of creation, You were there. Before our hearts reached out to You, their Source, You were there. Before we knew we could not be whole without You, You were seeking us out, coming to us and calling us to come home.

So it is, O God, that our hearts overflow on this third Sunday in Advent. Amid all the clatter and the noise, we hear Your still, small voice and the pure music of the angels. Amid the rush and hurry, we sense the quiet approach of Your Presence, the insistent nudge of Your Spirit. Amid our preoccupation with our pursuits, our projects and all those ego trips which build us up, we sense that life—indeed, our lives—are in the care and control of powers far greater than those of our devising.

Today we pray that we may put ourselves back in Your hands, learning how to do our best, and leave with You the rest. Today we seek a stability of soul that comes when we are at home in Your presence. Today we seek the wholeness which Christ can bring.

Grant, O Lord, Your blessing upon our land in these times. Amid the disquiet and unrest, may we gain a sense of purpose and perspective as we allow ourselves to be led to the Christ. We pray for all the peoples of the world, and our relation to them, that we who have so much may learn the ways of sharing with those who have so little. May we ever know that blessings come to those who know that to whom much is given, much is expected. Especially this week, we pray for our land as we enter into new relationships with China, restoring ties that were broken so long ago. Bless the Chinese people, both in China and Taiwan, and enable us, as the people of two great continents, to find those ways that can bring peace and harmony to this world. We pray for all leaders of state, that they may know their first obligation is to You. We pray for all who are faithful to Your word, refusing the temptation to exploit Your people and leading them to the freedom that is in Christ. We pray that all of us here on earth may be united with Your children in their heavenly home. And as we approach the holy birthday once more, open our hearts to receive the grace of our Lord Jesus Christ, who taught us to pray (The Lord's Prayer)

December 19, 1976

Almighty God, Before there was a universe, You were.
Before we began to think, You thought.
Before we could live, You were.

And when all our commotion is over, and our lives (along with our civilization) settle into their niche on history's shelves, still You will be—
the source from which we come
the magnet toward which we are drawn
the energy propelling us
frustrating us
encouraging us
mocking us when we have lost our contact with our Source.

In this holy season, let the miracle happen, O God. Put mystery back in our lives, that we may breathe deeply of existence, and meaning and direction. Come among us that we may know who we are, why we are, what we are. Stay among us to correct us and direct us, to comfort us and encourage us, to challenge us and chasten us.

Make us whole again as Your children, because we perceive Your presence in our midst. May we know that our inmost yearnings and aspirations find their match in the signals You send to us. Unite us to You once more, O God. Give us the simplicity of the shepherds and the perception of the wise men. The best we can cast at Your feet is our attempts—and our failures—to be what we want to be. The most we ask is that You take these broken lives and heal them, You take these fractured situations and make them whole, You take our self-appointed self-determination and mold us into Your servants, mindful of Your will, ready to heed Your call.

In this Christmas season, may Christ's reality come among the nations, so distraught and consumed in their own cunning. May Christ's power prevail in the church, so weak and beset by human frailty. May the Spirit breathe upon Christ's ambassadors in distant lands, in troubled areas, in places of need; and may we, His mystical, living body, be His hands and feet and mouth, to go forth to give and to proclaim and to do our Heavenly Father's will.

Now, as our Saviour Christ hath taught us (The Lord's Prayer)

Advent Prayer

O Heavenly Father, who makes us glad with the yearly remembrances of the birth of our Lord Jesus Christ, we give thanks for the strength which His presence brings to us.

For the rich memories treasured forever in these holy days, for the eager expectancy of little children, for the release which comes as we find it more blessed to give than to receive, for the rich fullness of the Christmas carols and the song in the hearts of even Your humblest children, we give thanks. But most of all, O God, amid the festivity which surrounds our Christmas, we give thanks for Jesus Christ, our Lord.

O loving God who in Jesus Christ sets us free and gives us strength: we pray today for the weak, that they may be made strong; for the sorrowing, that they may be comforted; for the needy, that their needs may be filled; for the sick, that Your Spirit may heal and bless.

O Christ, who came to bring peace on earth and goodwill among men: humble us until we are willing to try Your way. Purify our motives, and give us something more to live for than self-preservation and self-justification. May the light of Your truth illumine our good and destroy our bad. Make us a nation which promotes peace and finds its strength in its compassion.

Eternal God who dwelt on earth that we might dwell in heaven: unite us with the angels in their song of praise, until the mortal barriers break and we become one with all the heavenly hosts, evermore giving praise, and finding that in Your presence is our peace. And unto Him who is able to do exceeding abundantly above all that we ask, or think, according to the power that works in us, be glory through all ages, world without end.

(The Lord's Prayer)

December 20, 1975

Once more we have heard the Christmas prophesies and the Christmas scriptures, O Lord.

Once more have we sung, "O come all ye faithful."

Once more have we heard the choral voices blend in praise.

Once more we celebrate Christmas.

Great God of mystery and power, don't let it be another round of the same celebrations. Let something happen to us because we let You into our lives. Let us let go and let God take hold.

O loving Father of infinite patience and concern, look upon our frantic endeavors, our easy panic, our incessant concentration on ourselves, and somehow come into the midst of this clamor to bring a peace, a purpose and a power which comes from outside us, beyond us, into us.

Bless all homes—all children, all parents. Spare them from the superficiality that ultimately haunts and undoes them. Bless all churches—here in this land and in all distant places—unite us in Spirit with millions and enable us to hear the words, "unto You is born a Saviour," as though they were directed specifically to us.

Bless our land and our leaders. Give us a new sense of national purpose and raise up leaders whose lives ring with an integrity all their own. Give us compassion for the oppressed and make us a people both mindful and worthy of Your many blessings.

Even as You entered into our world long ago in the Middle East, enter there once more to bring reason and mercy, justice and love. Hear our prayers for planet Earth, that out of these times there may emerge the possibilities of peace and understanding among all people.

(The Lord's Prayer)

Christmas Eve, 1968

On this eventful night, O God, we lift up our lives and our land to Thee. Even as tonight we have rejoiced in the reunion of our families, so tonight, as Christ becomes real, knit us all together as one family, so we feel and hurt, love and laugh, work and play together as Thy children.

Even as we have beheld man probing outer space, tonight, may we marvel at all Thy creation, not only beyond this earth but on this earth. And as Thou didst come among us in the child Jesus, so come among us now and cause us to dignify and exalt all humanity, as Thou has in Christ.

For the strange year of turmoil about to leave us, we thank Thee. For the new year with promise, we praise Thee. For the possibilities in us, on our earth, in our relationships—possibilities which become clear in the simplicity and tangibility of Jesus Christ whose birth we celebrate—we thank Thee.

Be near to all this night. Not only to families and children but to those who grieve and ache, to those who have been injured and suffer, to those who need the healing touch of Thy presence and the calmness of Thy Spirit. Somehow may we hear the angels sing again, and may we follow the star again, and may we find Thee in the Christ again, and at last, amid our sophistications and our superficialities, may life be good and real again, and may we live again in Thee, now and forever.

(The Lord's Prayer)

Christmas Eve, 1970

Almighty and eternal God who fillest the earth with Thy presence: At all times and in all things that dost speak to us, but only occasionally do we listen or hear. In times past Thou hast spoken through prophets and seers, and in the right time, Thou didst speak to us in all the fullness of Thy reality in Jesus Christ. Forgive us, Lord, for not perceiving what Thou hast done and for not recognizing what Thou dost continue to do with His living presence. May we be thankful for the ways that His coming shatters our little worlds and disturbs the harmless sentiment with which we have surrounded that great event.

Even in our shortsightedness, we thank Thee for the light that breaks through, the truth that begins to dawn, the reality that challenges our fictions, when we perceive what it means to have Thee among us, as one of us. Enable us to be honest with Thee until we are honest with ourselves. In sensing the mystery which life never fully fathoms, give us the will to follow him whom wise men and shepherds adored long ago. Take our religion out of its bland agreement with our notions and let the Christ reshape our lives as we allow him to penetrate the walls behind which we protect ourselves. Relate us to our world even as Thou didst involve Thyself in our world when Christ came. Enrich our homes with something more than ourselves and our self-defeating, fleeting preoccupations, until the mystery and majesty of Christmas break through, and the earth and sky and world sing with the music of the angels. Make us one with the heavenly hosts, that we may rejoice to know that Thou hast entered our life and dost give it direction.

With the awareness of Thy love and presence, may we accept the comfort and courage, the strength and stability which Thy Spirit brings. Surround the suffering and the perplexed with Thy peace and give Thy hope and encouragement to those who are afraid. Bless our nation with a true pursuit of peace and fulfillment, and grant, in this holy season, a new awareness of Thy presence to all men, that all of life may become good again because it responds to Thy Spirit.

As Thou dost bind us to one another as mortal human beings on this holy night, bind us also, Heavenly Father, to the host of witnesses who have fought a good fight, finished their course, and are at rest in Thee. Help us to abide in their Spiritual fellowship that our lives may glorify Thee.

O Lord, support us all the day long until the evening comes, the shadows lengthen, the busy world is hushed, the fever of life is over, and our work is done. Then in Thy mercy grant us a safe lodging, a holy rest, and peace at the last.

(The Lord's Prayer)

Christmas Eve, 1971

Lord of glory, God of Bethlehem, with awe and wonder we stand where the shepherds stood to hear the angelic chorus. In mystery crammed with meaning, we bow at the manger stall, offering Thee our inexpressible thanks for the goodness of Thy gift to us. For coming among us, we thank Thee. For loving us, we praise Thy name. For sharing our lot in life and tasting what all mortal men must taste of life's bitter and sweet, we bless Thee. For redeeming us from our lot and restoring us to fellowship with Thee, we give Thee thanks.

O Thou who hast come so many times and found no resting place and no room, forgive us for our overcrowded lives which push Thee out; our vain haste which misses what we really are after; our preoccupation with ourselves, which blinds us to Thy glories. Grant in this Christmas season, O God, that we may be quiet and receptive to Thy Spirit. Our hearts are restless 'til they rest in Thee. We can but follow; enable us to be teachable so we may learn how to follow.

May we worship before Thee, not only because Thou art beyond, above and in all things, but because Thou hast spoken in the language of our flesh and form. In all our sophisticated splendor, make us smart enough to be humble and to see Thy glory in relating to one another. May we become tender once more. May we have faith once more, not to presume to know and understand Thy ways, but to trust the deep calls to our depths.

O Lord who didst suffer for us and assure us of Thy help, we pray especially for those to whom these Christmas days bring sadness. Comfort them with Thy presence and the blessing of rich and precious memory, and assure them of the Spiritual bonds which unite them with Thee and the hosts unseen. Be near to those who are ill and who must suffer, and bring them the blessings of Thy Spirit. As Thou, O Spirit, didst dwell in man, so dwell in them; and as Thou didst overcome all that overtakes us, so grant them both peace and power. Be with our nation in these days and our president and our country's leaders, that this land, so blessed by Thee in resource and heritage, may be worthy of Thy continued blessing, and may be used by Thee to spread the compassion and love which Thou hast so bountifully bestowed upon us.

Hear our prayer, O God, for we ask it in Christ's name, even as he taught us to pray, saying (The Lord's Prayer)

Christmas Eve, 1979

As we enter Christmas, O God, we see Jesus again and marvel at Your greatness. With shepherds and simple folk who want to express their souls with glory and wonder, we bow before the mystery of the manager.

With wise men and pensive people who seek to probe life's meaning and find their own significance, we follow the star to our spiritual home.

With Your children living eternal in the heavens we unite our hearts, along with the heavenly chorus, in singing Glory to God in the highest— and as we turn our gaze heavenward.

O Christ, who came to bring peace on earth, goodwill among men: humble us until we are willing to try Your way. Purify our motives, and give us something more to live for than self-preservation and self-justification. May the light of Your truth illumine our good and destroy our bad. Make us a nation which promotes peace and finds its strength in its compassion.

Eternal God, who dwelt on earth that we might dwell in heaven: unite us with the angels in their song of praise, until the mortal barriers break and we become one with all the heavenly hosts, evermore giving praise, and finding that in Your presence is our peace. And unto Him, who is able to do exceeding abundantly above all that we ask, or think, according to the power that works in us, be glory through all ages, world without end.

O Lord, who entered into our lives so that we might enter into Your presence. We commend to You our loved ones from whom we are separated. We give You all those who feel the pang of loss in the holiday seasons, and pray that the gift of memory and the sense of Spiritual presence may give them joy. Bless those who are sick, those who struggle, those who fail, those who seek, those who cry and those who pray.

As You came to bring peace, grant that our nation and all nations may find the motivation to want peace as much as we talk about it. In the love poured out at Christmas, may all of us find the pathway to goodness and mercy. In the compassion of Christ, may we find the will and way to brotherhood. And unto Jesus Christ our Lord, who is able to do exceeding abundantly above all that we ask or think, according to the power that works in us, unto Him be glory in the church through all ages, world without end.

(The Lord's Prayer)

Christmas Eve 1984

In the silence of this moment, our hearts reach back to their source and stretch forward to their destiny, O God. Once more, the elemental sense of mystery and wonder envelops us, reminding us how much we have caged our spirits in the narrow limits imposed by our minds and our experiences, oblivious to the broader dimensions that You intend us to have.

For the rich memories treasured forever in these holy days, for the eager expectancy of little children, for the release which comes as we find it more blessed to give than to receive; for the rich fullness of the Christmas carols and the song in the hearts of even Your humblest children, we give thanks. But most of all, O God, amid the festivity which surrounds our Christmas, we give thanks for the grace of our Lord Jesus Christ who unites us with our Source in You.

Our hearts are heavy this Christmas, O Lord, for we seek peace which the Prince of Peace can bring in a world filled with hate and fear. Even as You came among us at Bethlehem, come among us once more, that peace and understanding and mutual goodwill might find a foothold upon our earth. We say a prayer for our nation and our leaders, that we may be guided in the ways of justice, mercy and peace. We pray for planet Earth and for our nation's role among all other nations. As You have visited Earth with Your presence before, visit us again, that these good gifts which You have given us may be a blessing to all.

Eternal God who dwelt on earth that we might dwell in heaven: unite us with the angels in their song of praise, until the mortal barriers break and we become one with all the heavenly hosts, especially loved ones, ever more giving praise and finding that in Your presence is our peace. And unto Him who is able to do exceeding abundantly above all that we ask, or think, according to the power that works in us, be glory through all ages, world without end. Amen.

(The Lord's Prayer)

December 26, 1983

On this cold Christmas Day, warm our hearts with Your love, O God, that Christ may be born into our lives so we may sense Your presence and draw on Your power.

As You led wise men to the manger long ago, lead us back to our Source, that we too may catch a sense of glory in our lives:

as You quickened the hearts and spirits of people in other times, speak to us in our time, that we may live our lives knowing that we are surrounded by the glory of the Lord.

as You opened the gates of reality and dissolved the sham and pretense, open to us the gates of new life, that we may accept ourselves and our situations as the places where Your glory shines.

as You fired ordinary, sinful people with new dreams and desires, burn Your Spirit into our lives, that we may be ablaze with the glory of Your presence.

as distraught and troubled people were able to overcome in the past, so enter our lives and unite us in spirit with our loved ones who have gone on before us, that together, in this very moment, we may be swept into the glorious presence of the children of light.

as You have knit Your children together in one fabric within families, so step into our families, that we may share and care, know and grow in those Christian virtues which bring the joy and love of Your glory into our lives.

as You have cared for us and given Yourself for our sins, may we care for others and learn the glorious blessing of being able to forgive.

as You have blessed the nation whose God is the Lord, so bless our land with honorable leaders, honest government, merciful understanding and a compelling commitment to make peace.

as You stand ready to heal and help all of those wait on the Lord, so bring the ways of peace to a world of so little peace; bring succor and help to those who are victims of celebrity and catastrophe; bring light to our darkened world through Him who is the light of the world.

as Your church continues to bear witness around the world in many alien cultures and in our own hostile situations, continue to bless those who carry on Your ministries of love and compassion, that we and all people may know to what depths you descended to lift us into Your presence.

And as we have an advocate with God the Father in Jesus Christ the righteous, may we have the grace to leave our lives in His hands. In His name we pray, placing before You those of our number who are ill, perplexed, anxious, those who mourn. Visit them with Your peace and give them Your power. Surround us all with Your presence, that with Your children in light eternal, we may feel Your Spirit and receive Your strength.

We pray through Christ our Lord who taught us to pray (The Lord's Prayer)

December 27, 1981

O God, You are from everlasting to everlasting with whom a thousand years can be as a day, or a day be made eternal in its significance; in your majesty and might You dwell with us in our smallness and our need: How can we thank You for all Your blessings, both known and unknown! We praise You for this gift of life with its constant choice and daily struggle; for the light shed upon our pathway by the brightness of Jesus Christ Your Son; for the release brought to us as we put all we have and are into his hands; for the faith which does not demand intricate answers from us but devotion and trust; for the sure knowledge that the Eternal God is our refuge, and underneath are the everlasting arms.

O God whose infinite majesty looks on us from the heavens and earth, but whose grace and truth shine in the face of Jesus Christ, enable us to trust You with His trust, to love You with His love, to feel Your power as He felt it. Quiet our sorrows with your inward peace. In the turmoil of this world and the failure of lower hopes, may we remember the real life which is hid in You, that where our treasure is, there may our heart be also. Keep us by Your mercy, healing our sins, helping us in our weakness, sustaining us through Your power, until we learn the secret of trusting You.

Eternal Father, You know no limit of time or space or race or class, but You are Lord over all: we pray for our world. In Your eyes we know a generation can be as nothing, yet You give us the opportunity to make it forever significant. This is our world, O Lord, and we can't live in any other just now. Then show us how to live, not only with ourselves, but with others. Give us the nobility of Christian compassion. Guide our president and congress, and all those who lead our land. We pray for all leaders throughout the world—in enemy lands as well as friendly lands—that Your Spirit may enter into our spirits. Hear our prayers also for our church family, that in the fellowship of kindred souls we may grow in our understanding and strength. Bless all teachers and leaders of youth, that they may become instruments of that which endures. Bless all students, that they may seize the opportunities these years afford to uncover and harness the talents You have given them. Bless all parents that they may live in this generation and bring to it the values which endure in all generations. And grant to all who mourn, all who suffer, all who endure pain and face difficulty the blessings of Your presence and the calm of Your Spirit.

And now, as our Saviour Christ has taught us, we humbly pray (The Lord's Prayer)

December 28, 1969

Almighty God who art always ahead of us, yet always ready to be where we are so we can communicate with Thee, we thank Thee today for so many things: for this remarkable Christmas when we looked again to the start the wise men saw and marveled at Thy love coming into our world, and for the remarkable year when we also looked out into space and marveled at the precision of this universe and the laws which have been operating all the time, even though we used them for the first time. Most of all, we thank Thee for the marvel that is man—the restless spirit, the deviltry as well as the divinity—and the possibility of what he might be if he became Thy man. Enable us to see what Thou art showing us in the man and Jesus, and to hear what Thou art saying to us in His crucifixion and living presence.

As this strange year draws to a close, we thank Thee for it, praying that it has taught us some lessons, humbled our haughtiness, and opened some doors for hope. Spare us from making another year like the last one, O God! Give us personal direction and make us feel our kinship with one another. Before this next decade leaves us, and before we have conquered outer space, conquer us and saddle that wildness which masquerades as individuality, that cock-sureness among the young or old which so conveniently covers our insecurities.

We ask for Thy blessing on Thy church, so torn and troubled—through this fire refine it as Thy tool. We pray for our schools—our pupils and teachers and leaders. Through this turmoil, let us exalt excellence and quality without parading the arrogance of the old or the insolence of the young. We pray for our land and our leaders, that a new spirit may open the doors to peace and that we may develop new ways to overcome poverty and injustice.

O Thou who dost neither slumber nor sleep: bless and protect the injured and the suffering. Comfort the bereaved and sorrowing. May they know that Thou art their shepherd who leads them. Support us all the day long, until the shadows lengthen and the evening comes, and the busy world is hushed, and the fever of life is over, and our work is done. Then in Thy mercy, grant us a safe lodging, a holy rest, and peace at the last, through Jesus Christ our Lord who taught us to pray saying (The Lord's Prayer)

December 29, 1977

On Christmas, O God, we see Jesus again and marvel at Your greatness. With shepherds and simple folk who want to express their souls with glory and wonder, we bow before the mystery of the manger.

With wise men and pensive people who seek to probe life's meaning and find their own significance, we follow the star to our spiritual home.

With Your children living eternal in the heavens, we unite our hearts, along with the heavenly host, in singing Glory to God in the highest—and as we turn our gaze heavenward, we see our earth light up with the power and the presence of spiritual awareness.

Heavenly Father, we admit that we stand somewhat breathless before the manager. It defies our own logic, yet it directs us to so much more. Forgive us for not investing our lives in Your life for not acknowledging the hunger and hurt in life when we have no more to turn to than the goodness in ourselves. Help us to discover that as we let go and let God, we are fortified and strengthened. Show us how to bow in humility. Let us express Your grace—the grace of our Lord Jesus Christ!

O Lord, You neither slumber nor sleep. We commend to You our loved ones who are away and from whom we are separated. We give You all those who feel the pang of loss in the holiday seasons, and pray that the gift of memory and the sense of spiritual presence may give them joy. Bless those who struggle, those who fail, those who seek, those who cry, those who pray, and may those who pride themselves in their strength and their goodness yield themselves to You and with all humility allow You to direct and manage their relationships. Spare us from the haughty pride which makes us think we can manage our affairs without You, and save us from the conceit that makes us too good to become Your obedient servants who follow Christ.

As You came to bring peace, grant that our nation and all nations of this earth may find the motivation to want peace. In the love poured out at Christmas may all of us find the pathway to goodness and mercy. Be present in those historic holy places of Bible times in our time today, O God, that, as the forces of our world concentrate in the Middle East once more, Your Spirit may attend the peace talks of President Sadat and Prime Minister Begin and all whom they represent. May peace come in our time for all times, and may Your Spirit find a lodging in the hearts of nations once more. And unto Jesus Christ our Lord, who is able to do exceeding abundantly above all that we ask or think, according to the power that works in us, unto Him be glory in the church through all ages, world without end. Amen.

(The Lord's Prayer)

December 12, 1976

Great and eternal God our Father, Thou source of all beings; Thou creator of all creations; Thou who hast come among us in so many ways but especially in the mystery of Him whom wise men sought out, whom shepherds adored, of whom angels sang; You have heard our praise of Your glorious and great name, You have accepted our confession and offered us pardon for those things which have separated us from You, You have heard our expression of thanks for all You have done for us; we have praised you, O God, and listened to Your word. Now we ask that You hear our requests as we pour out our particular needs.

How much better You know us than we know ourselves. How deeply You probe into those motivations and drives which lure us on. How quickly You understand the frustrations and the cover-ups around which we build our lives. How close You are to each one of us. Hear us, O God, as we bring ourselves before You in openness, in honesty and humility, acknowledging that we belong to You and that in You we find the wholeness and meaning we seek.

We also bring to You, O God, the larger family of all of Your children everywhere. Unite us with them. May we feel that we are a part of this struggling humanity around this earth, where there is hunger and hurt and hardship, may we be the instruments of Your peace, of Your love, of Your goodness and Your compassion. We pray, O God, that You will be with all the servants of Your church everywhere, with those who witness in distant places in difficult times and with those who carry forth the honor and glory of Your name in the midst of our everyday life. Align us with them. Link us with all by whatever label they carry who confess You as Lord and seek to be Your disciples.

We pray also for those who suffer, those who undergo heartbreak and hurt and those who need help. Hear their earnest prayers. Break through all of the facades, all of those things that cause them to keep themselves from Your presence and allow the onrushing power of Your Spirit to fill their lives with something new and strong and good and beautiful, that they may go forth in their place, in their time, in Your strength.

These mercies we pray for through Him who came among us, even Jesus Christ, who taught us when we pray to say (The Lord's Prayer)

December 30, 1979

O Lord God our Father, in Christ You have laid down Your life for us, and through Christ we pray for the power to lay down our lives for each other.

In Christ You have revealed the secret of a fulfilled life as He gave Himself in love and service to others. Through Christ we pray for the release which enables us to give ourselves away to each other.

In Christ You put Your kingdom among us and called us to care for the oppressed, the unfortunate and those in need. Through Christ we pray for the clarity of purpose in our lives so that we find ourselves as we lose ourselves in Your service.

In Christ You carried our burdens and bore our sorrows. Through Christ may we receive the comfort and solace, the strength and stability we need to carry on.

In Christ You healed the sick and pointed the way, the truth and the life. Through Christ may Your healing Spirit surround us and bring us the confidence of Your presence.

In Christ You blended heaven and earth, body and spirit, life and death, temporal and eternal. Through Christ unite us with all Your children in heaven and earth that our lives may be spent in praise to You.

We give the old year to You, O God. Take it from us and set us on a fresh path with Christ as our guide. Bring comfort to the sorrowing, healing to the sick, hope to the despairing, grace and peace to all who let go and let you enter.

With these prayers we offer our plea for Christians everywhere, that the Holy Spirit may strengthen them. We pray for our country and our world, that in Your presence we may discern our purpose and find our peace.

And now, as Christ has taught us, we humbly pray (The Lord's Prayer)

January 9, 1966

O Thou who art our refuge and strength, a very present help in time of troubles, to whom a day can be as a thousand years or a thousand years as a day: We give Thee humble thanks for Thy leading and guidance throughout the past year: for the joys sustained and the problems overcome; for Thy help in time of trouble and the assurance of Thine unfailing concern. Chiefly do we thank Thee for Jesus Christ, through whom we feel Thy love and find Thy peace, and with whom the way, the truth and the life becomes a bright and shining light in our darkness. As we progress into another year, fresh, clean, and new, we thank Thee for the gift of the new year and the promise of Thy help as we fashion it. We thank Thee that You art the God of the present, as well as the future and the past. With our gratitude, cause us to see the limits Thou hast placed on mortal life—not only confining us to one place and situation, but holding us within the bounds of time from which we cannot escape. Make us sensitive to the laws, which we can neither make nor unmake, which govern life and cause us to see that our joy comes as we learn to live within those limits and conform to those laws.

Thou who art peace—perfect peace—and canst drop Thy still dews of quietness even as we strive for the larger peace of Thy world, grant us Thy calm and confidence as we face our personal needs. Help us this year to believe that Thou art actually capable of keeping Thy promise to us, and give us enough common sense to live up to our part in doing each day our best and leaving with Thee the rest. As we commit loved ones to Thee, those who are ill or in difficulty, may we have the faith to know that Thou hearest heartfelt prayer and dost surround them with Thy spirit. As each new day dawns, may we greet it with praise to Thee, live it in love to Thee, and close it cradled in Thine everlasting arms.

We pray for our president and our leaders, that they may be judged and guided by Thee in the days and months ahead. Give maturity and wisdom to congress as it convenes, and unite us as a people with those causes which relieve oppression and dissension. We pray for our men who must fight abroad in Vietnam, that they may know the reality of Thy Spirit and Thy presence, even as we pray for all our leaders who seek the avenues of peace.

Eternal God who makest all things new and abideth ever the same, grant us to begin the year in Thy faith and to continue it in Thy favor; that, being guided in all our days, we may spend our lives in Thy service, and finally by Thy grace, attain the glory of everlasting life, through Jesus Christ our Lord, who taught us to pray (The Lord's Prayer)

January 9, 1983

Almighty God, before whose face the generations rise and pass away: age after age the living seek Thee, and find that of Thy mercy there is no end. Our fathers in their pilgrimage walked by Thy guidance, and still we see Thy cloud by day and fire by night, pointing us to that destiny which is both blessed and a blessing. We give thanks for this heritage, for the host of witnesses surrounding us, for our citizenship which is in heaven, for the dazzling mercy which spends itself in our humanity. We give thanks that even though we may waste our years, waste our life, waste our opportunities, You forgive us until life is restored and renewed.

As we contemplate Your greatness and goodness, O Father, we pray to You to take from us our superficiality which makes a mockery of the penetrating demands You make upon us. Astound us by Your mercy and grace, O God who has lived among us in Jesus Christ! Surprise us as we see how simple and obvious, yet how veiled to our eyes, is the joy of the kingdom of God. Assure us of forgiveness until we center our life in Your Spirit. Deliver us from the false gods we worship, and restore us to wholeness in Thee.

Then send us forth as servants of Your word, forgiving because we have been forgiven, understanding because we have been understood, helping because we have been helped.

Hear our prayers for others, O God: For Your Church that She may have the pure spirit of Her Lord; for Your ministers and missionaries, that they may be instruments of compassion and heralds of truth; for Your people everywhere, that in this turbulent age they may not lose heart but hold fast to that which is good, looking unto Jesus, the pioneer and perfector of our faith. Expand the outlook and broaden the horizons until all of us feel linked together as Your children on earth, united with the children in light eternal in the heavens.

Bless those who mourn; comfort those who are afflicted; strengthen the sick and assure us all of your care. Your healing and help attend those facing great physical difficulties, that Your Spirit gives them strength. May Your blessings attend our nation and may Your Spirit guide and direct our president.

These prayers we ask through Christ our Lord, who taught us to pray (The Lord's Prayer)

SECTION 2

Lent and Easter

March 1, 1981
Prayer before Lent

At the beginning of this new day, we come into Your house to offer You our praise and thanksgiving, O God. You are our refuge in the time of storm, and our strength in our daily walk. In You is wholeness, completeness, meaning. For the gift of another day, for the gift of this bright day and this good hour, we give thanks.

At the beginning of the month of March, we offer You our praise, O God. As we rely on the seasons to come and go with dependability, so also do we rely on Your constancy. We turn to You because we depend on You, O God. As winter gives way to spring in this month, so does Your love melt the coldness and indifference in our lives.

At the beginning of Lent, we offer You our praise, O God. From You we get our direction. Like the needle of the compass, like the North Star, You point the way when we wander and stumble. May we approach Lent this Wednesday with expectancy, O Lord, eager for Your Spirit to touch our spirits and bring us alive. May we go through the weeks of Lent with a sense of discovery and renewal, O Lord, anxious to make this holy season into something special for ourselves. As Lent moves toward Easter, may we find our Lord entering our lives, just as He entered the lives of the people around Him. As He approaches the cross, may we approach Him, that He may carry us with Him through His suffering and sacrifice. As He arose on Easter, may we rejoice that our lives are of everlasting meaning in Your sight, and thereby may we take on those values that bring vitality to our days, and as we learn about the significance of the life of our Lord, may we discover our own significance and live our lives in praise and joy for Christ Jesus.

In His name we commend to You the grieving and the hurting, the sick and those in need. In His name we pray for our president and our leaders and for all the peoples of the world, that we may pursue the paths of justice and compassion and learn the ways of peace. In His name we pray the prayer He taught us (The Lord's Prayer)

March 19, 1972
Lent I

O Lord, who in Your tender love toward mankind has sent Your Son Jesus Christ to bring us back to You, we praise and bless You for life and its provision, but today we thank You for the season of spiritual quickening known as Lent. Bless us in these days, that we may search our hearts, not by standing before a mirror and defending our opinions, but by standing before Your cross and facing the gaze of Jesus Christ. Guide us in our spiritual disciplines, that we may come to the end of this season with a clearer grasp of what matters.

Eternal Spirit whom to know is life eternal: bless, we pray, all those who seek You with special needs this day. To the lonely, the bereaved and those feeling forsaken, be the good sheperd. To the anxious, the despairing, the doubting, be the Rock which cannot be moved. To those who are sick in body, mind or soul; to those in hospitals, those for whom this earthly body has asserted its limitations, be the good physician and the Lord of all life. To those separated from us, be their refuge and strength in whom they find calm and courage.

Almighty Father, who has made of one blood all nations of men to dwell on the face of the earth, we pray for our national unity at home and abroad. By Your Spirit, open our minds to things which unite rather than divide. Give leadership to our president and congress that in this day of responsibility we may be strong in the right, humble before You.

O Lord of all worlds, before whom stand the spirits of the living and the dead, we bless Your holy name for all Your servants who have finished their course and kept the faith, and who are now at rest with You: grant us grace to follow that we with them may be partakers of Your heavenly kingdom. Take now the veil from every heart, and unite us in one communion with all the saints on earth and saints in heaven, through Jesus Christ our Lord who taught us to pray together (The Lord's Prayer)

March 4, 1979, Lent I
March 9, 1980, Lent II

Eternal Father, who has loved us with a love too full for human expression, who speaks through every experience, but ever so clearly as we gather as Your expectant children: we approach Your presence with gratitude for all Your mercies and blessings, and chiefly for Your love in time of stress, for courage in time of crisis, for Your companionship in critical hours. Accept our thanks for all the good gifts of this life, and for Your overarching presence which makes us to know that in joy or sorrow, in sickness or health, in life or death, our times are in Your hands, and we need fear no evil, for You are with us. We give thanks for the Christian love which binds us one to another, for our common humanity and common concern which call forth our uncommon Spirits. We give thanks for this Lenten season, with its encouragement toward earthly disciplines which develop eternal capacities.

O God, when we seem alone and when life centers in upon ourselves only, make us to know our Father who art in heaven.

When we treat life carelessly and cheaply, bring us back as we affirm, hallowed be Thy name.

When life turns sour and we become bored or broken by it, fire us with zeal as we live the prayer, Thy Kingdom come, Thy will be done, on earth as it is in heaven.

When we become fearful for the day's demands and needs, may we find faith and courage as we pray, give us, this day, our daily bread.

As our past mistakes arise to haunt us, and as our emotional imbalance strikes to harm us, give us a peace and poise the world can neither give nor take away as we pray, forgive us our sins as we forgive those who sin against us.

As our problems become bigger than our convictions, our weaknesses stronger than our willpower, make us to pray the more fervently, lead us not into temptation, but deliver us from evil.

And as we feel utterly insufficient for such a faith, and find our world too much for us, return to us the courage we were meant to have as we affirm in body, mind, and soul: Thine is the Kingdom, and the power, and the glory, forever.

Almighty God, we pray for those of our number who are sick, lonely, facing problems and difficult decisions, and those who have felt sorrow's darkened way. Surround them all with Your Spirit and breathe into them

Your guidance and assurance. Hear our prayer for our nation and our leaders, that we may do justly, love mercy and walk humbly with our God. And now, as our Saviour Christ has taught us, we humbly pray (The Lord's Prayer)

March 1985
Lent I

Eternal God who sows the seed of new life in our hearts, we give thanks for fresh beginnings such as come with this Lenten season. We are thankful that we are not mere animals, biological specimens simply reacting to social environment. We give thanks that You have made Yourself known in so many ways—through nature and this world, through sacrifice and compassion, but, supremely, through Christ our Lord. We give thanks that Lent comes to us as a means of grace, when we may discipline ourselves and stretch our lives.

Grant, O God, that we may direct our Thought toward our Spiritual sources in the Lenten season. May we stop making excuses and devising explanations, and may we simply, humbly, sincerely lay our lives before Your piercing presence. Grant that we may not come to the end of this holy season exactly as we are now, but changed, and even born again, into the life of the Kingdom.

O loving shepherd, restore the souls of the sick. Lead them beside the still waters. Grant them goodness and mercy. To those who are carrying heavy burdens, grant Your grace. To those who sorrow over the loss of loved ones, grant the vision of a world greater than they or we can imagine. To those from whom we are separated, be their refuge and strength, a very present help.

Bless the Church throughout the world. Restore to it the Spirit in which it was born, that it may be a holy nation, a royal priesthood, God's own people set in the midst of the world. As You have spoken and acted in ages past, speak and act in, through, and within the church in this upheaving age. And grant, O God of all, Your grace and guidance to our nation, that we may do justly, love mercy and walk humbly with You, our God.

Especially, we lift our hearts in prayer this week as the talks begin in Geneva. May Your Spirit, which brings peace, rest upon the Russians, as well as upon us, that somehow we may become Your children once more and pursue the things that make for peace.

Now as our Saviour Christ taught us to pray (The Lord's Prayer)...

March 2, 1980
Lent II

Dear Lord our Father, in the surprises of the seasons and the variety of our daily experiences, we are aware of Your presence, reminding us of the infinite possibilities in this adventure which we call life. Accept our thanks this day for this knowledge of Your nearness, this awareness of Your care.

On this Sunday, as again we celebrate faith instead of fear, hope instead of despair, love instead of hate, life instead of death—on this Lord's day when each week we celebrate the resurrection and the living presence of Christ—accept our thanksgiving for the deeper meaning within the daily happenings in our lives.

And as we give thanks for our many blessings and for those whose lives reveal Your Spirit here and there and everywhere, we pray for those who shed Your mercy all around us, for those who minister to Your people in special ways, for each person in his or her profession or occupation, giving of self to the service of others, opening self to the wider world beyond self and family. Grant, O God, Your blessing upon us all.

Bless our president and our leaders, that they may be enabled to share in a new day of purpose and peace, with all the nations of the world. Give us a sense of responsibility in this world. Even as we pray for our country, we pray for our enemies, and we pray that they and we may somehow discover our common humanity again and learn how to live in this world. Surround with Your Spirit our loved ones, and enable all—those who sorrow, those who suffer, those who seek, those who are sick, those who are in need—to know their Saviour and their friend Jesus Christ and unite us in Spirit with all Your children in heaven. These mercies we pray through Christ who taught us to pray together (The Lord's Prayer)

February 27, 1983
Lent II

Great God who neither slumbers nor sleeps, we offer thanks for Your constant love of us, even when our love of You grows distant or indifferent. For mercy mingled with judgment, for direction and correction, but most of all for stepping into our frame, living among us, and bearing our sins on the cross, we give heartfelt thanks.

Quicken our spirits in this Lenten season, O Lord. Lead us through our own expression of discipleships, onto the highs of Palm Sunday and the lows of Good Friday, to the refreshing rebirth of Easter, that we may say of our lives, "Whether we live or whether we die, we are the Lord's. Praise be the Lord!"

Today we give thanks for Your church here and around the world. We thank You for persons and families, for Boy Scouts and youth groups, for youth and adults who seek and search, and who find Your grace sufficient for their need when they put their lives in Your hands. Bless us here at home, O Lord, and use us to be a blessing.

And bless us as Your family in churches around the world—churches in developing nations of the third world; churches in lands of revolution and uprising; churches in lands controlled by Communist forces; churches in the Middle East, where ideologies clash against one another; churches everywhere, where Christians are persecuted for their faith and where nations are reshaped because of their witness; churches in Asia, newly budding in China and flourishing in Korea. May our oneness in Christ overcome the barriers that divide us, so that we may link arms in furthering the peace and purpose of Your kingdom.

We pray for our land, O Lord, that we may become aware of one another's needs and seek the common good. May Your blessings be with our government, our president, his cabinet, our congress and leaders, that the welfare of all Your people will be paramount in their minds. Hear our prayers for the sick of our number, and those who are discouraged and need help. Be the good shepherd who leads them beside the still waters and restores their souls through Jesus Christ our Lord.

(The Lord's Prayer)

March 18, 1979
Lent III

Like the disciples of old, we behold Your wonder-working power, O Lord, and come into Your house on Your day to offer You our praise and gratitude for Your constant concern for us. Hear our prayers of thanksgiving as we move from the winter of disbelief and separation from our source into the springtime of new hope, new promise, new beginnings.

Today, we lift our hearts in prayer for those of our members who are in trouble and need help; those who are perplexed and need guidance; those who are sick and need health; all those whose load is heavy because they bear it by themselves and do not turn to You. To each of us with our particular need, come, O Lord, that we may experience the reality of Your Kingdom in our midst. In these days of global decisions, we pray Your blessing upon our leaders and upon the peoples of the Middle East, that the ways of peace and new hope may become a reality. Bring to our world a sense of common purpose and unite us in the pursuit of peace. In truth may our nation be one of many instruments which makes vivid our prayer that Your Kingdom come, Your will be done on earth as it is in heaven.

Now let us continue in prayer as we turn to the front of our bulletins and pray responsively the Lord's Prayer:

[2]"O God, when we feel homeless in the immensity of this universe, may we experience your love as we pray

Our Father who art in heaven.

When we become confused about our standards and lose our sense of values, enable us to pray

Hallowed be Thy name.

When our life becomes full of conflict and confusion, steady us as we pray

Thy Kingdom come, Thy will be done, on earth as it is in heaven.

When we become proud and selfish, remind us of the source of all our gifts until we are able to share with others as You have shared with us. Then hear our prayer

Give us this day our daily bread.

When anger, impatience or hatred overtake us, remind us of Your understanding of our own weaknesses as we pray

Forgive us our sins, as we forgive those who sin against us.

---

[2]   From Fourth Presbyterian Church, Chicago

When life becomes too much for us and we become the victims of forces that war around us and within us, hear us as we pray

Lead us not into temptation, but deliver us from evil.

And when we assume center stage and expect life to cater to us as though we were your special exceptions in the human race, put life back in perspective as we pray

For Thine is the Kingdom, and the power and the glory forever. Amen.

March 25, 1973
Lent IV

Eternal Lord, source of light and giver of love, who in Your greatness need not bother with us but have told us to call You our Father; You created us with powers greater than all other animals, so that we <u>must</u> dream and dare, choose and plan: today we give thanks for the many mercies we receive. Accept our gratitude for this span of years called life, which You have given to us though You owe us nothing. We give praise for its joys and for its yearnings, its struggles and its problems all reminding us that existence alone can never satisfy us, all beckoning us to admit the reality of our spiritual life and replenish its springs from Your unfailing fountains. Today we give thanks also for those earth disciplines which bring heaven into our lives; for this Lenten season whose simple habits can call us to closer prayer and contemplation; for the church here and for our relation to the larger church family of all kinds of people throughout the United States and around the world.

O loving Father, who understands us better than we understand ourselves, all things betray us when we betray You and try to live outside Your love. Look down on our foolishness, our blindness, our prejudice, our problems. Give us that simple, childlike trust which enables us to share our personal problems with You. Then give us courage to let You show us how to unravel the tangled knots we have made. Then give us power to weave the pattern You have shown us for our lives; and then, O Lord, give us a quiet patience to leave the results in Your hands. Quiet down our self-vindicating excuses and the clamor which hides our insecurity, until we turn to You and relate to each other.

Shepherd of our souls, You are the way, the truth and the life. Our prayers go beyond ourselves and to our loved ones. Bless those who are separated from us, and with the archway of prayer unite us to You and to one another. Comfort those who mourn and sorrow. Uphold the sick, the weak, the needy, that they may ever know they are not alone. Bless the church that it may point all nations to Your ways of justice, mercy and compassion for fellowman. Be pleased to grant unto our president and the leaders of state, the wisdom and the calm of Your guidance. And bring to us—as persons, as homes, as communities, as nations, as united nations—a concern to understand and care until the miracle of a new life and a new world is performed. And now as our Saviour Christ hath taught us, we humbly pray saying (The Lord's Prayer)

April 1, 1979
Lent V

Eternal Father who enters into our lives with deep compassion and understanding: we boldly enter into Your presence in the full awareness that You understand us, see through us, care about us and forgive us. For the knowledge that Your love is at the heart of the universe and Your peace can be at the center of our lives, we give You thanks, O God. As we draw near to the events of Holy Week and the crucifixion, we pray that You will draw near to us, that we may be cleansed of all superficiality and restored by Your grace as human beings who can embrace the life You have given us.

Great God who speaks through the earthquake, wind and fire with the still, small voice of calm: speak to us now, in this time, as we unleash something of the awesomeness of Your creation in our onward struggle to explore and harness the remarkable energy of Your universe. In particular, our prayers reach out to all families and persons in the area of Three Mile Island and Middletown.[3] Spare them and us from catastrophe and give to us all cool heads, strong minds and stout hearts, that such difficulties as befall us may show us how to care for one another and how to use our ever-expanding knowledge of this fabulous universe. In all that we do, may we ever know that humanity is our first priority; and in these days of crisis, grant us the strength of Your steadying hand.

We pray also for our nation in these days of global unrest, that all of us may regain a sense of confidence, and credibility as we perceive our national purpose. May Your Spirit open our minds and hearts to the ways that make for peace and fulfilment, that we may learn how to live as Your grateful and forgiving children.

We pray for the suffering and the sick, and for all who seek peace and do good, for all who bear the name of Christ in difficult and troubled places, for all who bear witness to Your reality at tremendous danger to themselves. Surround us all with the cloud of witnesses of Your children in light eternal, and unite us in Spirit with all who have kept the faith and finished the course here on earth. For these mercies we pray through Christ (The Lord's Prayer)

---

[3]   Dr. Watermulder references the partial nuclear meltdown of March 28, 1979.

April 3, 1977
Palm Sunday Prayer

With the jubilant people of the first Palm Sunday and with our own children today, we blend our voices in praise and Thanksgiving, O God.

Even as new life bursts from the trees, so You bring new awakenings to those who lift their lives to Your presence where Your Spirit may restore and renew.

For this we give thanks, and for the immense fact that You are ready to uphold us and direct us, and even use us for plans and purposes far bigger than we realize.

Lord Jesus Christ, King of our lives: rule now in those where joy has turned to mourning, that they may receive the blessings from the same Spirit who ministers to those they have lost for a while. Rule in the lives of those whose earthly bodies have asserted the inevitable limitations of our mortality, that, confident of Your presence, they need not be depressed or afraid. Rule in those places where tragedy has struck and reminded us of the tenuous nature of our life, and enable all of us to reclaim our meaning as we share with one another. Rule in this nation that all our government may be judged, directed and corrected by Him who is King of Kings and Lord of Lords. Rule in Your church here, across this nation, and the world. Rule in our lives, O King of Kings.

(The Lord's Prayer)

March 30, 1979
Palm Sunday

Almighty God who designed this world to be full of joy and gladness, reflecting Your majesty and power: may the music of this day form a melody of earnest praise to Thee. "The company of angels are praising Thee on high, and mortal men, and all things created, make reply." Instinctively our spirits blend with Your Spirit, naturally our hearts open to Your love, longingly our souls crave Your forgiving understanding. In deep, profound thankfulness, we turn to You, our Father. May our Palm Sunday praise be no hollow mockery that give way to Good Friday scorn, but may our outer joy be sincere expression of inner desire and devotion.Take from us now the veil of self-deceit and self-sufficiency, that humbly and like little children we may lay our lives at Your feet, there to see them as we have not seen them before, there to receive the grace that enables us to remake them into something enduring.

O Christ, who didst set Your face to go to Jerusalem, give us the courage of conviction that we may not shrink from the harder paths of a dutiful life. And grant that having confessed and worshipped Thee upon earth, we may be among the number of those who shall have Your eternal triumph and bear in their hands the palms of victory. With this prayer go prayers for our president and our nation, for our world in turmoil and need, for our own members who are sick or sad and grieving. O God of love and life, visit us with Your power and grant us Your peace, through Jesus Christ our Lord, who taught us to pray (The Lord's Prayer)

Good Friday 1974

Almighty and Everlasting God, before whom the generations rise and pass away, age after age the living seek Thee and find that of Thy mercy there is no end. In the company of the faithful in all ages and places, we thank Thee for the truth made flesh in Christ our Lord; for the wonder and variety of the gospel as it brings us to Thee and relates us to our world; for men of old whom Thou didst use in preserving and proclaiming Thy truth; and for the many facets of Thy church today which enable us to grow in faith and bear witness in our time.

Quicken our conscience, we pray, that we may not go through life bogged down in the ruts of our self-dug prejudice, the mire of our personal whim, the slipperiness of our self-exalted opinion. Ever expose us to Christ. Make us sensitive to His beckoning call. Disturb us and haunt us until we respond to His summons, whatever it may be.

O Thou who dost honor our wistful, undeveloped faith: in our misgivings and doubts, give us the assurance that Thou art our refuge and strength. May we be forgiving and understanding in our relations with others, knowing how every person cries out for understanding. With Christ may we see the gallantry and courage in others, rather than the crudeness and smallness. May we feel our kinship with each, as we behold Thy love which went all the way for us; and as we give out of ourselves, may we find the springs of significance rising within us, refreshing and purifying.

Eternal Father who lovest us with a love too full for us to grasp, direct us as a nation and people. In our darkness help us to see Thy light. In our perplexity, help us to feel Thy presence. Be to our president and our leaders a Refuge and a Strength, and to our land a lamp unto our feet and a light unto our path that justice, mercy and love may be shared by all. We commend to Thee those who sorrow, those who struggle, those who seek. To us all, O God, be the good shepherd who restores our souls through Jesus Christ our Lord.

Let us join in George Washington's prayer for the nation:

Almighty GOD; we make our earnest prayer that Thou wilt keep the United States in Thy holy protection, that thou wilt incline the hearts of the citizens to cultivate a spirit of subordination and obedience to government; and entertain a brotherly affection and love for one another and for their fellow citizens of the United States of America at large. And finally that Thou wilt most graciously be pleased to dispose us all to do justice, to love mercy and to demean ourselves with that charity, humility and pacific temper of mind which were the characteristics of The Divine Author of our blessed religion, and without whose example in these things we can never hope to be a happy nation. Grant our supplication, we beseech thee, through Jesus Christ Our Lord. Amen.

Easter, April 17, 1976

Everlasting Father who has never yet been put down by the chaotic whims of Your children and whose remarkable patience lets us attempt to express ourselves, knowing all the while that someday we must come to terms with the spirit You have breathed into us:

We thank You for the freedom You give us. Although our ways may become so ingenious that we are baffled by our own behavior toward one another, and sometimes, like a petulant child, we actually presume to blame You for the pitiful way we've handled life because of our self-protecting attitudes, from the depths of our being we really praise You because You have not given us up, however alienated we may be from ourselves, from others, and from You. In profound amazement we view the significance of Easter and all You have been trying to tell us, even though our incredible preoccupations with our own notions have shut You off altogether! Almost in embarrassment, we marvel at the power of the risen Christ over the lives of once-hopeless and rather futile people. If He became like us that we might become like him, we pray for the good senses and wisdom to worship something bigger and better than our own selves; for the needed cleansing and therapy of knowing we are known, and understood, and still loved. Our jaded lives are ready for something new, like resurrection and new life.

May it happen, O Lord: Happen in the games we play with ourselves and our friends, our society and our world. Happen as our great country once more turns to the spiritual roots of its greatness. Happen as those who have special needs today find in You their strength, a very present help in times of trouble. Happen as we join in spirit with saints, heroes, loved ones precious to us, who in their time and way fought the good fight, kept the faith, finished the course.

O blest communion, fellowship divine!
We feebly struggle, they in glory shine;
Yet all are one in Thee, for all are Thine.
Alleluia.

So, O Lord, support us all the day long. And now, as our Saviour Christ taught us, we humbly pray (The Lord's Prayer)

April 6, 1980

In deep humility we come before You today, O Father, for You have given us so much and we have acknowledged so little; and Your patience with us so totally outdistances our patience with each other.

Make us aware that we figure into your scheme of things, O God. Don't let us go on pretending we are the center of the universe, so intent on grabbing and protecting our possessions, as though they actually belonged to us!

Make us alert to this universe, O God, recognizing that we are but travelers on this earth. Give us maps for the journey, and in Christ may we find the guide for the way and the One who rescues us from our own failures.

Make us attentive to Your Spirit, O Father. There are so many restless urges in us—all the way from resentments and alienations, to frustrations and exasperations. Somehow may we simply put ourselves at Your disposal. We give thanks that Christ paves the way for us, opens the doors, and brings us back to our spiritual reality.

And now, O God, enable us to join the communion of saints—that great cloud of witnesses of all Your children in all places and ages who surround us. In spirit, may we and they be as one before the reality of your Presence. Bring blessings to those who mourn, help to those in need; grant a sense of presence to those who feel alone. Our prayers extend to our nation, that we may draw from those spiritual roots which once made us great. Enable us to do justly, love mercy and walk humbly with our God, that we may exalt the Prince of Peace.

So, O Lord, support us all the day long, until the shadows lengthen, the evening comes, the busy world is hushed and the fever of life is over. Then in Your mercy grant us a safe lodging, a holy rest and peace at the last, through Jesus Christ our Lord who taught us (The Lord's Prayer)

Easter, April 10, 1977

Almighty God who calls us by name and asks us to call You our Father: again we respond to our deepest longings and return to our spiritual home, there to rediscover our roots, there to feel your love, there to join Him who is the way, the truth and the life. In our darkest perplexities, as well as in our moments of ecstasy, You enter into our lives, bearing the cross we should shoulder and overcoming the disasters that are too much for us to handle by ourselves, but which are not beyond us when we have put ourselves in Your hands.

For all this we are grateful, O God. Forgive us for treating You so lightly and for allowing our lives to become so messed up in our self-worship. You know us better than we know ourselves; give us the good sense to turn to You and learn from You. Above all, pick us up and place us in Your hands, O Saviour of the world.

As we pray for ourselves, we pray for those in need—those who grope, those who suffer, those who sorrow, those who aren't even aware of their needs. We pray for our nation and our leaders that we may be a people worthy of your blessing. We pray for Your church everywhere and in this place. Here may the faithful find salvation and the careless be awakened. May the doubting find faith and the anxious be encouraged. May the tempted find help and the sorrowful comfort. May the weary find rest and the strong be renewed. May the aged find consolation and the young be inspired, through Jesus Christ our Lord:

(The Lord's Prayer)

Easter 1982

Almighty and loving Father who continually reminds us that we are created for fellowship with You, and who made our hearts restless until they rest in You: with all the company of heaven and the multitudes of earth, we gather around the throne and exclaim. Blessing and honor, glory and power be with God and to the Christ the lamb of God who takes away the sins of the world. So we offer our gratitude.

For Christ, the way, the truth and the life;

For Christ, in whom we see God and in whom God shows us who we are;

For Christ, the redeemer who restores us to life with You and one another;

For Christ, who tasted death for everyone and overcame its curse:

For Christ, who by his death destroyed death, by His rest in the tomb sanctified the graves of the saints, and by His resurrection brought life and immortality to light; for the many ways You speak to us within the human heart, in our relationship to others, and our attitude towards the problems of our world; for these and many more blessings we offer our thanks on this day of resurrection.

O Lord of boundless love, the comforter of the afflicted: send Your strength to those in need and Your comfort to those for whom this day brings piercing memories. Visit us with the presence of the living Christ, that all of us may find in Your presence the companionship which brings joy and the triumph which brings victory to life once more. Bless those who mourn. Be with those who today experience the ravages of this mortal life. We give thanks for all who have made the world richer for their presence, and who are now abiding in light eternal. Grant that we may enter with them into the fullness of Your unending joy.

In the midst of the stirrings of war, give us the spirit of peace. Where we would glorify national anger, hatred and power, give to us the mind of Christ, the Prince of Peace. We pray for our leaders, for Alexander Haig in Argentina; for all stirrings for peace in Argentina, and Lebanon, and Israel. We pray that we may learn how to wage peace and not war, and bring hope to a world so rapidly falling with hopelessness. We pray for peace in our hearts: peace with God, through the grace of our Lord Jesus Christ; peace with ourselves, through the transforming power of the Holy Spirit;

peace with all others, through the love of God which outloves us all. So may Jesus Christ be risen today—in our lives and in our land—and may all creation sing the praise of the Creator who waits to give us life through Christ.

(The Lord's Prayer)

March 15, 1981

O God, Your strength is sufficient for every need, and You meet us where we need You. Therefore, we gather in Your house to give You our praise.

O Lord God Almighty, heaven and earth join in praise. All Your works blend their voices in song to Your glorious name, for You are high and lifted up, beyond our highest thoughts, our deepest joys. You are infinite and eternal, and we are but finite and cast in the fleeting mold of time. Yet, O God, You have made us for Yourself, and our hearts are restless till they rest in You. In Your majesty You have given us hearts to seek You, minds to know You, hands to please You, and wills to follow You.

In Your mercy You have met us in Christ Jesus and welcomed us home. So we dare to presume upon Your presence and beseech Your guidance, O God. Bless us in our work and play, our pain and sorrow. If anxiety or fear strike this day or week, dispel it with Your Spirit, and cause Your light to shine upon us. As another Easter season returns, prepare our hearts to receive the gift of Your sacrifice for us, and in this Lenten season, open our hearts and minds to new truth. Accept our thanks, O Father, for what happens to our lives when we put them in Your presence and live by Your power.

Be to our president and our leaders a refuge and a strength, and to our land a lamp unto our feet and a light unto our path. May Your blessings be upon those who seek Your will through this church, that we may grow together in grace, as we make our pilgrimage. May Your consolation and comfort be with those of our number who mourn, that they may be strengthened and kept in Your care. Guide our decisions and purify our motives, until the world of our human relationships becomes a world touched by the peace of Your Spirit.

Lord of all worlds, before whom stand the Spirits of the living and the dead: we bless Your holy name for all Your servants who have finished their course and kept the faith, and who are now at rest with You. Unite us in one communion with all Your saints on earth and in heaven, through Jesus Christ our Lord.

(The Lord's Prayer)

March 20, 1981

Great God our Father: in these days so suggestive of spring's freshness, hinting so strongly of life's renewal; in this Lenten season so useful in bringing us into spiritual contact, so helpful in making us aware of the presence of the Spirit; in this day, this hour, this world, we simply give thanks! We offer our praise because of Your greatness and our need, because of Your inexhaustible resource and our exhaustion, because of Your clarity and our confusion.

In our struggle for righteousness and truth, may we heal rather than hurt, help rather than hinder the cause of a just society. In our zeal; may we not overlook our own shortcomings; and in all our thoughts and acts spare us from the malice that destroys not only our society but ourselves as well. Where we are separated from one another and from God, may Christ reconcile us to You and to all others.

We pray for our nation, our leaders and all those who ought to be our leaders. We pray for the church and its ministry and all of those places where it ought to minister. We pray for ourselves and all those needs and longings we feel and those we ought to be aware of. Particularly today, we pray for those whose physical health threatens their spiritual and emotional health. May they put themselves in Your hands, and having done their best, leave You with the rest, and may they and we sense that "underneath are the everlasting arms." Surround us with Your children in light eternal, that together we may drink from Your unfailing fountains and live to give You glory. In this Spirit send us from strength to strength in affirmation of life as Christ gives it to us.

(The Lord's Prayer)

Easter 1981

Great and good God who set these planets into motion and devised these laws of life, then breathed Your Spirit into us so we could discover them and use them on Easter: we marvel at the immeasurable possibility of life. We give thanks for keeping faithful to us even when we have been unfaithful to You. With gratitude we consider the adventure of living today and dying tomorrow, the challenge of opportunity that comes each day, the drive of great causes that make us instruments of Your Spirit, and all those things unseen which give meaning to all we see and do.

Today, on Easter, we give thanks for coming among us in Christ. We know You are Spirit, quite beyond our grasp. We give thanks for getting into our life-size in Christ and for taking our sins and raising us to the newness of life. We know You have made us to care and share. We give thanks for sharing so totally with us in Christ. We know You have made us restless to be, and to realize what we are to be. We give thanks that You have met our need in Christ, assured us of your forgiveness, and brought eternity into our time.

As memories flash into our minds, give us joy, rather than sadness, because we know that our lives and the lives of our loved ones are in Your hands. As our days are faced with difficulties and decisions, give us encouragement because we have been raised with Christ into newness of life, and found His living Spirit directing us. As perplexities cloud our world, we call upon you, O Father, to become so vividly present that our lives will find stability and strength. May Your healing Spirit be with those who are ill. May Your Spirit bind us together with those who are separated from us. Together may we look to You for help and find in You our life. May our nation humbly look to You and seek Your ways of justice, truth and peace.

So,

O Lord support us all the day long,
Till the shadows lengthen
And the evening comes
And the busy world is hushed,
And the fever of life is over,
And our work is done.
Then in thy great mercy,
Grant us a safe lodging,
and a holy rest and peace at the last.
Amen.

March 29, 1981

All people of faith in the U.S. have been asked to join in a National
Weekend of Prayer for the people of Atlanta, and especially
for the families directly touched by the tragedies there.

Eternal God who speaks to us out of the burning bush, or out of the
budding flower; who comes to us in good times and bad, who loves us not
because of who we are but often in spite of who we are, and whose love,
mercy and power are poured out to us in the person of Jesus Christ, our
Lord and our Saviour:

On this springtime day, we offer You the best we can give You—our
praise.

On this Sunday in Lent, we put ourselves before You in penitence,
dedication and commitment.

On this holy day when Your people gather together and with one voice
lift their hearts in praise and thanksgiving, we join in the communion of
saints—that great multitude which no one can number in heaven and on
earth, declaring in awesome wonder, "Blessing and honor and wisdom and
power and might be with our God forever and ever."

"Like as a father pitieth His children" so do You love us; "as one whom
His mother comforteth," so do You enter into our needs. Hear, then, our
prayers for our land, and especially for the people of Atlanta, so haunted
by senseless crime, so fearful of the sins we commit against each other and
against You.[4]Our prayers reach out to bereaving parents whose children
have been snatched from their homes; to bewildered brothers and sisters
and families whose joy has been turned to mourning; to police officials and
all others who seek the ways of peace and justice. In our mortality and in
the limitations of our humanity, hear our prayers, O Lord.

Eternal God, You have called us to the ways of peace and justice. We
pray today for the people of Poland, so besieged by the threats of invasion,
so uncertain about their future.[5] We pray for our enemies who stir up war
and conquest, and who destroy the aspirations of peoples and nations, that
they and we may seek primarily the ways of unity, so that a climate of trust
may develop. Wherever we add to the ways of war, correct us, O Lord; and
wherever we make for the ways of peace, direct us.

---

[4] Dr. Watermulder references the Atlanta Child Murders

[5] Dr. Watermulder references the warning strike in Poland held to protest violence

Hear our prayers for our own number who are sick or troubled or bereaved, that they may experience the blessings of Your peace. And now, as our Saviour Christ has taught us (The Lord's Prayer)

Easter, April 19, 1981

This is the day the Lord has made: we will rejoice and be glad in it.
This is the day which dramatically discloses the meaning of life in the Spirit: We stand in awe before the living Lord.
This is the day, Lord; this is the day!
With the disciples of long ago, we stand in amazement at the day's meaning. With wise men of the ages, we recognize that there is something being said about the eternal scheme of things. With Christians we fall before Jesus Christ and for the first time see all of life's meaning caught and captured in Him.
Make us spiritually mindful, O God, of the cloud of witnesses who surround us. Unite us in spirit with your children in light and life eternal. Relate us in spirit to people of all races and places. Help us use these physical lives to express spiritual truth.
Above all, O God, may we affirm life over death, joy over grief, hope over despair. Let all our fears and sins die now. Nail them to your cross! Then raise us up into new life with Christ.
We affirm it, O God! May we live this resurrection life. May our nation reflect its values. May those in trouble or need find restoration in its reality. May those who feel the ravages of our mortal earth draw on Your spirit.
So,
O Lord support us all the day long,
Till the shadows lengthen
And the evening comes
And the busy world is hushed,
And the fever of life is over,
And our work is done.
Then in thy great mercy,
Grant us a safe lodging,
and a holy rest and peace at the last.
Amen.

Easter 1982

Captured by the dazzling light of Christ, who could not be contained by our world of space and time but who breaks through the veil and exposes the power and reality of the Spirit to us, we bow in praise. We give thanks for the quiet of this place, for the hush of the holy, for pensive reconsideration of so many notions, and for the breakthrough we find in Christ.

As we think on these things on Easter day, O Lord, our prayers turn from thankfulness to prayers which ask your forbearance with us. In this place we're somewhat appalled at the way we've tried to manage Your affairs in our way. We admit our spiritual growth may have stopped long ago, and we feel rather inadequate as we realize how deeply penetrating and broadly inclusive is this Christian faith which we have handled so lightly. So even where we are spiritually tongue-tied and don't know how to pray, hear our wistfulness, hear our anguish, hear us—and understand!

We can't pray for ourselves without praying for others, O God. Even as You inspired Your children in other difficult times, enable us not to bemoan these days and add to their problems but to embrace Your presence in our midst and draw on Your Spirit. Thus we pray for our president and our leaders; for those who have felt the ravages of this mortal world; for those who seek peace that You will lead them and bless their endeavors; for those who mourn today that they may experience the spiritual communion of all your children; and for those who are ill, that they may achieve a calm confidence because You are with them.

Catch us up in this hour with all Your children of all races, classes and places. Blend us in spirit with all your children who live in light eternal, triumphant in the heavens; unite us all together in one spirit that they who have gone on before and we who follow after may share your presence and trust your love through the power of the risen and living Christ.

So,
O Lord support us all the day long,
Till the shadows lengthen
And the evening comes
And the busy world is hushed,
And the fever of life is over,
And our work is done.
Then in thy great mercy,
Grant us a safe lodging,
and a holy rest and peace at the last.
Amen.

March 7, 1982

Almighty God who neither slumbers nor sleeps: in Your presence darkness becomes light and winter turns to spring. With You there is joy and hope which brings abounding love.

For this good gift of life: its time and its seasons, its joys and sorrows which beckon us beyond our mortal world into the realm from whence we come and into which we return; for Your consuming care as we walk this earthly sphere, and for the glimpses of grace which sustain us, we give thanks.

Especially in Lent, we give thanks for Christ, our companion and guide, our Saviour and Lord. Enable us to put ourselves in His hands with total abandon and utter confidence, and derive from Him a joy in creation and a delight in life that spring from a sense of Your transcendent Spirit around us.

We pray for those whose joy is turned to sadness and those for whom life seems to be closer to gloom than to glory. Whatever their state, minister to them with the peace that passeth understanding, and lead them beside the still waters to restore their souls. May we all know that nothing in our life or death—adversity, calamity, infirmity—can separate us from the love of Christ, and may we rest in that love and enjoy the peace and power it brings.

May Your blessings be on Your church, here and across this land and around this world. Through its ministries of compassion and its declarations of salvation, may healing and hope come to all. We pray especially for this congregation, as we gather here to worship and to praise. Lift us beyond ourselves; support us with strength greater than our own; open our eyes and hearts to all the wonders You have prepared for us—and may we know what it is to glorify God and to enjoy him forever.

And now as our Saviour has taught us, we humbly pray together, saying (The Lord's Prayer)

March 14, 1982

Everlasting God our Father, You feed us as the vine supports life to the branch. In the wintertime of our soul, Your life-supplying strength continues to support us, until a new springtime bursts within us and our lives become fruitful and good once more. We praise You that we may abide in You, ever mindful of the peace and power You bring us.

We gather in Your house on Your day with Your people, to praise You and thank You, O Father, even as Your children have gathered throughout the centuries. Unite us in Spirit with all Your children who are in heaven and all Your children on earth, that we may worship as one great family.

Your goodness has created us; Your discipline has corrected us; Your patience has borne with us; Your love has redeemed us.

Grant unto us with these gifts a heart to love You, and enable us to show thanks for all Your benefits by giving up ourselves to Your service and delighting in all things to do Your will. Let Your forgiveness make us willing to forgive all wrong we have suffered, and to ask forgiveness for every wrong which we have done. Give us the Spirit of Christ who dwelt among us in great humility, and let the same mind be in us which was also in Him. Let our love and concern be abundant as our joy, that our hearts may be tender to all needs and our hands give freely for the sake of Christ. And grant that being rooted and grounded in the mystery of the Word made flesh, we may receive power to overcome all that would hinder us.

Bless all who serve—in our nation, our world, and in the church. In days of despair, give us hope; and in times of preparation for war, show us how to wage the battle for peace. Be near to those who are sick, those who are sad, those who have need. In waiting on the Lord, may they find strength; and through the patient waiting may they find that peace which the world can neither give nor take away.

And now as our Saviour taught us, we humbly pray together, saying (The Lord's Prayer)

April 7, 1985

With the voices of children, we praise You in this holy place on this holy day, O Lord. With our earthly families, we join the holy family of Your children on earth and in heaven, praising You for the goodness and greatness we find in life when we see it through the eyes of our risen, living Lord.

We come as very fallible human beings, O Lord, not quite adjusting to dimensions of life which differ from those we know. We are so used to figuring things out by our own measurements, and yet as we look over the centuries, we realize what mistakes we make when we limit ourselves to our present knowledge.

May we come before You with believing hearts, peering beyond the Easter message to the truth it declares about Your love for us, Your suffering for us, and the victory You bring to us. May we see our lives—and the lives of our loved ones—as being led by You over the mountaintops and down through the valley of the shadow of death and into the celestial light of life no longer encumbered by our frailties.

On this glad Easter morn, we pray for people everywhere: particularly for our loved ones and those we know who need Your encouragement, Your help, Your power; also for our nation, that we may learn the ways of peace and become a beacon of hope and promise to peoples everywhere; also for the peoples of the world who struggle in the midst of poverty and revolution which we do not experience, that they may find the ways of life abundant. As You commanded, O Lord, we pray for our enemies, that they may understand us and we may understand them, so that together we may live as the children of Your family on planet Earth.

We reach upward as well as outward on this special day, linking heart and hand with loved ones who have gone on before us, thanking You for their lives and praising You that in death, as in life, You are with us to bring us into the fullness of eternal life.

We trace the rainbow through the rain
And feel the promise is not vain
That morn shall tearless be.

Hear our prayers through Christ our Lord and Saviour, who taught us to pray (The Lord's Prayer)

April 8, 1973

Almighty God, in a quiet moment like this, we gather apart from the noisy world and ponder on all our blessings. We give thanks for the goodness that surrounds us, the opportunities that beckon us, the hopes that spur us on. For the inspiration of this day, for this awareness of your presence, for the blessings we receive, we give thanks.

Great God of Life: how much You understand about us, and in how many ways You call us back home! For a world brimming over with possibility, so that we have a right to have hope and to plan; for the choice of becoming open to Your Spirit rather than bitter and cynical; for Jesus Christ, so terribly human, so new and real for today, so far ahead of us; for what He does to put shape in our life and a sense of direction in our living, we give thanks.

Have mercy upon us, O Lord, and help us to feel at home once more with our world, with our fellow human beings, and with You. Send some kind of purifying stream which will release our spirits and will restore the joy of struggle and effort together.

So we pray for our world: for the old that they may appreciate what the young are going through, and for the young that they may recognize the added experience of the old. We pray for Your church, that it may be the agent to reconcile the diversities and the polarities that grow among us, until we find our deepest love for country in our love for Your way and Your truth and all your children. We pray for our president and our leaders, that their awesome responsibilities may spare them from the smallness of factionalism. Deep in Lent as we move toward the Easter victory, we pray for all who suffer in body and spirit, all in physical or emotional pain, all who sorrow over earthly loss and separation. May Your presence bring new joy and hope and lead them through their valley of the shadow, knowing all the way that the Lord is their Shepherd, and they shall not want. As He taught us, we now offer His prayer, saying together:

(The Lord's Prayer)

SECTION 3

Pentecost and Ordinary Time

November 11, 1962

O Thou who dost bestow the peace which the world can neither give nor take away, we thank Thee for this sacred hour, when our words are winged in the flight of prayer to Thy presence, and Thy Spirit hovers over us to open our eyes to the true nature of this world and our place within it. For the opportunities of this sacred hour, for Thy daily revelation in the world about us, surpassed only by the revelation through Thy word and Jesus Christ Thy Son, we thank Thee.

O Thou who dost speak through the earthquake, wind and fire, but who dost become most real in the still, small voice, who art with us wherever we go, whatever we do, and whenever we seek Thee: teach us how to pray so that we may use the capacities that lie buried within us. Make us know that Thou dost honor honest doubt and sincere seeking. Grant us the assurance that if we truly seek Thee, we shall find Thee. Thou hast made us for Thyself, and our hearts are restless until they rest in Thee. Since Thou hast created us with so many different moods and temperaments, may we not become discouraged in knowing that each must find the road that best leads to Thy presence. Touch us with Thy Spirit until we know that however we differ, we shall never find Thee until we come before Thee humbly, freely admitting that Thou owest us nothing, and that we are not worthy of the many blessings Thou dost bestow. Then, O loving Father, pour Thy Spirit upon us, that where we are weak we may become strong, where there is cowardice there may come conviction, where there are problems we may be blest with guidance. Like the scientist humble before the facts of the universe, make us humble before Thee. Like the child looking up to his parent, grant us reverence toward Thy power. Like the pupil looking up to his teacher, grant us a willingness to learn of Thy way and truth and life. Like an apprentice learning from the master, grant us obedience to Thy counsel.

Thou hast called us, O Lord, to pray for others; and Thou dost work wonders through heartfelt prayer. Hear, then, our prayers for the sick, that they may find comfort and courage in the good physician who canst release Thy healing power. Hear our prayers for those of our number who are separated from us. Bring us together around Thy throne of grace and give to them Thy companionship and counsel. Hear our prayers for our church, that her officers, teachers, and leaders may know they are doing Thy work and exalting Thee, and that all who worship here may find that in this place Thou givest peace, even as Thou dost also disturb us whenever Thy light casts its shadows on our self-opinionated, narrow ways. Our prayers are for our land and our leaders, O righteous Father, that we may become worthy of our blessings and humble in our leadership, acknowledging that Thy blessing also brings Thy judgment. These prayers we offer through Jesus Christ who taught us to pray (The Lord's Prayer)

September 8, 1963

As the deer pants for the water brooks, so our thirsty souls pant for Thee, O God. How great Thou art! How marvelous is Thy creation—the earth, the sky and sea, and man! For such blessings, so often unnoticed, we thank Thee.

Today we also thank Thee, O God, for the restfulness of slow summer days, and the verve and vigor of autumn adventure. We thank Thee that life is not dull or stale. We thank Thee for the opportunities we have to deny ourselves and to respond to duty—for what these things do to us and make of us, for the glorious fun and force life becomes when we find ourselves as we bow before the cross of Christ.

Also, we thank Thee for this Church: for its heritage and witness; for its determination to relate Thy saving faith to the demands of today's world; for the creation going on around it and within it. We thank Thee for these members. O Lord, all of us make mistakes and often look a trifle foolish. We blunder. We are proud. We save face. We would like the world to be like it was in our childhood—or at least we want things to be as we have decided they are. Yet beneath it all, we seek Thee. We want Thee. We need Thee. We thank Thee for the ties that bind us one to another, for willing, sacrificial, cheerful workers; for responsible people who shoulder their responsibility; for our common ground as disciples of Jesus Christ.

Also, we thank Thee for the communion of saints, O Lord: for the host of witnesses who surround us, and for those of our church family who have kept the faith, finished the course, and are at rest with Thee. Help us to abide in their fellowship, and here in Thy house may Thy Spirit blend heaven and earth.

Thou art our good shepherd, O Lord. With our thanks to Thee, we mingle our prayers for ourselves and others. Ourselves, that we may lay hold of faith and play God a little less as we form our opinions until we learn the secret of surrendering ourselves, our physical conditions, our outer circumstances, everything to Thee. We give Thee all these things, O God. Give to us what is best for us, of courage and comfort, of peace and power, until we know of a truth that the Eternal God is our refuge and underneath are the everlasting arms. Bless those who suffer, those who are ill, those at home and in the hospital who find their body too limited for their spirit. Give them Thy presence!

We pray for our land. For all teachers, parents, pupils as schools begin and new opportunities arise; for our national leaders in this day of destiny; for people of all races and classes, that we may sense the moment in history in which Thou hast placed us, and respond with a faith which identifies us with the sufferings of others and uses us to witness to the reconciliation which must come among Thy children—a faith which leads us to the cross, the cross which leads us in suffering love into our world, even the cross of our Lord Jesus Christ, who taught us when we pray to say (The Lord's Prayer)

April 19, 1964

Eternal God who art ever powerful and all wise, but who didst come among us not to be served but to serve and to give Thyself for us: we magnify Thy holy name for the many blessings Thou dost constantly bring us. As we see apparently dead trees and bushes burst forth into life, and as springtime's warmth finally begins to soften the chill, we behold Thy constancy and learn how to depend on Thee. As we behold Thy power to bring life out of apparent death, may we learn to leave all life in Thy keeping. Above all, may we learn the patience of Thy laws: first the blade, then the ear, then the full grain in the ear, and may we not demand of January what can only come in June, nor demand of self or situation what can only come through long periods of growth.

O Lord, teach us to pray! We come to Thee as children turn to loving parents, but forgive us, O Lord, for being crudely chummy with Thee, Thou who art high and lifted up, creator and judge of all life. In reverence and awe, and utter assurance that Thou dost listen, we approach Thee. Forgive us, also, O God, for acting like spoiled children who think Thou wilt give us anything if we whine long enough. We want to be sincere and real in our prayers, O Lord, and we would not insult Thy truth. Forgive us when we have played God and worshipped ourselves! Help us to listen as well as to speak. Give us confidence and courage, born of conviction, to do our best with the resources Thou hast given us; then give us the faith to leave with Thee the rest. May we put ourselves with our strange mixture of base desires and holy aspirations, into Thy hands and keeping; help us to put our life situations, with their tangled knots and perplexing problems, as well as their joyful moments, into Thy hands; then make us humble, simple, and gracious enough, O Lord, to accept and receive what Thou wouldst give back to us, so that every day we may face life clean, fresh, restored and understood.

O Lord, bless our land with concern and responsibility, that we may be worthy of the blessings of being the most materially favored on the earth. Direct our leaders that they may be responsible to Thee. Bless our church, not only here but everywhere, that it may transmit Thy grace and transform life through Thy Holy Spirit. Bless those who mourn; those whose faith wavers; those for whom illness has dimmed the luster of life; those baffled or beaten. Take them all in Thine arms, and cradle them with Thy love. Thus may we face ourselves and our days because we have faced Thee and Thou hast claimed us as Thine own.

And now, as our Saviour Christ hath taught us, we humbly pray (The Lord's Prayer)

October 11, 1964

Almighty God, whom the heaven, even the heaven of heavens, cannot contain, much less temples built by human hands, but who yet delightest to dwell with Thy children, we thank Thee for this holy place and for the opportunities Thou dost give us to grow in our faith and our relationship to our world. Particularly today, we thank Thee for this church and the noble heritage our fathers have bequeathed to us. Grant that we may be worthy in our day and world, as they were in theirs, O God.

Today also we thank Thee for the life of Thy servant and our pastor emeritus, Andrew Mutch. For all he has meant to so many, for his long and fruitful life, but above all for the tender compassion of his faith which pointed us to Christ our Lord, we praise Thy holy name.

O God and Father of us all, grant Thy comfort and Thy courage to those who are in need. Bless those who have met with accident or illness, those who face perplexing days. Guard our nation from hatreds and ill tempers which weaken our fabric. Strengthen our nation in justice and mercy, that we may walk humbly with Thee our God.

This prayer we offer through Christ our Lord (The Lord's Prayer)

September 12, 1965

Eternal God our loving Father, whom to know is deep peace within, whom to love is constant concern without, whom to serve is release, fulfillment and satisfaction: we worship Thee, Thou God of the universe, lord of all life, and lover of our souls.

As the deer pants after the water brooks, so pant our thirsty souls after Thee, O God. Thou hast led us beside the still waters to restore our souls: for these experiences of Thy presence we thank Thee; and for the many times we have refused to let Thee lead us, we beg Thy forgiveness. For quiet summer days, for seasons of work and seasons of play, for the dependability of Thy laws both physical and spiritual, we give Thee our thanks. For this church, as human as we are and as divine as our Lord, striving and yearning to be identified with our living Lord in our world today; for the persons who make up this church, as mortal as any flesh and yet sincere in their seeking to be Thy children and to serve Thy cause; for the fellowship of sharing we have with one another as we forget ourselves and see the larger picture; for all of life, beckoning us to daring and adventure, pleading that we not busy ourselves in safety and security alone:, for all these things—blessed, sanctified, transformed in Thy hand—we give Thee thanks.

Grant Thy blessing upon us as summer gives way to fall, as easy days become active days. Give us wisdom and discretion to see the futility of so much of our motion, and give us the strength to be selective in the places we put our time and energy. Bless the leaders of our church—the elders, deacons, trustees; the young people of all ages as they find in Thee the sense life needs; the church, schoolteachers and leaders, and all groups of men and women as they open themselves to Thy Spirit.

O God in whose hands is the destiny of all nations and people: may the Spirit be with our president and the leaders of our land, may we be a people of calm judgment, clear vision, high purpose, that our land may be blessed with those qualities that unite and strengthen us.

O God our help in ages past, our hope for years to come: we are mortal and cannot know the secret things which belong to Thee. But Thou art our shepherd, and Thou dost lead us through the valley of the shadow and into the light of Thy peace and presence. Surround with Thy Spirit those of our number who have met with unexpected difficulty or the immeasurable loss of loved ones; unite us with the communion of saints who worship Thee in light everlasting. In the limitations of our mortality, may we rest in the knowledge that Thou knowest our needs and hearest our cry. And now, as our Saviour Christ hath taught us (The Lord's Prayer)

October 10, 1965

O God, who art, and wast, and art to come, before whose face the generations rise and pass away: age after age the living seek Thee and find that of Thy faithfulness there is no end. Our fathers in their pilgrimage walked by Thy guidance and rested in Thy compassion; still to their children be Thou the cloud by day and the fire by night. Where but in Thee have we a cover from the storm, or shadow from the heat of life?

For these abundant blessings made so vivid in Thy church, we give Thee thanks, O Lord. For the blest communion that binds us to Thy children in light celestial; for the tie that binds our hearts together in Christian love; for the ways we may find ourselves as we lose ourselves in Thy service; for the salvation Thou hast given us, and the redeeming, restoring work Thou wouldst do through us, for the host of witnesses who surround us, and particularly the valiant souls of this congregation who fought a good flight, finished the course, kept the faith, and received their crown of righteousness; for feeling ourselves one with Christians of every country, class, color around the globe; for so much more than we can begin to mention, we thank Thee today, O Lord.

O Thou King eternal, immortal, invisible, Thou only wise God our Saviour, who didst send the Holy Spirit upon the apostles: pour out that same Holy Spirit upon Thy Church today. Make us the instruments of Thine outgoing redemptive concern. Make us glad in the joy of the faith, and bold in the power of the Spirit. Take us out of our cozy corners and tear us from our pious platitudes, that we too may translate Thy Gospel into our contemporary tongue and bring its verve and vitality wherever we are.

Even as we thank Thee for the past and strain towards the future, we remember those of our number who are ill or in sorrow; those who are disappointed or in despair; those who are alone or confused. Bless them all, O Loving Father, that they may know that nothing can separate them from Thy love. Grant to our president and national leaders a sense of loyalty and responsibility to Thee, that they may face the complexities of our day in the spirit and with the guidance of Him who came to bring deliverance; and return to us a sense of dependence upon Thee, thou God of all nations and Lord of all life. And now, as our Saviour Christ hath taught us, we humbly pray (The Lord's Prayer)

April 17, 1966

Thou Spirit of life, unfathomable and unchangeable who in Thy majesty dost ask us to call Thee our Father: we praise Thee that in the immensities of this world we may feel at home because Thou art the creator of all, and hast made us for Thyself. We thank Thee for the love which Thou dost shower upon our lives: the friendships which turn us from ourselves; the sacrifices which develop our larger souls; the companionships which mellow through trust and sharing; the social nature of our being which blends into a heavenly harmony as we share our hopes and fear; the memories of homes and loved ones dear to us and the creation of new homes in each generation; the heavenly home toward which we move in the communion of Saints; the Divine Companion Thou dost give us in Christ, so we need never walk alone.

O loving Father, whose everlasting arms uphold us and whose Spirit enfolds us in Thy bosom, as little children do we come to Thee, admitting our needs and seeking Thy help. Teach us to confide in Thee. Move us to talk with Thee daily, listening for Thy still, small voice and feeling the firmness of Thy power. Thou knowest our weaknesses over which we have so little control. Thou knowest our tendency to get in our own way and trip over ourselves. Thou knowest our problems and the situations we have created for ourselves. As we cast these burdens upon Thee freely, may we know that Thou dost not only sustain us, but dost show us how to bear one another's burdens in Christian love.

Be with our members who are sick and ill, that those powers of health may flow once more and life be made whole. Bless all who are sick, all who are alone, all away from us who serve in the military, all who have trying times and special needs, until they find new strength and hope flowing into their lives as they abide in thee and Thou in them.

Thou Lord of all worlds and all men, who hast made us different and yet all alike, open unto us the avenues of love and peace in this world of hate and war. Truly give our leaders a sense of divine guidance and work through them, using them to establish peace. Help us and all men to see one another as brothers, and lead us beyond our proud and clever ways to a common humility before Thy throne. Through Jesus Christ our Lord, who taught us when we pray to say (The Lord's Prayer)

June 12, 1966

Almighty Father, who art concerned about us Thy children, even when we rebel in childish adolescence, we thank Thee for the winsome ways Thou dost show Thy love to us, and the wisdom with which Thou dost discipline us. Accept our gratitude for those realities we cannot touch or see: the warmth of friendship and understanding; the meaning and memory of home and loved ones; the spirit of kinship which brings us together as Thy children; the wholesome feeling that life is good whenever we place it before Thee for inspection, correction and direction. We give Thee thanks for the Lord's day set apart for worship of Thee: for that uncanny atmosphere which fills the beauty of holiness until we sense that Thou art here; for the sense of overarching awe which comes as we know our spirits are linked to those of millions of others who also worship Thee; for that great cloud of witnesses which sees Thee in a light purer than we shall know until we join them in the greater world beyond space and time. For all these blessings—so many, so simple, so penetrating—we thank Thee.

Eternal God who lovest us with a perfect love and hast revealed Thy full measure of concern for us in Christ Jesus our Lord: as the shepherd doth seek the lost sheep, so Thou dost seek us. Hear each of us as we bring our heartfelt needs before Thy throne of grace: the haunting and doubting and cynical suspicions; the gnawing defeats and failures; the strange sense of our need for something more than we are, and our inadequacy to provide it alone. Hear us, Lord, even when our pride makes us boast that we are quite capable without Thee. And have mercy, O Loving Father! Understand our needs, our calls for faith, our yearning for light, our need to reach beyond our narrow walls.

Thou art our refuge and strength, a very present help in time of trouble. Therefore we lift our hearts in prayer for those around us. Be near to those whose sickness or heartache has altered plans and brought discouragement, those who need the power of Thy Spirit and the assurance of Thy companionship. Send forth Thy healing, that spiritual and emotional strength may bring new life and open the channels which bring healing and health once more. Grant Thy blessing upon our nation and her leaders, our president and his advisors, until we shall sleek Thy will and do it, and shall receive the blessings of Thy kingdom. And now as our Saviour Christ hath taught us, we humbly pray (The Lord's Prayer)

September 4, 1966

In the quiet of this hour, surrounded in spirit by Thy children of all ages and places, we rest in Thee and receive strength from Thine unfailing fountains of life. We contemplate on Thy power and goodness, we lean on Thine everlasting arms, and our hearts spill over in thanks to Thee for all the possibilities that life affords. We thank Thee for the added reflection of quiet summer hours and the renewed anticipation of busy autumn days; for the beauties in nature and the opportunities within human nature; for the world around us so much bigger than the small world we so often inhabit in our introspection; and for the fresh new life which comes as Thou dost find us in Christ and cause us to be lost in causes and concerns far bigger than ourselves.

Thou hast been our God in ages past, and Thou art our help for years to come. As we face the uncertainties of our day, give us the certainty of Thine everlasting concern. As we retreat into our safe little cages, open the gates and set us free in Thy world of people, events and issues. As we dwell nostalgically over the past, set our eyes on our present world, assuring us that the future, too, is in Thy hands. May we be a people who care and share, a people who strengthen one another because our strength comes from Thee. May we embrace our world as the arena where our faith is acted out because Thou has so loved our world as to enter into it as one of us.

Give to our land, O Lord, a sense of compassion for the oppressed, and mold us into a people whose joy and happiness come from our common endeavor to lift the level of well-being for all. May Thy Spirit comfort Thou who are anxious, and those who grieve and sorrow. May Thy presence be with those in the danger spots of life, whether they find themselves in Vietnam or waging the battles for a better, fuller life at home. Grant to our president and our leaders a compassion borne of love, mercy and concern, and a wisdom shaped by the perspective of Thy righteous judgment in all history. Open to us the gates of new life and lead us through the world around us, and into the abundant and eternal land, through Jesus Christ our Lord we pray (The Lord's Prayer)

October 16, 1966

Almighty God whom the heavens, even the heaven of heavens, canst contain, much less temples built with hands, but who delightest to dwell with Thy children and dost call them together in praise: with all the hosts of earth and heaven, we blend our spirit in thanksgiving to Thee for life and its goodness, for memories of the past, hopes for the future, and strength for the day. For the adventure of life even in the midst of adjustment and change for Thine everlasting arms to support us and Thy tender mercies which forgive us. For Christ our Lord and Saviour, in whom all things become new and fresh, we thank Thee.

Eternal Father who art acquainted with all our ways! Give us the vision to see life as Thou dost see it and the perspective to see ourselves in the light of causes and concerns greater than we are. Grant us the joy of losing ourselves in more than ourselves, and the willingness to put every intention and motive before the mirror of Thy truth. Enable us to let go and let Thee take command. So fill our hearts with trust in Thee, that by night and by day, at all times and in all seasons, we may without fear commit ourselves and our loved ones to Thy never-failing care, and give us the joyful abandon of seeking to know Thy will, however it may disrupt our present thought, and to seek to follow thee, however Thy path may direct our steps onto new and different roads. Above all, enable us to be honest before Thee, that we not add to our confusions with the audacity of trying to pretend in Thy presence.

May Thy blessing and Spirit be with all who are ill and those who minister to them. May Thy confidence go with those who mourn. May Thy light shine on those whose path is dark with conflict, with decision, with difficulty. Bless our land, that it may be worthy of its heritage and willing to examine its purposes in Thy light. Direct our president and those in authority that they may feel their responsibility to Thee, the ruler of all. Be with those who lead us in this church, that all of us may catch a vision of what Thy church should be. Here may the faithful find salvation, and the careless be awakened; may the doubting find faith and the anxious be encouraged; may the tempted find help and the sorrowful comfort; may the weary find rest and the strong be renewed; may the aged find consolation and the young be inspired—through Jesus Christ our Lord who taught us to pray (The Lord's Prayer)

October 30, 1966

O Thou who hast given us a place of quiet rest within our hectic world, and who dost ever enfold us within Thine everlasting arms, we give Thee thanks for this holy hour, and for Thy church around the world, gathering Thy sinning—yet striving to be faithful—children together in one great family. For spiritual resources to turn stumbling blocks into stepping-stones; for the inner calm amid the outer confusion; for Thine outgoing love which is more than a match for our ingrowing pity; for the bonds of prayer which link us to Thee; for the wonder of each day and the adventure of an outreaching life; for all Thy blessings so manifest in Jesus Christ, we thank Thee, O Lord.

O Heavenly Father, who has called us to find ourselves by losing ourselves in Thy cause, hear our prayers for our personal needs. We know not how to pray as we ought, but Thou dost hear our prayer if we but seek to express it. Teach us to pray, and having done our best, give us grace to leave with Thee the rest. In our restlessness, give us Thy rest; and in our anxiety, grant us Thy peace, that we may face any outer turmoil or trouble with the resources of Thy Spirit.

We pray not only for ourselves, but also for those we know who need our prayers, as we bring them before Thee now, one by one. Thou art their refuge, as well as their strength. Therefore, O Father, give peace to the troubled; guidance to the confused; direction to the despairing; help and healing to the sick. In all conditions, may they and we know that if Thou art with us, we need fear no evil. Be to us all the shepherd who leads us beside the still waters, and restore our souls!

Even as Thou hast commanded us to go into all the world to preach the gospel, we pray for our family of believers around the world. May our comfort not dull our compassion. Increase our opportunity to be involved in the witness of Thy Church in all areas of our nation and the world.

We pray for our president and the officers and leaders of our nation, state and community. In this telling decade, speak to and speak through those who lead us, that this nation may be an instrument of justice, and peace and compassion. These blessings we ask in Jesus's name, who taught us to pray together, saying (The Lord's Prayer)

June 20, 1965

Almighty Father, who hast searched us and known us and understandest our thought afar off: Thou hast laid Thine hand upon us, and fashioned us with the breath of Thy spirit. For such spiritual creation, and for capacities to receive Thy power and peace into our lives, we praise Thy name. For all those impulses, quite beyond our control, which call us to Thee and haunt us when we separate ourselves from Thy spirit; for the soul within us that transforms existence into happy living consumed with service; for Thy Spirit which can bring the best out of us when we would settle for the worst, we thank Thee, Thou God our creator.

We lift up our hearts in thanksgiving for Thy Church everywhere, as she opens the gates for new life to souls imprisoned; for Thy truth which makes people free and accountable only to Thee; for this church, her officers and leaders, her instruction and witness which opens the channels through which Thy mercy and peace flow into life. For all ways Thou dost speak to us, we thank Thee, O God.

Open my eyes, that I may see glimpses of truth Thou hast for me;

> Place in my hands the wonderful key that shall unclasp
> and set me free.

Eternal Father, we pray to Thee to be near not only to us, but to all Thy children. Bless the youth of this church with an alert awareness of Thy reality, and be with those of our number who participate in summer church camps, conferences and projects. May those who have tried to flee from Thee know that it is impossible—but even more, may they know their happiness is only in Thy keeping. Give us the will to do Thy work; but even more, give us the wisdom to wait on Thee. Give to the troubled and tense, the sick and the seeking, the lonely and the longing Thy refuge from the storm, Thy strength for the day. Lead those who walk through the valley of the shadow of death unto Thine everlasting light. Open for us the doors of peace and understanding, and give us a national pride whose strength is humility before Thee, Thou judge of all people. Surround us with Thy Spirit, quicken us with Thy compassion, until we awaken to the possibilities within us and within every event surrounding us. Grant to our president and our leaders cool judgment and sound wisdom, and unite us as a nation dedicated to truth and righteousness, until all men may know their common brotherhood under Thy sovereign guidance. And now as our Saviour Christ hath taught us, we humbly pray (The Lord's Prayer)

October 8, 1967

Almighty God who hast blessed us with life in this good land, and hast brought us out of many backgrounds to the present day: we thank Thee for the many ways Thou dost ever renew our lives—in the beauty of the seasons, the adjustments of the years, the demands of the times. Above all, we thank Thee for life's blessings and the limitless love of Christ Jesus our Lord. For the knowledge that Thou dost still love us, forgive us, accept us; that Thou art waiting to make something far more out of us, we praise Thy holy name.

O Lord of all men and nations, we pray for our land in this day of destiny. May we not only be aware of the forces playing around us, but may we become the instruments Thou dost use to fashion the days to come. Save us from futility and spare us the agony of protecting and defending viewpoints which we know must wither if we dare expose them to Thy light. In losing ourselves in causes greater than ourselves, may we find who we are; and in opening ourselves to Thy truth, may we discover the fascinations of living as Thy children.

Bless and guide our president and our congress. May the presence of Thy spirit be with those who must fight in Vietnam. Be with all in our government and our United Nations, who seek the means of peace. Be pleased to comfort those who are sick and those who sorrow. May they, and all who face difficult decisions and anxious moments, find that "underneath are the everlasting arms," and having done their best, may they have the faith to leave with Thee the rest.

And now, as our Saviour Christ hath taught us, we humbly pray (The Lord's Prayer)

September 22, 1968

Eternal Father, who in Thy power and might doth yet tenderly enfold us within Thine everlasting arms: we lift our hearts in thanks to Thee, Thou who art the author of every good and perfect gift. We praise Thee for life, and for its secrets revealed in Thy word and in the face of Jesus Christ. We thank Thee for love, and for the heartache and hope it stirs within our hearts. For the peace of summer days and the stirring of autumn breezes, for the restless quest of men in the social conscience born of the Spirit, we give thee our thanks. We pour out our gratitude to Thee as we rejoice in the reunion of friends, in the ties that bind us one to another, in the common labors within this church which knit our lives into holy purpose and shape our attitudes. For this community and city, for this land of abundance in which we live, but chiefly for Jesus Christ our Saviour, we rejoice and give Thee praise.

Thou everlasting Lord who doth neither slumber nor sleep, we bring to Thee our personal petitions for Thy grace and help, knowing how helpless and deceived we are without Thy Spirit. As Thou hast given to each of us different gifts, give us the will to use those talents for some good end. Prevent us from concentrating our gaze upon ourselves; enable us to experience the joy of losing ourselves in sacrificial concern for Thy kingdom and, thereby, find our real selves. Give us strength to bear our burdens, and the faith to cast our burdens upon Thee when we have done all we can do. Give us intense compassion and concern for all Thy children on the earth, and direct us to use our talents and resources to uplift all mankind.

O loving God, who hast gathered us together in the holy family of Thy church upon earth and eternal in the heavens: we pray for the officers and leaders of this church. Direct us as our church officers meet this Saturday. Guide us in church school and our various activities. Prepare us to be of service and significance to Thee. We give Thee thanks for loved ones departed who have kept the faith, finished the course, and now are at rest with Thee. Help us to abide in their spiritual fellowship. To those of our number who are sick, be Thou the good shepherd who doth lead beside still waters. To those who are perplexed, be Thou the everlasting arms which uphold them. To those who grieve, be Thou the resurrection and the life. May Thy blessing be upon all children and youth as they begin their school and college training. May Thy nurture be with every mother and father, as they share with Thee in the miracle of life, and become Thine entrusted servants to mold and make the generations to come. Bless this land and her leaders; in this election year give us cool heads and clear motives. Hasten the day when justice, mercy and peace will be the desire of all people and the strength of our land. And now as our Saviour Christ hath taught us, we humbly pray. (The Lord's Prayer)

October 29, 1967

Within the blessed walls of Thy church, etched with eternity and surrounded with Thy Spirit, we join our hearts in thanks unto Thee. When Thou didst form the world, Thou didst fill it with light. When men chose darkness instead of light, Thou didst call to them in the cool of the evening, sending Thy patriarchs and prophets to let Thy light shine once more. In the fullness of time Thou didst come to earth as a man to dwell among us, and in the blackness of our sin, the light of Thy resurrection glory illumined our pathway once more. For Thy constant, caressing love, we bless Thy holy name, thanking Thee that even in our own time Thou hast not left us without a witness in Thy Church; and in the Christ, the firm foundation upon which Thy church is built. Our fathers in their pilgrimage walked by Thy guidance, and Thou hast surrounded us with a cloud of holy witnesses for them.

Almighty Creator, whose glories fill the earth and who hast called on the works of men to praise Thee: Thou hast given us minds to fathom the secrets of the atom, but we destroy ourselves, as well as the glory of Thy world, as we harness Thy mighty power. Thou hast given us wills to live together as siblings in love and law, but our very systems become channels of mockery instead of praise. Yet Thou dost brood over us and suffer for us and with us. Therefore, we implore the presence and power of Thy Spirit among us. Grant a holy guidance to the president and to all his advisors, that ways may be found to unify the land and restore a sense of law and dignity. Give to us all, O Lord God of men and nations, a humility of heart and mind.

These prayers for peace and strength we offer as we remember the sick and suffering, the lonely and the discouraged, and the men who must do battle. In an awareness of our national heritage and our reformation ancestors, as well as the memory of all good men of all ages, we offer our prayers within the communion of saints, thanking Thee for Thy servants who have kept the faith, fought a good fight, and now live in light eternal before Thy face. Help us abide with them in Thy fellowship and link us together by Thy Spirit, through Jesus our Lord, who taught us to pray (The Lord's Prayer)

September 8, 1968

Eternal God, who art ever the same and yet canst make all things new: how often Thou must have watched Thy children in their frantic motion and wondered when they would come out from the shadows into Thy light. Today, as another summer ends and another season of effort begins, we thank Thee for Thy light which no darkness can put out, Thy compassion which no indifference can smother, the opportunities Thou dost present to us in this day which can bring harmony out of our confusion. Most of all, we thank Thee that Thou art both a refuge in the storm and our strength for the battle. For many mercies and blessings, many opportunities and moments of refreshment, contemplation and companionship, and even for the hard conflicts which shake our settled ways, we thank Thee, O Lord.

Today, O God, we come asking for Thy help. Our country is confused, and so are we. We stand baffled at the many things that are happening, not knowing whether to cry or strike back. We need Thy Spirit, Thy presence, Thine insight, so we may understand what is going on; and we pray that we may be receptive to some truth which may break upon us as a new idea. Help us to be a part of the answer rather than the problem, and to sense the new age that is bursting upon us which calls for new understandings from us.

We pray for our nation—for the oppressor and the oppressed, the young and the old, the Democrats and the Republicans, the mean and inferent as well as the soft and sentimental. Somehow, restore to us the glory of life. We pray for our president, our congress, our leaders of state, as well as our boys who must fight, and those who negotiate at the peace table. Somehow, make us instruments of Thy peace. We pray for Thy church everywhere and Thy church here, that it may be sensitive to every human need and see the face of Christ in every suffering face. Somehow may Thy church be the channel to shed light, hope and new possibility; and may we in this church here rise to the occasions to be a force for good and a source of strength. Bless all who worship here, all who work here, all who witness here, and unite as one with Thy children everywhere on earth and the children in light eternal in heaven. Hear our prayer through Christ, who taught us to pray, saying (The Lord's Prayer)

September 15, 1968

Eternal God, our loving Father, who art ever the same and yet dost make all things new: age after age the living seek Thee, and find that of Thy faithfulness there is no end. Our fathers in their pilgrimage walked by Thy guidance. So to us in our time be Thou the cloud by day and the fire by night. For Thy many mercies, too numerous to number, we offer Thee thanks and praise. For the faith of our fathers, living still, and thrusting us into the issues and problems of our world, we glorify Thy name. For Thy Church around the world proclaiming Thy truth—sometimes silently, sometimes gloriously, we adore Thee. For this Church with its heritage and promise, its devoted disciples and earnest concerns, we give Thee our heartfelt thanks.

O Lord, who dost surround our lives with divinity and dost direct us to the destiny we are to fulfill, may Thy Sprit fall upon us and favor us with Thy guidance. Spare us from the false piety which makes our religion another worldly masquerade. Open our eyes that we may see how fascinating the adventure of life may be when we draw on Thy wisdom and courage. Allow our faith to expose ourselves to ourselves, until we fall before Thee penitently, acknowledging that Thou art the Lord who dost visit us with judgment and mercy, and art ready to make all things new as we lose our lives into Thine.

Almighty Father, who dost hold the whole world in Thy hands: grant Thy blessing upon our land, our president, the congress, and all those who lead. Be pleased to be with all schools and teachers, and pupils of all ages, who adventure afresh into the limitless world of the mind and spirit. May Thy peace rest upon those who are ill and troubled, and those who grieve and sorrow. We commend to Thy loving care and to the power of Thy Spirit all who suffer in body and soul, all who need strength to face new problems, all who need Thy companionship so they do not walk alone. And now as our Saviour Christ hath taught us, we humbly pray (The Lord's Prayer)

September 29, 1968

Thou who art infinite and eternal and who canst not be contained in temples built by hands, but who dost delight to dwell with us because we are created for Thee: we thank Thee for Thy Church universal, speaking in all places to all people; we give thanks for this church where Thou dost make us responsible to Thee. We thank Thee for its work among the former generations. We thank Thee for all whose labor here is to serve Thee in their place and time. As we embark into another year of worship and work, grant us Thy grace and Thy guidance. Bestow upon these, Thy people, Thy benediction which the world can neither give nor take away.

O Thou who art the light of the minds that seek Thee, the life of the souls that know Thee: in Thee do we find the way and the truth. In troubled days when emotion burns up intelligence, grant Thy grace to all, especially to our parents and homes, our teachers and school faculties, that they may lay hold of truth until truth lays hold on them and all whom they influence. Grant wisdom to all who guide our youth. Endue all teachers with love of truth and devotion to it, with balance of heart and mind. With brilliance give humor, with wisdom give insight, with responsibility give humility. Cause Thy light to shine upon all who learn, that they may know the voice of the people is not necessarily the voice of God. Give our students a sense of excellence in their work, that whatever they do, they may do it well. (Fill them with conviction, honor, and determination.) Save them from worshipping things, lest in gaining the world they lose their souls.

Our prayers reach out to the rest, O God. Where there is sickness or anxiety, despair or trouble, bring comfort, causing Thy children to know that they that wait upon the Lord shall renew their strength. Where there is sorrow, open eyes and hearts to life far greater than this, and give vision to see beyond this moment into Thine eternal future. Where there is doubt and confusion, be Thou the way, the truth and the life.

O Lord of history and father of mankind: grant the calm of Thy wisdom and direction to our nation and our world. Give to our president and leaders a commitment which reflects Thy truth, and to all who work for peace and concord, bestow the presence of Thy Spirit. May Thy presence be with our men in Vietnam, and may Thy power for peace and brotherhood move through our hearts and land and world once more, through Jesus Christ our Lord, who taught us to pray, saying (The Lord's Prayer)

September 14, 1969

In the beauty of this day, the fresh adventure of the fall, the glories of Thy Church, we lift up our hearts to Thee in thanks, O Lord.

For memories of home and parents, for children growing and grown, for homes and household problems, for the family of God within Thy Church, for responsible parents, eager children, devoted teachers, conscientious leaders, we give Thee thanks, O Lord. For answered prayer and hopeful days, we bless Thy name.

O loving Father, who in times past did create for Thyself and Thy world a people of God, and didst give to them Thy clear word and the fellowship of Thy Holy Spirit, we raise our hearts in thanks to Thee that amid our confusion, our shallow goals and shabby performances we may return to Thy house for acceptance, forgiveness, understanding and direction.

We pray Thy blessing upon us as we move into a new year in school and community, in church and activity. Temper it with Thy spirit and correct it by Thy judgment. Expose to us our prejudices. Open to us the adventure of commitment. Spare us from the futility of existence. Today we pray for this church, her teachers and leaders, pupils and parents. May she be true to Thy word as a living, disturbing, upsetting word. May She call forth service and sacrifice, commitment and concern.

Today also we pray for our president and our leaders, that Thy spirit may transform our spirit. Enable us to be good Americans because we are, first, good Christians. Keep us as individuals and a nation ever under Thy judgment, and allow us to see our needs and receive Thy help. Guide those who make for peace and be near to those who must be in Vietnam. May Thy Spirit be with those who meet today, and that we make peace and not war.

O divine shepherd, lead beside still waters those who are ill or lonely, perplexed or in need. Unite us with the communion of saints in life eternal, now as our Saviour Christ hath taught us (The Lord's Prayer)

September 28, 1969

O Lord our Lord, how excellent is Thy name in all the earth! What wonders Thou dost perform! What difficult tasks Thou dost transform with Thy Spirit! How gloriously dost Thou speak in the tang of autumn air, in the constancy of the seasons, in the immense powers which, though unseen, surround us! O loving Father, how good Thou art to us in understanding us. What companionship and courage come from Thy nearness! O Lord our Lord, how excellent is Thy name in all the earth. For life so adventuresome, for truth so durable, for power so plentiful, for friends and opportunities, we give Thee our unworthy though heartfelt thanks.

Dear God our help in ages past, our hope for years to come: We seek Thy help, here in our homes and work, here in our day as we buckle down to the tasks of another fall season. Grant that we may not routinely go into another year, simply repeating the same blunders. May we seize this season as a gift from Thee to gain new vision. May we seek out Thy way so Thou canst go to work on us. May we keep still so Thy voice may be heard. May we be receptive so Thou canst make something out of us. Make us aware of the possibilities within us and around us. Spare us from making ourselves into little gods: rigid, brittle, and opinionated. Help us to worship ourselves a little less, and Thee a little more. May we welcome our doubts as expressions of our quest for truth, and hence through them be led to a firm relationship with Thee. May we gain strength from a faith which allows us to be confident that Thou art real and Thou dost understand.

May Thy blessing be upon Thy Church and upon this church where Thou dost use us. Be near to those who are sick, those who mourn, those who grope: be their Good Shepherd. Be near to bless and surround our loved ones away from us, particularly those in the armed forces, both at home and abroad in Vietnam.

Bless and direct our land and our leaders, that we may use our immense blessings to heal the division of the world and witness to a way of life and peace. Put us under Thy corrective judgment until we become the channels through which truth, righteousness and peace may increase. Temper these supplications through Christ, who taught us to pray, saying (The Lord's Prayer)

October 12, 1969

Almighty God, who art stability and strength in our worlds which seem to fall apart: we thank Thee that we may bring our perplexity to Thee and wait on Thee for clearer perspective. We praise Thee, that these times may bring a sense of adventure and inquiry into our lives until we are able to participate in Thine unfolding creation. We thank Thee for the landmarks Thou dost give us in Christ and for the humanity we learn to share and struggle with because of the high regard He had for all humanity. For the blessings of this past week; for failures placed at Thy feet and successes turned over to Thee; for purpose and direction and for this hour to draw apart and be caught up in something so much more than ourselves, we thank Thee.

O God, our Father, our Source and our Hope: we bring our perplexities to Thee. We pray for frustrated students who desperately need to discern Thy way and will in this contradictory world. We pray for bewildered police who are at a loss to know how to fulfill their duties. We pray for a fermenting society whose very soul is churning and whose people often strike each other rather than share with each other. We pray for every person who is seeking to be a person in this age when so many voices try to tell him what to do, who to be. We pray for our men who must endure battle in Vietnam and for students whose desperation expresses itself. We pray for our president and his counselors, and for the health and hope of our nation whose once-clear purposes seem so clouded over in the dust of today's turmoil. We pray for every Christian in the midst of such times, that we may seek to be channels of Thy Spirit, people who bring reconciliation in the midst of innuendo and charge and countercharge. We pray for a sense of responsibility and for a recognition of those processes which alone will save us.

O divine Shepherd, we also pray for those whose personal and private battles make them desperate; for those who feel they have no place to turn even though Thou, through Thy children, art ready to minister to them. For those who grieve, those who mourn, those who suffer, may all of us be caught up in a world bigger than ourselves become aware of a presence which brings meaning to our days.

And now, as our Saviour Christ hath taught us, we humbly pray (The Lord's Prayer)

May 17, 1970

Thou all-wise Creator and Father, who dost use everything to reveal Thyself to us and who dost speak to us both directly and indirectly, in subtle suggestions as well as in clarion command: we thank Thee for life in this good earth, and for all the ways it relates to Thee. For the sermon of the springtime, for the constancy of the seasons, for the adventure of continued change with an orderly sameness behind it all; for the message of the physical year with its bursting buds and new life; for the message of the church year as we move from the resurrection fact to the coming of Thy Holy Spirit among us at Pentecost; for so much more than we can name, we thank Thee, O Lord.

Grant the blessings of the same Holy Spirit upon us as we face our individual tasks, O Lord. Where decisions must be made; where memory burns and days haunt because of grief and loss; where illness thwarts and life's joy has turned to mourning; where there is a loneliness or insecurity, an arrogance born out of inadequacy or a pride born out of inferiority—in every complicated problem, O Lord, surround us with Thy Spirit, undergird us with a peace and sense of purpose which the world can neither give nor take away. So may our individuality be exalted because it is the channel of Thy Spirit and manifests Thy power.

We pray again for Christians everywhere. May we, being sustained by Thy Spirit, be drawn closer into the same faith, and be living testimonies of Thy power and evangelizing witness in every complicated contemporary problem of this century. Especially, O Lord who didst send Thy Holy Spirit, do we pray for our General Assembly in Chicago this week. Bless those who lead and who represent us. In these tormented times when tempers tear our national fabric, restore to us and our nation a sense of our meaning and a capacity to listen to each other. May Thy presence be with our boys who must fight abroad; may Thy presence be with all who strive for peace at home. Be with our senators and representatives, our president and his advisors; give us as a nation an awareness of our heritage in freedom; and may all of us be drawn together by great hopes and lofty causes, through Jesus Christ:

(The Lord's Prayer)

June 21, 1970

Almighty Father who hast painted nature with vivid hues and filled it with the breath of Thy peace, who dost provide us with the freshness of rain, the brightness of sunshine and the calm stillness of the night, as the seasons come and go and the earth moves in its orbit, so dost Thou move among Thy children and minister to their needs. For Thy love and goodness, for Thy challenge and hope, for giving us blessed memories and aching aspirations, for Thy glory made understandable in Jesus Christ, we thank Thee.

Eternal Spirit, who art nearer than breathing, closer than hands or feet, our souls are restless till they rest in Thee. Hear us as we pour before Thee our individual and private needs. Make us sensible and realistic, O Lord, so that we recognize the call of Thy voice, the knock of Thy hand. Make our faith so implicit that we may trace Thy nearness in every situation. In our fondest joys and success may our happiness be complete because it is in tune with the promptings of Thy Spirit. In our lowest depths, and in our deepest problems, may our confidence be strong because we have learned to look to Thee for help. In our sadness, lift our eyes to the eternal realm where there is no death nor sorrow. In our righteous dealings, may we rejoice in Thy holiness; in our inhumanities, may we behold the justice of Thy wrath and the immensity of Thy mercy.

O Creator and Father, whose morning stars sang together at the joy of Thy creation, and who didst freely give us a good world: stab us with the responsibility Thou didst give us to care for and use such sacred gifts. Thou who has blessed us with freedom of choice, show us the consequences of our choices and cause us to choose Thy will. Thou who didst give us friends and neighbors and a world full of relatives, show us how to express our gratitude by helping us to live together as we ought. Make us see how much we have and how little we have done with it; how much Thou canst do for us and how little we let Thee do; how great and wonderful is our world and how small and miserable we make it when we worship our ideas rather than Thy Spirit. Send Thy Holy Spirit upon us, upon thy church, upon this land. Thou canst get along without us, but we can't get along without Thee, O God. Use us, then, as the tools of Thy hand, until our noblest achievement but reflects Thy skill and power, and people glorify Thy name and enjoy Thee forever. Grant to our president and our leaders the blessings of Thy presence, the light of Thy truth as the judgment of Thy justice, and give us the strength to be Thy servants, through Jesus Christ our Lord and Saviour who taught us to pray saying (The Lord's Prayer)

June 28, 1970

As the deer panteth after the water brooks, so panteth our souls for Thee, O Lord. We give thanks unto Thee, for Thou art good, and Thy mercy endureth forever. Mindful of the joy of quiet summer days, we praise Thee for the contrasts in life of night and day, summer refreshment and winter endeavor. Hurt by the pangs which strike us in our daily round, we thank Thee for the healing that comes by Thy streams of living waters. Yearning for a faith that fulfills our lives, we bless Thee for thy word and thy word made flesh in Jesus Christ. Knowing how frail we are, we give thanks to Thee that Thou knowest it too, and dost reward us not by our virtue but by our endeavor, not by our outer pretense but by our inner struggle. Linking ourselves with others and seeing our dependence upon one another in almost every action of life, we thank Thee for the fellowship of Thy Church and the communion of saints which enfolds us in Thine arms as children seeking the strength of their home. We thank Thee for this church—the comfort she sheds and the challenge she imposes, the restless dissatisfaction she gives us with ourselves, the compelling witness she calls us to make.

Not only do we thank Thee for so much, O Lord, but we seek Thy help, until the horizons of thankfulness reach out to wider, broader worlds. Take us as we are, O God, and give us the faith to put ourselves, as we are, into Thy hands. Beholding Thy love in Christ, give us courage to gamble our lives on Thee and to follow into these days of the 1970s with all their needs. Keep our faith fresh. Make it contemporary. Spare us the caretaker role of defending a past good while losing a present battle for Thee. Thou who art the good shepherd, may Thy calm and peace, Thy strength and blessing, be with all who are sick, those who mourn, and are in need. Direct our nation and our leaders with the power of justice mingled with mercy, and grant that we, as Thy children, may be equal to the shattering times in which we live, until both we and all others may know what it is to live as children of God. These prayers we offer through Jesus Christ; who taught us to pray (The Lord's Prayer)

September 13, 1970

Almighty God our Father, in every age Thou dost take us into Thyself, and gather us as Thy children. In every stage of our development Thou dost meet us, hear us out, and help us. Therefore, as we gather in Thy house after a quiet summer, and before the quickened pace of the fall, we come to thank Thee for Thyself and Thy goodness; to express our gratitude that we may turn to Thee and that, always, Thou art ready to give us help. Hear our prayers of thanks for this summer, for the church, for these other people who seek Thee in this house of prayer. Even where we have walked through the valley or in despair, we thank Thee that we are not alone. Accept our thanks for the adventure of life, as with the apostles of old, we too experience the teaching, the fellowship, the prayers of this Christian community.

Eternal God who dost know us so well: do not let us go off alone, as though we were substituting ourselves for God. Do not let us break with the company of the faithful, however impatient we may be. Help us to share together in the agony and the opportunity of these days, and enable us to draw strength from one another, as together we see ourselves as Thy children, nurtured in Thy house.

We pray for all the children of the church. At whatever age they are, may they know they are Thy children, and may we know that we are brothers and sisters to one another. We pray for all teachers and leaders. In a world of change and challenge, may our relation to Christ grow so positive, so deep, so compelling that we will be able to cope and to confront the needs before us. We pray for parents and for homes; for youth and for schools; for adults of every age and condition in this land, that we may look at each other and see one another as members of Thy family. We pray that we in our health may be used by Christ as His agents, and that all of our members who have illness may be strengthened by the awareness of His presence. May Thy blessing and guidance spread to our land, to our president, and to our leaders, that we as a people may meet the challenge of this day. And now we pray (The Lord's Prayer)

September 27, 1970

O God of life and seasons, Lord of the moment as well as the year, Spirit from whom we came and to whom we return: we thank Thee that we may call Thee Our Father. We praise Thee for our creation, and for the adventure of living in an ever-changing, always recreating world. We bless Thee that Thou hast given us eternal truths so that our lives may be fashioned by them. We thank Thee for coming among us in Jesus Christ— the way, the truth and the life—and for assuring us of Thy forgiving love, through Him.

O Thou who hearest every heartfelt prayer: we bring our supplications before Thee knowing that Thou art near. Grant Thy blessing on this church as the year's program gets under way, that worship of our whims, prejudices and opinions may leave us, and we may seek only to be channels of Thy Spirit and power, Thy love and life. Bless the officers of all groups within this church that they and all of us may be caught up in the larger company and broader vision of Thy holy family, the Church. Bless all boys and girls, all youth, all teachers and leaders, that our church school may be an adventure into the wonderful world of Thy love for us. Make us know that faith is not our frenzied attempts to prove our strength but our humble bowing before Thee in anticipation of what Thou canst do, even in spite of us. Bless all those in the colleges and universities of our land; all who teach and all who learn, that we may stand before Thee eager and expectant to fathom the mysteries of Thy marvelous universe, anxious to love Thee with our minds as well as our hearts.

In this holy place we bless Thee for the communion of saints and the host of witnesses who surround us. We pray to Thee to be with those who are sick or depressed, and with all who face trouble. We offer our prayers for our land, our president and leaders. Under their burdens give them judgment and understanding, as well as strength and courage, which are born of the Spirit and reflect that care for people and their needs which filled our Lord with such understanding. May the calm of Thy presence be with those separated from us, and may the compassion move us all to find the ways of peace and brotherhood. And now, as our Saviour Christ hath taught us to pray (The Lord's Prayer)

October 18, 1970

Eternal God whose morning stars sang together at the joys of creation, we grasp this new day Thou hast given us and thank Thee—thank Thee for the day, while being sorry that we so often take a day for granted. We thank Thee for the life we can live today and for the whole life that can be packed into this hour of worship in Thy house, where with other human beings, other persons, we may thank Thee for the breath of life, the breath of this day, and the new life and new day Thou dost give us in Jesus Christ.

Make us grateful for simple blessings, O Father. Grateful for each day in our life, and each person in our life. Grateful for the events and the strange patterns those events weave. Grateful that Thou dost understand us and forgive us. Grateful that we therefore may let go of everything behind us that haunts and hurts us, because Thou hast taken it over; grateful that we may leave the future with Thee, and simply affirm today, and today's possibilities, and today's people.

So today we also pray for those who have immediate needs. Today, right now, bring calm, and peace, and a certain assurance to those who bear loads of anguish, suffering, trial. May they know that Thou dost help them. Today be with those who are ill and those who have special needs and face immense troubles. May they know that the eternal God is their refuge, and underneath are the everlasting arms. Bless our land in these days—our president, our leaders, and those who influence our days. Use us to overcome the hatreds and enmities that eat at us like a dreaded disease, and bring to us a healing, hopeful new possibility for peace and clear purpose. Now, as our Saviour Christ hath taught us, we humbly pray (The Lord's Prayer)

November 15, 1970

Almighty and most merciful Father from whom cometh every good and perfect gift: we give Thee praise and hearty thanks for all Thy mercies; for Thy goodness that hath created us; Thy bounty that hath sustained us; Thy Fatherly discipline that hath correct us; Thy patience that hath borne with us; and Thy love that hath redeemed us. Grant unto us with Thy gifts a heart to love Thee; and enable us to show our thankfulness for all Thy benefits, by giving up ourselves to Thy service and delighting in all things to do Thy will.

O Thou who hearest every heartfelt prayer, we boldly bring ourselves before Thy throne. Thou knowest us better than we know ourselves. We have our fears and doubts, and so often they become thundering clouds of doom; we have our blind spots and our prejudices, and so often they blot out all else. Through all of our moods, speak to us, O Lord, and remind us that Thou didst give us such sensitivities so that we might be sensitive to Thy presence, Thy power, Thy peace. Enfold us within Thine arms until we hear Thy still, small voice which shatters all the clatter surrounding us. Give to us the peace the world can neither give nor take away, and grant us the assurance that Thou art our shepherd.

O Lord, at Thy command we bring before Thee every problem: not only our personal ones, but those affecting our business, our family, our plans. Shed light, grant guidance, assume control. Thou God from whom we came and to whom we return. Be near to all whose physical bodies have reminded us once more that our souls have bigger plans than our bodies can handle. Surround Thy loved ones and bless those who mourn loved ones whose life now encompasses a larger wall. Comfort those in hospitals and on sickbeds, and give them the inner peace and healing power of Thy presence. Give the spirit of wisdom and godly fear to our president and to all in authority, that our land may be sensitive to the new opportunities to bring dignity and liberty to all people. And now as our Saviour Christ hath taught us, we humbly pray (The Lord's Prayer)

January 17, 1971

O God our Father, how immeasurably remarkable it is to call Thee Father and to know that Thou dost care about us. How good it is to know that the occasional bewilderment which besets us with all its petulance and demands, its fears and misgivings is more than matched by Thy love and care. For the fact that Thou art here and we may come to Thee: for Thy love as a Father who hast given us Christ, we pour out our hearts in thanksgiving today. We are grateful that continually Thou dost speak and give us directions for living, that Thy grace is available to us, and that we belong to Thee. We thank Thee for giving us a conscience which reacts in sensitivity, and that our concerns may be sharpened for us to be aware of the next person and the next need. There is so much to thank Thee for, O Father. Accept our attempts to express it!

O Lord, Thou hast searched us and known us. Thou knowest our downsitting and our uprising. Thou understandest our thought afar off. Therefore we won't hide from Thee any longer. Therefore, we will put the needs that make their demands on us before the masks that hide us from our true feelings. Lift us into Thy presence and give us that release and renewal which attends the presence of Thy Spirit.

We pray for all who mourn and grieve, all who are saddened and sorrowful. May they experience Thee as the shepherd who leads them beside still waters to restore their souls. We pray for the sick and the suffering, that Thy Spirit may attend them and Thy calm may encourage them. We pray for those with problems that they may find new strength, new hope in the knowledge that Thou dost care and that they are not alone. We pray for our president and our nation, that this year may be a time when Thy spirit of justice, mercy and peace may move through the hearts of our leaders and become a reality in our world. Support those who struggle for peace and those separated from us, that they may know that in thy mercy they are not alone, and hasten the day when we become instruments and channels of Thy peace and purpose, through Jesus Christ our Lord who taught us to pray (The Lord's Prayer)

January 24, 1971

Almighty God who art our refuge and strength: even when the earth seems to shake and the mountains seem to tumble into the midst of the sea, we know Thou art still with us; that this is Thy world and in Thee is our refuge in weariness and our strength for facing the day. For such assurance, we praise Thee. For the knowledge that Thou dost overlook our arrogance and our presumption, we thank Thee. For Thy constancy in our wavering, Thy strength in our weakness, Thy light in our darkness, we bless Thy name.

Today we come to Thee, O Lord—very mindful that we are mortal, very aware of our precarious world, mystified at the way so much good can go so wrong. Today we come to Thee in bewilderment, and sometimes in despair; in despondency, and sometimes in cynicism; in restlessness, in hurt, in fear.

We implore the blessings of Thy Spirit upon us personally and individually, so that we may not crack or crush under our loads, and so we may see ourselves as Thy children, waiting on Thee, receiving from Thee, finding renewal in Thee. In sickness and in health, in joy and in sorrow, in plenty and in want, may Thy blessing attend us.

We also come before Thee collectively as a nation and people, mindful of our heritage and blessing and aware of our present dangers. May Thy wisdom guide and direct our president and his advisors, and spare us, O God, from partisan loyalties which prevent the greater good to occur. Be with our nation as our new congress convenes, and enable us to understand each other, work with each other, and plan together for a life of peace and opportunity for all.

We ask the presence of Thy Spirit to be with those in hospitals; those who suffer; those who grieve; those who fear heavy loads this day or week. Come into their presence and bring the peace of Thy calm and the power of the Spirit. And now, as our Saviour Christ hath taught us, we humbly pray (The Lord's Prayer)

September 19, 1971

Great God of this universe, Father of our spirits who hast given us this age and place to live in: we come before Thee both individually and as Thy family to thank Thee for the blessings of life. We know how self-sufficient we are, yet we also know how much we depend upon each other, and how much our lives depend upon the awareness of Thy presence and Thy power. So we thank Thee, O Father, for friends, for work, for this church, for broader and bolder visions, and for tasks to do. We thank Thee for the fresh beginnings of the fall season and the opportunities which beckon us into the days ahead.

O Father in whose hand are the destinies of men, yet who dost not leave us without the responsibility of choice and decision, we seek Thy help. Show us how to get ourselves out of the way of Thy Spirit, that we may receive power. Reveal to us the false gods of pride and prestige, of prejudice and smallness, that shackle us and frustrate our days. Give us an understanding of Thine undeserved grace, that we may yield to Thee our lives and receive from Thee our answer to our needs.

O Lord who dost protect our going out and our coming in from this time, and even forevermore: we give to Thee our students who are returning here or are leaving for college and work. Enlighten their minds, direct their wills, fulfill their deepest needs, as they find that in Thee is truth beyond all truth. Bless our universities and colleges, our professors and teachers, that they may be ambassadors, of all that is good and true. We pray Thy blessing upon our public and private schools and teachers, that unhampered or burdened, they may be used to develop the minds and personalities of our children. May Thy Holy Spirit be with our church schoolteachers and leaders, that they may be channels through which Thy grace flows.

O Lord of all worlds, before whom stand the spirits of the living and the dead, we commend to Thy care all who grieve and sorrow, all who are suffering and sick. Unite us in one holy communion before Thy throne, there joining in fellowship with all Thy children and receiving Thy power. Especially we pray for those who grieve in Athens. May the types of concerns and compassion we find in Christ safeguard and dignify human life in the future. We pray for those who suffer loss from floods—may agents of compassion alleviate the strain on them. Our prayers extend to our president and our leaders as we pray for those who strive for peace and thereby enable us to become a nation of peace. We also pray for our youth who are serving in the armed forces, that they may know the blessing of Thy presence.

Now, as our Saviour Christ hath taught us, we humbly pray (The Lord's Prayer)

October 10, 1971

Almighty God who hast talked to Thy children in times past, and who hast always been more than equal to the times, today we gather to praise and to thank Thee that we may hear Thy voice in these times. For this capacity to stop taking ourselves so seriously and to reflect on how much our brief lives are related to Thine eternal Spirit; for the blessings that surround us and the avenues of rest and new resolve we find in prayer; for the fact that our lives belong to Thee and Thou art ready to give them direction and strength, we thank Thee. Above all, we thank Thee for the meaning we find in Jesus Christ our Lord, whose presence gives us the way, the truth and the life we need.

Everlasting Father, our times are in Thy hands. Enable us to respond to our awareness of Thy presence, and to pause before the reality of Thy Spirit. Don't let us get so involved, or so exasperated that we think everything is up to us, or that it all rests on our shoulders. Show us how to put our lives in Thy hands and, having done our best, to leave with Thee the rest.

Give to us all a sense of Thy presence in these times, so we may be both Thy agents of change and those who know how to put their trust in thee. Be with those who are sick, that they may experience a healing power. Be with those who sorrow, that they may know the possibility of new beginnings. Grant Thy direction to our nation, that in these strange times we may find a new sense of national purpose and unity as our compassion responds to our day and we give a new expression to our heritage. Bless Thy Church, O God, that She may feed Thy people and be the agent of Thy blessings, through Jesus Christ who taught us to pray (The Lord's Prayer)

October 31, 1971

Almighty God whose ways are past finding out and whose love is immeasurable: with all Thy children in heaven and on earth we gather in Thy presence this morning to praise Thee. We thank Thee that we can take our gaze off ourselves and our preoccupation which often becomes self-pity. We thank Thee that we can relate to a Source and Force far greater than ourselves, where our lives can be corrected and directed. Above all, we thank Thee for Jesus Christ in whom we catch a vision of Thee and Thy kingdom. We thank Thee that we enter Thy presence in the company of Christ, resting on His love for us rather than on our own credentials.

Knowing how much Thou dost care about us, we bring all these puzzling questions about ourselves and our world to Thee. Teach us how to hold in proper balance the spiritual and material forces in our lives. Show us how to pray and how to let go and be willing to leave our lives in Thy hands. Lead us beyond this unmerciful preoccupation we have with our feelings, so that we respond to Thee with a healthy sense of duty and an awareness that Thou dost place demands upon us. Somehow show us how to find who we are as we try to follow Thee. Teach us what prayer is and how to pray.

Always Thou dost assure us of Thy care for us, even beyond the bounds of our vision and our experience. Therefore we respond to that care by offering our prayers for others: for loved ones away and for those who are ill; for everyone who is hurt or haunted by this war—the ones who have had to do battle, those who are taken as prisoners of war, those who are conscientious objectors; those who are parents, friends and helpers— Almighty God, give to them all a new hope for purpose in their lives and a new awareness of Thy presence in our midst. We pray for our land, O God, that its attempts at democracy and humanitarian concern may ever broaden. In particular, as another election approaches this Tuesday, we pray that the noble motives of democracy and dignity may find new opportunity to be expressed and grow.

Hear our prayers for Thy Church in these times, O God, that She may once more be like a compass to all who are confused about directions. Once more, may Thy people find in Christ Thy love reaching out, until the forgiveness and healing we find in Christ will be shared with all others too. Hear us now as we offer the prayer He taught us (The Lord's Prayer)

November 14, 1971

O Lord of the whole world, we come before Thee expressing our wonder with it all! When we behold Thy heavens, the moon and stars, what is man that Thou art mindful of him? When we detect the accuracies of science, the certainties of the laws by which this universe operates, we stand astonished. When we see Thee take on a human body, walk among us in Christ, we marvel. When we behold Thee suffer, share our agony and go through our valleys, we fall at Thy feet and confess, "My Lord and my God."

So here we are, O Lord, attempting to express our lives but often confused and bewildered as we face our days and our world with all these situations we had not bargained for and had not planned on. Here we are, not always certain how to proceed, how to respond. Here we are, terribly aware of our humanity with its weakness and our inhumanity with its cruelties. Here we are, back to Thee the Source, hungry, hurting, seeking to be made whole again. Hear us, O Father, and understand us.

These same blessings we pray for those who sorrow and grieve, those whose illness takes them through the valley, those who need an extra measure of assurance just now. Accept us, O God, and grant us Thy Spirit. Feed us, O Lord, and give us strength. These blessings of justice mingled with mercy, of purpose caught up in peace, we pray for our nation, for our president and our leaders, and all whose decisions can restore to us the joy of being a people who seek a higher will and way. May Thy mercy attend us and Thy blessing direct us, through Christ who taught us to pray (The Lord's Prayer)

November 21, 1971

Almighty God who continues to gather us together in Thy Church to receive Thy teaching and experience Thy fellowship, and who sends us Thy witnesses into the world around us and beyond our bounds: We praise Thee for the wonder of life and the joy of salvation. We thank Thee that we may be gathered together with the communion of saints—those who have gone on before us—and with Thy confessing children of every continent on the face of the globe. Most of all, we thank Thee for this place of quiet rest, near to the hand of God, where we are cleansed and fed.

In such troubled times, O Father, enable us to find ourselves by being caught up in Thy concerns. Help us to find life larger and more liberating by losing ourselves as we give ourselves to those who suffer, those who struggle, those who need a friend. Enrich our lives by an awareness of Thy Spirit. And when we have done our best, may we have the good faith and the good sense, O Lord, to leave with Thee the rest.

Bless our land and leaders with a new sense of Thy mercy and compassion, that once more we may represent the place of hope, renewal and fresh beginnings. Bless Thy Church that She may match these times with Thy Holy Spirit, until Thy reconciling spirit pervades us and brings Thy love into our lives. Bless those who suffer, those who struggle, those with special needs, and grant us all the peace and power of Thy presence through Jesus Christ who taught us to pray (The Lord's Prayer)

April 30, 1972

Everlasting God our Father, ever the same yet always new: whenever we feel that drab and dead winter has settled upon us, You always surprise us with the spring. For this we give thanks. That we can count on the constancies, even when we concentrate on the changes; that things are not what they seem, even when we get caught up in our fantasies; that You are sufficient for our needs, even when we rely on ourselves; that this world isn't such a bad place after all, even though it overwhelms us at times; that this world becomes so much brighter when we share the next man's problems in it, even though we like to be preoccupied with ourselves; that You have made us restless until we find rest in Your presence and power in this world and in its needs—for all we give thanks for Your love which gave the world Your Son that we might have life through Him.

Grant that we may see what He sees, hear what He heard in this world around us.

We pray for those for whom this world is not so bright and good: Those who peer inward and miss the outward delights of life. Those who look outward but meet with despair. We pray for those sick in body, or mind, or spirit. Be to them and those who watch over them the great healer and helper.

We pray also for those who suffer from heartache and heartbreak and who need to know that life is more than grim fate; we pray for those whose plans have not worked as they hoped, that they may find a new beginning. We pray for those troubled or saddened, that they may look beyond themselves to their source of strength. We pray for those who make peace and seek justice, that their cause may be strengthened and endorsed. We pray for the church here and everywhere, that it may be worthy of our Lord—neither caving in to the fears, those who hold on to the past, nor being broken by those who would make it the instrument of the fads of the moment. We put before You our nation, with our many fears and frustrations, and ask for divine guidance for all our leaders of government as we meet with governments around the world. Shed forth Your peace and surround us with Your purpose. Through Jesus Christ:

(The Lord's Prayer)

May 21, 1972

The heavens declare the glory of God and earth shows His handiwork. As we give thanks for such glimpses of grace, we bow in astonishment and appreciation for Your full revelation, O God, in Jesus Christ our Lord and Saviour. Grant that being yielded to Him, we may be lifted by Him into that bright world of fulfillment and release where we find the courage and conviction we need because of His companionship.

O God, You are strong and mighty. Make us strong. Give us strength of body, that we may do our work well and cheerfully. Give us strength of mind, that we may fearlessly accept Your truth with all our powers, and love our neighbor as ourselves. And give us patience, that we may, with our Lord and Master, be made perfect through struggle, knowing that they who wait upon the Lord renew their strength. Comfort the afflicted; heal the sick; strengthen those who sorrow. Unite with Your Spirit those who are separated from us.

Lord God of hosts:

In the midst of uncertainties give us the certainty of your presence.

In the midst of war give us peace.

In the midst of panic and confusion give us calm and deliberation.

In the midst of national turmoil give us all that guidance which enables us to work things out.

Grant to our president the quality of leadership he needs.

Grant to our people the capacity of understanding and the power of expression they need.

Grant to all who strive for peace the assurance of Your presence.

Especially today, we seek an outpouring of Your Spirit upon all people everywhere, that even though we speak in different languages, we may understand each other. In the midst of international dealings, may Your Spirit make us realize our oneness as humanity. Bless our president and all those with whom he deals this week; bless all efforts to bring this world into peace; restore to our land a sense of purpose and respect, that we may find joy in life once more and discover the opportunities which await us.

(The Lord's Prayer)

June 11, 1972

Almighty and everlasting God, whose light shines out of darkness, and whose fullness shines in Jesus Christ: we give thanks for the multitude of mercies around us. Especially today, we give thanks for children and homes, for family and loved ones. For all they have meant, and for treasured memories, we offer thanks, O God. For all they demand of us as we seek to grow into responsible individuals, we give praise. For the warmth of love and relationships, for the adjustments they bring as life's adventure unfolds, we express gratitude, O God.

Today we give thanks for the larger family, the Church, as it binds us in mutual concern and sheds upon us the power of the Holy Spirit. Enable us to grasp its length and breadth, depth and height. Show us the expansiveness of church membership, uniting us with little children here, with kindred souls less fortunate in places far away, with Christians around the world—and cause us to feel ourselves a part of a universal company, as well as a part of the heavenly hosts.

O loving Father, You neither slumber nor sleep, so we pray for the Church in this day. Give it prophetic voice. Make it equal to the days' demands. Unite us as one family, serving one Lord, and make out of us the family of the faithful who are loved, understood and forgiven, and who now are agents of understanding, forgiveness and reconciliation throughout the world.

Bind the entire family together, O God: the sick, the despairing, the perplexed. Give us abundantly of the Holy Spirit. And now as Christ has taught us, we pray (The Lord's Prayer)

November 12, 1972

Today, O God, we give thanks for so many things, but especially for life itself, and for life lived in the shadow of the everlasting, drawing strength from the unfailing springs, and finding renewal in Jesus Christ. In everything, by prayer and supplication, with this deep, profound thanksgiving, we give thanks.

Accept our prayers for others, O God. We bring before You those who suffer and seek, and those who live in a wilderness way; those who face difficulty, and even death; those who are uncertain; those whose reliance on themselves has caved in and who need someone to turn to, something to hold on to—all who are in need. Surround with Your Spirit, uphold with your love, strengthen with Your presence, O God of our Fathers, our God and our Father!

Grant to us in our national life a new sense of purpose and a new desire for unity. Help us heal the fractured body of our land, and direct us toward goals which are unselfish—which bring hope, life and fulfillment to many. May those of us who have so much be sensitive to those who have so little, for we both need so much of the Spirit. Abundantly surround us with the Spirit of Christ who is the way, the truth and the life. Bless the Church of Jesus Christ, that it may call us from our small and petty preoccupations and set our feet on high places. Unite us with all who search after Your Truth and grant us Your Spirit.

And now, as our Saviour taught us, we pray (The Lord's Prayer)

November 19, 1972

Eternal God, whom we know in every age so that divine light continues to shine even in our darkness, we give thanks for the many ways we have sensed Your presence. As we seek refuge within the quiet of the church, we feel the strength of Your Spirit touch our souls and restore the needed power we lack. We give praise for the indications of Your presence; for the ever deeper truths that lie hidden behind laughter and tears; the glance of a little child and the faith of a friend; the work of the church in the ministry of teaching and serving to which it calls us; the joy of new discovery when we find who we are and what we can be; the demands which call forth new Christian judgments and discretions, until we know what things matter and what things are passing shadows, the beauty of creation and the joy in believing, until body, mind and spirit blend into the all-consuming presence of Your Spirit. Lead us, O Lord, as we face our problems and our needs. Bless those we love. We remember those who are sick and suffering, lonely and longing. Undergird them with the assurance of Your presence and the confidence that they are not alone. When their faith is dim, shed light; where they have a task to perform, grant them help.

Almighty Father, restore our souls in Jesus Christ, that we too may be merciful and kind. Let Your forgiveness make us willing to forgive all wrong we have suffered, and to ask forgiveness for every wrong which we have done. Give us the Spirit of Him who dwelt among people in great humility, and was meek and lowly of heart. Let the same mind be in us which was also in Him. Let our love and charity be abundant as our joy, that our hearts may be tender to all need, and our hands freely give for His sake.

Our God, our help in ages past, our hope for years to come: we remember before Thee our nation; our president and leaders; and the United Nations to which we belong. As we recall our nation's heritage in our Thanksgiving celebration this week, we also recall our nation's concern for all men, that the good life might be shared. Make us worthy of the heritage which is ours and equal to the explosive demands of our day, that the mind of Christ may be in us and our world. And now as our Saviour Christ taught us, we humbly pray (The Lord's Prayer)

February 4, 1973

Great God who continually comes among us to restore us to life abundant and eternal, and who in Christ points out the way, the truth and the life for us: on this Sunday, we gather with these fellow Christians and fellow human beings to offer praise for Spirit, for Life, for God, for Christ.

We also express thanks, O Father, for the way we have been led in the past, and for that certain settled assurance we have because we leave the future in Your hands. Help us O God, to get out of the way, so that we may put our lives, our needs, and the whole world in Your hands.

But don't let us escape the work You have cut out for us, O God. Help us to see ourselves as Your servants. Make us the channels by which Your Spirit of peace, joy, reconciliation, compassion flow into our world. God, there are enough problems! By our words and deeds, our acts and attitudes, make us a part of the answer, not a part of the problem.

We put Your whole family in Your hands—our loved ones departed; those who are ill; those in need; those who suffer and those who strive for good. We are humbly thankful for peace, and pray that we may become a part of the climate in which it may flourish. May Your Spirit find such new channels of expression that all people will come to acknowledge our common humanity and need. Now, as our Saviour:

(The Lord's Prayer)

February 18, 1973

Great God, source of love and light and life: we have come here to put ourselves in Your hands, for we are mindful of the fact that our spirits come from You and return to You, and we need to establish a right relationship with You so that we may perceive our purpose in life and receive the support and guidance to make their accomplishment possible.

Even as we say this, O God, we recognize all that separates us from You. We are mortal and fickle; You are eternal and stable.

We are consumed with self, drawing people and things unto ourselves like a magnet; You are outgoing and self-giving, radiating life and energy like the sun.

We exact our sense of judgment and justice; You pour out mercy and grace.

God, we give thanks for this hour together, and especially, we give thanks for Jesus Your Son, our Lord and Saviour.

For the way he loves us in spite of our little arrogances;

for the way he makes our relation with You possible, in spite of the blockade we put in the way;

for the way he gives substance and style to these often-fussy and whimsical selves;

and for the way we find ourselves by forgetting ourselves and being lost in Your service:

For all these blessings all around us, we give thanks.

Be pleased to give special grace to all the Youth of our land who have felt the pangs of this war. As families have been reunited this week, so reunite us as a loving, hopeful, helpful people. Direct our president and all our leaders, that the days ahead may mark a turn from cynicism to constructive concern. May Thy Church proclaim the hope there is in Christ and His way, and may all who need Your peace and presence find it in abundance as they let go and let Your Spirit take command:

These mercies we ask through Christ our Lord:

(The Lord's Prayer)

April 29, 1973

Almighty God, our Father, these are the days when the heavens declare Your glory and the firmament shows Your handiwork. Therefore, we come into Your house today to link our spirits with other Christians across the world and give thanks

for life
for renewal
for hope.

We feel something like those early disciples, O Lord. We are perplexed with so much futility, so much duplicity, so much hatred.

So here we are in Your house to gain Your perspective, and then in finding our purpose restored to experience the blessings of patience and persistence. As You came to the disciples, come to us and give us light and life.

We pray for all who despair; for all who grieve; for all who are troubled; for all who seek, for all who agonize for a new awareness of Your presence. May the living Christ become known to them, and may new life come to them.

We pray for our nation and our leaders in these days. Restore to us the grandeur of great dreams and high ideals. What does the Lord require of us but to love mercy, to do justly and to walk humbly with our God! God of our Fathers, our fathers' God, our God and our Father: come again among us with healing and hope and purge us of all our dreadful preoccupations with our own devices until once more we may become the instruments of Thy Spirit and hope may return to our land once more.

And now, as Christ has taught us, we pray (The Lord's Prayer)

June 10, 1973

God, our all-wise Creator, who uses everything to reveal Yourself to us and who speaks to us both directly and indirectly, in subtle suggestions as well as clarion command: we give thanks for life in this good earth, and for all the ways it relates to Your Spirit. For the sermon of the springtime, for the constancy of the seasons, for the adventure of continued change with an orderly sameness behind it all; for the message of the physical year with its bursting buds and new life; for the message of the church year as we move from the resurrection fact to the Holy Spirit at Pentecost—for so much more than we can name, we give thanks.

Grant the blessings of the same Holy Spirit upon us as we face our individual tasks, O Lord. Where decisions must be made; where memory burns and days haunt because of grief and loss; where illness thwarts and life's joy has turned to mourning; where there is loneliness or insecurity, arrogance born out of inadequacy or a price born out of inferiority—in every complicated problem, O Lord, surround us with Your Spirit, undergird us with Your peace and sense of purpose.

We pray again for Christians everywhere. May we, being sustained by Your Spirit, be drawn closer into one faith, and be living testimonies of Your power and evangelizing witness in every complicated contemporary problem of this century. Especially, O Lord, who didst send the Holy Spirit, do we pray for our nation and her leaders in these tormented times when tempers tear our national fabric. Restore to us and our nation a sense of our meaning, until justice rolls down like water and righteousness as a mighty stream, in a land which has learned compassion and mercy and seeks its meaning as a servant of Your will and way. Now, as Christ taught us, we pray (The Lord's Prayer)

September 16, 1973

Almighty God in whom we live and move and have our being: we return to Your house on Your day to offer our praise and our heartfelt thanks for this life—for its wonder and mystery, its joy and struggle, its meaning and purpose which unfold as we put it in Your hands.

As another fall season begins, may the fresh breezes of Your Spirit spread over our lives, enabling us to affirm our life and its daily round; our opportunities and their challenge; our struggles and the strength which You supply. Enable us to do our best and leave You with the rest, O God, until we learn that the secret of a happy life is to live in Your presence and seek to discern Your purpose for us.

Today we pray especially for teachers and all who influence youth, even as we pray for all who enter schools. With knowledge impart wisdom, and with wisdom grant the humility to become disciples of Christ our Lord. Especially, support those who sorrow, those who struggle, those who seek, that the reality of your Spirit and the power of Your Spirit may rule. Purify our land and leaders that we may be instruments of truth and righteousness, and restore to us the joy of life lived in Your presence, through Christ who taught us to pray.(The Lord's Prayer)

October 21, 1973

Great God of power and might, who has seen empires rise and fall, nations come and go: we turn to Thee today in humble hope and prayer. Our resources have run out. Our cleverness has overtaken us. Our great ideas lie shattered. Our beloved land stands in turmoil.

Lord God of hosts, be with us! Make Thy face to shine upon us and be gracious to us! Show us the way of life. We know the words of the prophet: "What doth the Lord require of thee, but to do justly, to love mercy and to walk humbly with Thy God." O Lord of all life, we pray for the capacity to do these things—to blend justice with mercy and to walk humbly before Thee.

Therefore we commend to Thee our executive, legislative and judicial branches of government, and all those who are in charge and authority. We put ourselves in Thy hands that with clear heads and calm emotion, we may be instruments of forces and powers far greater than ourselves. In this day of national crisis, revive in us the springs of greatness which burst this nation into being, and fortify us with Thy Spirit.

We pray not only for our nation, but for every individual who has a special need—especially those of our number who are sick, who face decisions, who are at a turning point, and who must decide whether Thou art the God they worship or whether they worship their self-devised Gods instead. Have mercy on us all, O God, and love us, that we may love Thee and so love one another, through Christ whose love took Him to the cross and whose sacrifice brought our redemption and hope.

As He taught us, we pray (The Lord's Prayer)

November 4, 1973

Almighty God whose love exceeds our highest hopes and deepest needs, we gather here in this holy place on this day to do what Christians have done for centuries—to offer our praise and thanks, to receive pardon and insight, and to be caught up with all of Your children in heaven and earth in this spiritual act of worship.

Surround us with Your Spirit. Bring us Your healing love. Infuse us with Your power. In these days of national crisis, call us back to that sturdy heritage which made us strong, and fortify us with the knowledge that God is our refuge and our strength, a very present help in time of trouble. As our land has stood for so much that is so good, so may she find herself in these times. Therefore, we are bold to commend to You our president and the executive branch of government; our congressmen and the legislative branch of government; our judges and the judicial branch of government; and all our citizens, that we may know we are called to do justly, to love mercy, and to walk humbly with our God.

We bring into the healing, restoring presence of Your Spirit all of our number who are sad or who suffer; all who need help; all who are looking for light. We give thanks for our members who have found fulfillment in Your nearer presence this week and commend to Your unfathomable and unfailing love their loved ones. We place this church before You—with all her members and all her concerns. May we be faithful, O Father, and seek to follow Him who is the way, the truth and life, in whose name we pray (The Lord's Prayer)

November 7, 1982

Eternal Father, whose morning ever breaks through the somber shadows of our darkness, and who watches over us as a mother protects her child, we give thanks for the signs of Your presence among us: for the precision and beauty in the natural world with its days and seasons; for the judgment in history wherever we forget to reckon with our source and destiny; for the craving within our hearts to be attached to something more than ourselves; and for the penetrating and shattering experience of Your Spirit as it comes to us through Jesus Christ. Accept our thanks, O God, for such a guiding hand, and for such clear markers to show us our way.

Almighty God, in whose light alone we know ourselves, without whose guidance we are distressed, in the obedience of whose larger will there comes a sense of completeness: grant us the spiritual resources which we personally seek and need. Be attentive unto those needs of ours which face us so painfully and so obviously: the faith we need where fear has now taken hold; the courage we lack where cowardice now reigns; the comfort we crave where anxiety haunts us now; the assurance that life is in Your hands whether we live it here or beyond the limits of our earthly understanding. May we awaken to the depths of joy which life can offer us even where it has not turned out as we planned. Awaken us to the explosive power within us, waiting only for Your Spirit to dry the human dampness which has settled upon it, needing only the spark of Your presence to burst it into a flaming light. Bless those who mourn and those who suffer the loss of loved ones, those who need Your arms about them just now.

God of all peoples: we seek Your cleansing, restoring Spirit upon us as a nation. Heal our wounds. Refresh our languid spirits. Replenish our faith, hope and love. Unite us as a people and fashion us as a nation with compassion and concern. Bless our land and leaders in all branches of our government, and unite us in common cause with peoples and nations around the world to bring dignity, integrity and peace to people everywhere. Hear our prayers for those who represent You in other lands and often under horrible conditions. Surround them with Your Spirit and use them to advance Your Kingdom of peace, justice and mercy.

(The Lord's Prayer)

May 26, 1974

Everlasting God who has taught us to call You our Father: we come as the children of Your family, thankful that we may feel at home in this world as we move on to our eternal home. On this day of memories, accept our thanks for all the goodness that has surrounded us, for all the opportunities we have had, for the fulfillment which may come as we accept the responsibilities of our time and for the rich heritage which has planted our lives in such fertile soil. Above all, as meanings seem to blur, we give thanks for Jesus Christ our Lord and Saviour, whose compassion, forgiveness and purpose surround our lives and show us how to make the world into a home once more.

Dear Father, hear our prayer for every parent, every son and daughter, every grandparent, every teacher, every friend and neighbor. Sweeten and freshen the stagnant streams which flow through our world, that healing and happiness may return to us all. Make us children once more—all of us at all ages—so we may lose our brittleness and become pliable in Your hands. Give us humility enough to learn and warmth enough to care, and sense enough to know we don't know everything.

On this patriotic weekend, enable us to affirm our heritage. Give us pride in the sacrifice and struggle that have made our lifestyles possible. Give us a sense of the past as it engulfs us, and make us grateful for all who thought more of a great cause than they thought of themselves.

We pray for the nations of the world, that we may be concerned for the good of one another. We pray for the church in the world, that it may be the channel of Your Spirit and power. We pray for all who have needs and face difficulties, that Your Presence may make the difference.

(The Lord's Prayer)

September 22, 1974

Great God, who speaks in the stillness and penetrates into the center of our souls, with saints above and all Your children everywhere, we gather today to offer praise, to confess our failure to accept Your love and joy, and to receive Your pardon, Your power and that peace which the world can neither give nor take away.

We give thanks that we can do this, O God—thankful that You are the Father who understands, who cares, who forgives, and who helps. Accept our gratitude, especially for the fact that we can turn to You, lean on You, and draw strength from Your Spirit. Above all, we give thanks for Your presence in Jesus Christ our Lord—for His love, His immeasurable sacrifice, for the new life He gives us.

And as we leave summer and move toward the fall, may there be something of new life moving into us—putting aside the old maladies and pettiness, but above all the old unwillingness to turn to You and let You reshape us for our daily tasks and our heavenly journey. We do not turn to ourselves, but to Your constant unfailing resources, O Christ our Lord.

Pour Your Spirit, O God, on those who grieve, those who suffer, those who struggle. Cleanse and clarify our nation's goals, that we may be a people who do justly, love mercy and walk humbly with our God. Raise up leaders and give us vision that Your goodness may sweeten our land. As families and youth participate in their various schools, and as all of us set our goals, give to us that stability and strength that enables us to endure, to achieve, and to be the people who have grasped Your Spirit and found joy in Your purpose for us. And now, as our Saviour Christ has taught us (The Lord's Prayer)

September 29, 1974

Every morning we seek Your presence, O God our Father, and every Sunday we gather with Your people in Your house to offer our worship and adoration. For such enrichment to change the flavor of our daily diet, we give thanks. For such new strength to enable us to face our need, we offer praise. For such a calming peace within and clarifying purpose without, we bow in adoration. Above all, Father, we give thanks for the ways we find You in Jesus Christ, our Lord, and for the ways You reach out to reclaim us through Him, His gracious, forgiving guidance.

Accept these prayers of thanks for all these spiritual intangibles, O God, and enable us to grasp even more the spiritual blessings around us. "For each new day, when morning lifts the veil of night," for friends and loved ones and for this world of imperfect people and far-from-perfect institutions, we give thanks; for the daily round with its duties and delights, we give thanks.

Eternal God, You know us so well: Do not let us go off alone, as though we were substituting ourselves for God. Do not let us break with the company of the faithful, however impatient we may be. Help us to share together in the agony and the opportunity of these days, and enable us to draw strength from one another as together we find our identity in the Church.

We pray for all the children of the Church. At whatever age they are, may they know they are Your children, and may we know that we are brothers and sisters to one another. We pray for all teachers and leaders. In a world of change and challenge, may our relation to Christ grow so positive, so deep, so compelling that we will be able to cope, and to confront the needs before us. May Your blessings attend the sick and those in need. May Your judgment and mercy and guidance be with our nation and our leaders. May we seek to do justly, to love kindness, and to walk humbly with our God.

These mercies we pray through Christ our Lord, who taught us to pray (The Lord's Prayer)

October 27, 1974

Everlasting Father, to whom a day is as a thousand years and a thousand years is as a day, and who has placed us in this day that we may grasp its opportunity and mark it for eternity, we give thanks for the world around us; for leaves in the crisp wind; for the seasons of the year and the seasons of life; for the message of this autumn with its adjustment and change; for life and our chance to live for something more than ourselves, and for all the blessings that surround us.

Eternal Power, you have taught us to call You our Father; we come to You as little children. We need Your comfort: enfold us in your mighty arms. We need Your guidance: point to us the way. We need Your strength: breathe on us, breath of God. Take from our eyes the scales that we may see the problems we create because we try to live as though You weren't around. Give us a robust thankfulness for being alive and a capacity to affirm life.

Heavenly Father, You know our frame and remember that we are dust, and You lead us beside still waters, through valleys, and into never-ending tomorrows. Be very near, we pray, to those of our number and our loved ones who are ill in hospitals or home; those who face crises and decisions; those who need the comfort of Your everlasting arms and the courage of Your presence. May we exchange our fears for Your faith, our timidity for Your strength; and, leaving self and situation and loved ones with You, may we live in calm and confidence.

Eternal light, immortal love, we bless Thy name for all Thy servants who have kept the faith and finished their course and are at rest with Thee. Help us to abide in their fellowship that we with them may receive the blessings of Thy Spirit and the strength of Thy presence. And now as our Saviour Christ:

(The Lord's Prayer)

February 9, 1975

Great God, we come to thank You for this time together, but also for this time when we can bare our souls and seek Your Spirit, for many of us come here today in great pain—maybe not physical, but personal, emotional, spiritual pain. Something seems to separate us from our source, and we feel cut off, alone, disturbed. Somehow this feeling builds massive defenses in us, and we have become brittle, bitter and without the hope of those who are rescued by Your Spirit.

Help us to get out of this kind of thinking, doing and being, O God. Enable us to look to You for the compulsions and commitments which will put our lives together instead of tear them apart.

Forgive us for our self-preoccupation, O Father. As Your Spirit touches our Spirits, may we find our real self as we submit to Your way and Your love. Even as You entered our life in Christ, reach down from the suffering and agony of the cross and touch us in our own struggle. O Christ who loved us and loves us still, we put ourselves back in Your hands, awaiting the cleansing, restoring, reshaping we need.

Even as we are occupied by our needs, occupy us with the needs of our world. In the midst of its suffering and sorrow, may we be the instruments of healing and help. Relate us to all Your children everywhere, and join us in one Spirit with Your Church in heaven and on earth, that our lives may declare and demonstrate Your power and purpose for us all.

(The Lord's Prayer)

February 23, 1975

Thank You, God, for this day: for its outer dreariness and inner brightness; for its surprises and possibilities; for the way it reflects the varieties within our lives; and for the fact that Your seasons come and go, Your sun rises and sets as always, no matter what we do to clocks or what clouds do to us.

We affirm it all, O God—this life we live in You, and Your Spirit lives in us; this sense of authenticity and identity we hold because You hold us.

Almighty God, You have given us so much more than we deserve, so much more than we remember, so much more than we can measure; and You dignify our days and our lives by requiring us to use these gifts for Your glory:

We give thanks for Your love, even when we grow bitter;

for Your dependability even when we are unstable;
for Your purpose at work in people and in events even
when we are aimless;

For so many blessings, we give thanks:

for the church triumphant and the church militant;
for the hosts of heaven who surround us and the friends
on earth who join us;
for Your church in this area and Your church in the
uttermost parts of the earth;
for Christ our refuge in stress and Christ our strength in
need.

Eternal Spirit, we remember all those in hospitals, all who are sick, all who sorrow, all who are lonely. Visit them with Your Holy Spirit, touch them with Your peace. Bring Your healing and Your help. Especially, we ask for Your blessings on those of our members who grieve and despair; lead them beside the still waters and restore their soul. Bestow upon our nation a Christian compassion and a love for justice and mercy. Direct us in our efforts toward peace. Grant to leaders of our nation and of all nations a new sense of our common humanity. And now, as our Saviour Christ has taught us, we humbly pray together, saying:

O God all-knowing, all loving, and ever present: You know us better than we know ourselves. Give us the strength to put our weaknesses in Your hands. Fix our gaze on You so we may see how foolish we are sometimes and how petty are the things which we turn into mountains and martyrdoms. And having brushed aside the trivial, give us that faith and trust which enables us to draw on Your Spirit. If we have important decisions to make this week, give us insight. If we have upsetting experiences to face, give us calm. If we are haunted by past mistakes and foolish blunders, assure us once more of Your love which forgives. Enable us to be agents of Your love and understanding.

(The Lord's Prayer)

April 20, 1975

Eternal Spirit who came among us to make our life blessed and to open up all the blessings which abound around us: accept our thanks for all the possibilities we have because we have Your Spirit. Cleanse us and refresh us by Your grace, and make the Christ to be that strong companion and solid support on whom we rely and to whom we look for directions.

As He showed mercy and compassion, enable us, as His servants, to do the same. As He found his identity in God His father, enable us to find our identity in Him. As He gave Himself in sacrifice and struggle, enable us to find great meanings and possibilities in the duties and disciplines which demand our response, and which mold and make our integrity and being. As He gave Himself for us and took upon Himself our own sin and alienation, bridging the gap between us and our Source in God, may we in return be able to exclaim with the disciple, "My Lord and my God," and rest ourselves in His power and presence.

Our hearts reach out to this fractured, broken world. We seek ways in which we, both individually and collectively, may minister to the hurt and suffering, the hungry and dying. We confess our failure, O God, as the citizens of 1975, to have been able to inspire and construct a world of joy and peace and love. We confess our need to turn about and to look to You for those motivations and efforts which alone can restore balance and sanity to our world. Bless the sick, the sorrowing, those with special needs.

We give thanks for all Your servants who have fought a good fight, kept the faith and finished the course. Help us to abide in their fellowship and, at the last, to be joined with them in Your eternal kingdom.

(The Lord's Prayer)

April 27, 1975

O God, how great Thou art! Our minds like to create You in our own image, tailor You to our size. But how great Thou art! Towering over us, seizing us, shaping us, shaking us—simply not letting us sink to the animal level of impulse and notion. How great Thou art! Putting Yourself in Christ, coming among us and becoming our advocate, leading us from our sin and smallness, our despair and depression, right into the cool breezes and broad vistas of Your Spirit! Seizing us, shaping us, loving us! How great Thou art!

Accept our gratitude even when we don't know how to pray. But even more, accept our awe and wonder at the dimensions of life which we have missed. Forgive us for being so self-centered, so possessed with our worlds. Thrust us into Your world. Hear our wistful, questful, plaintive cry, O Father. Take us, use us, reshape us. We ask not for mighty special favors. We do ask to be Your servants, Your channels, Your instruments. We do ask to be whatever You want us to be—and to be happy and content in being that. Show us how to suffer, how to endure hardship, how to live for more than ourselves, how to represent the good and the true.

Bless our land, that we may reclaim our trust in Thee. Bless those who mourn, who struggle, who need help. Once more, visit us and give life great goals, O God. Accept our love. Hear our prayer:

(The Lord's Prayer)

September 28, 1975

Great God of the eternities, Lord of all time and of our time: in spiritual company with all Your children, we bow before You in praise, offering our deep thanks for the wonder of life and the possibilities of fresh beginnings. Your ways are past finding out, O God, but You have found us in Christ and called us home to the company of all Your children on earth and in heaven. For such a fellowship, and for the warm, embracing earthly expression of it here in Your church, we give thanks.

And now, O Father, filled with the joy of life in the Spirit, we bring before You our petitions:

For our nation: Give clarity to us and integrity to our government. Support our leaders with Your laws and Your love, that in seeking Your will and way, we may be spared the ravages of human cleverness and cunning, and may draw from Your endless resources. Give us great visions of a world where Your way is our way, so we may dream once more, and hope and work and pray.

We pray for our church: not only here in Bryn Mawr but your Church everywhere. Save it from narrow, divisive directions, that it may be the channel through which Your Spirit cleanses and heals. Bless the ambassadors of the cross in all lands and cultures—and especially here in our land, that the Church may be a light and a way.

We pray for those with special needs: especially those who today are feeling the ravages of storms. Even as we are constantly reminded that we are mortal and life on this earth is not permanent, so help us to help one another; and when all help is done, help us, O God, and be to those who today are destitute a source of courage and strength and hope.

We pray for all families and all persons, particularly within the reach of this church. Where there has been death, may the joy of life and light eternal shine. Where there is sickness, may the presence of the Spirit bring new life. Even as our hearts reach out, may Your Spirit reach out in compassion and companionship, in strength and in new life. Bless those who are sorrowing and strengthen those who are suffering so that the healing powers of Your Spirit may pervade all of us. Where there are troubles and hard decisions, may Your love be so encompassing and so compassionate as to enable us to overcome. Where there are families and children, students and leaders, may Your grace and joy, Your peace and purpose pervade all of us.

Now, as our Saviour Christ has taught us, we humbly pray together (The Lord's Prayer)

January 18, 1976

Dear Lord and Father of Mankind, whose Spirit joins with our Spirit as we wait for the still, small voice: in the midst of the thunder and tumult of our lives, enable us to wait and watch for Your still voice. In the midst of our own preoccupations with ourselves, may we be aware of Your presence and power. And then, O Lord, may we know how to say "Thank You" for our life, for its associations and possibilities, and for the way You enter into our failures and move us beyond them.

Hear our prayers for others, O Lord. Give us some clear guidelines, along with an abundance of Your Spirit, to discern these times. May we affirm our world, O God, without becoming enslaved to its fads and fancies. May we embrace our lives with their drives, without becoming victims of life that is neither disciplined nor directed.

In the midst of today's confusion, bring insight and raise leaders sufficient for the day. May our land, so richly blessed, seize hold of its opportunities and find how to share them and develop them with all Your children. May our world, so caught up in faction and fear, find new paths to righteousness and peace. Spare us the hatred and name calling that so readily enters into times like these. We pray for Your church everywhere—beginning here with us, reaching into our city and nation, and across the seas. May Your messengers bring the good tidings that help and heal and save us from ourselves. Especially, we pray for the missionaries of our church and for their ministries, that all of us may be channels of Your Spirit, bringing Christ's love and salvation to all. In Christ's name we ask for these mercies:

(The Lord's Prayer)

March 28, 1976
9:30 AM service

Great God our Father: how much better You know us than we know ourselves! With what delicacy You refurbish the earth in springtime, and with what sensitivity You fashion our spirits to seek their source in Your presence! For this gift of life and this seasonal renewal; for this time of Lent and its deepening disciplines; for the mirror of Your word held up to the image of our lives, we give You thanks.

As we live the experiences of those first disciples, we pray that we may live with You, O Lord. As we perceive our lives in their circumstances, we pray that You will enter into our lives and make us very aware of Your presence. Amid so many tangible, material things, may we not lose contact with the spiritual spark that lights our lives by Your Holy Spirit.

Today we pray especially for all young people—our ninth-graders who have returned from their retreat, all youth who seek to find direction, all college youth who now set the shape of their days to come, and in particular, the members of the Hope College choir who lead us in worship today. Nor would we be less mindful, O Lord, of those whose age has dimmed their days, or those whose health has slowed their pace. Be pleased to be with them, that they may know You are the Lord for all seasons.

In this world of so many misplaced enthusiasms, we pray for the people of Your Church, here in our midst and in our land and on across the seas. Unite us one in Spirit as those who drink from Your fountains. Feed us with Your spiritual food, that everywhere, among all people, Your church may proclaim our Lord and witness to His power to help and to heal. Hear us as we pray the prayer He taught us.

O Lord God, the light of the faithful: we give thanks for those who have faithfully lived and died. Grant us, with them, to abide in Your fellowship and to affirm this faith which overcomes the world. Send us forth with Your light and life, and ever uphold us with Your love, through Christ our Lord who taught us (The Lord's Prayer)

March 28, 1976
11:00 AM service

Eternal God who brings us the brightness of a new day and the recurring spring freshness out of winter's drabness: pour on us now Your Spirit to restore our souls and revive our spirits. For this awareness of Your nearness and this assurance of Your faithfulness, we give thanks, O God. As we gather here in Your house, surrounded by the communion of saints of all times and places, all ages and races, accept our gratitude for Your love.

Even as You ministered to the first disciples and made them servants of Your purpose, so enter into our lives, that in our sense of discipleship and service, we may find the fulfilment and the satisfaction for which our spirits crave. In our time of trial and testing, fortify us with Your Spirit and power, that we may not only endure but also overcome and achieve.

Our prayers reach out to Your people everywhere, O God—to the youth in our service today, and to all youth who with their leaders and guides seek to find the life that fulfills. Bless the servants of Your church in this strange new culture and in every culture around the globe. Unify our motives by Your Spirit. We pray for our president, our leaders, our government and its people, that we may rise to the hopes and promises You have given us. Minister to those in need, those who suffer loss, those who cry for help. May they experience the presence of the Good Shepherd who leads them beside the still waters.

O Lord God, the light of the faithful: we give thanks for those who have faithfully lived and died. Grant us, with them, to abide in Your fellowship and to affirm this faith which overcomes the world. Send us forth with Your light and life, and ever uphold us with Your love, through Christ our Lord who taught us (The Lord's Prayer)

May 9, 1976

Great and loving Father, with joy we come into Your house and join our family because we are Your family. With thanks we offer our prayers because Your love is so constant and Your help is so real. With hope we blend our spirits with all the hosts of heaven, mindful that we are indeed a spiritual company, a household of faith.

O Lord Christ, who cares for us beyond our comprehension and knows us better than we know ourselves: come into our midst with Your healing Spirit. Make us into Your disciples who finds the wholeness and help we need, because we are receptive to Your Spirit. Direct us in areas of responsibility where our living may make a difference in this world.

You have made us one family, O God. We pray for those so less fortunate than we, and pray that we may use our resources, our compassion and capacities to lift their lives. O God who has placed us in a world of cause and effect, and natural forces and mortal limitations, we pray for those ravaged by earthquakes in northeast Italy, and for all who daily feel the hardships and hazards of this earthly life.[6]

We pray for our nation, that we may be one nation under God, who can join hands together because we live under Your sovereignty. We pray for Your family the Church, that it may minister to the needs of Your children both here and through our missionaries who enable us to share the faith around the globe. We pray for our own families, that we may be united to one another in the faith, hope and love that flow from Your Spirit in Christ.

(The Lord's Prayer)

---

[6]   Dr. Watermulder references the earthquake in Friuli, Italy, of May 6, 1976

June 13, 1976

Eternal Father, who knows us so much better than we know ourselves: we give thanks today for the simple fact that You do know us, that You put up with us, that You restore and redeem us and remake us. We give thanks also that You have equipped us for this earthly trip and added splashes of delight as well as probing depths along the way.

Today, O God, we give thanks for Your church, for the way She has become the mother of us all, carrying us in her womb, nursing us into this world, instructing and equipping us for our tasks, loving us when we have been lost, restoring us when we have gone bad. We also give thanks for the varieties in your Church, O God—for babies and old people, for eager children and passive adults, for anxious, alert persons and quiet, resigned persons. Today we give thanks for our students—for students of all ages in schools, in colleges and graduate schools. We also give thanks, O God, for those of our number who have gone to seminary and graduated and are now serving in churches throughout this land, for the five students who are in seminary now, for those who are planning to enter after their years in college and other experience.

We pray Your blessings upon all these people, O God, and upon all of us—that each of us may minister to the other and each may receive your ministries and blessings. So we pray, O God, that You will hear our prayer. We will give the prayer not only for ourselves but for our whole church family, here in our own membership with its own particular needs, beyond these walls to Your family around us, Your family across this world, Your family eternal in the heavens. Unite us with them all. Supply us with that grace and strength sufficient for every need. These mercies we pray through Christ, who taught us to pray together, saying (The Lord's Prayer)

June 20, 1976

Eternal God our Father: we gather in Your house on Your day as Your children, praying that we may recognize the blessings we have and give You thanks. We are aware, O Lord, that the more we have, the less we appreciate, so somehow help us to stop and remember whose we are—from whom we come and to whom we return. Then let gratitude for life—with its goodness and toughness, its difficulties and decisions, its hardships and its joys—in all these areas be reflected in the way we live it. With the apostle may we say, whether we live or die, we are the Lord's. Praise be the Lord.

As your understanding is so broad and your forgiveness so deep, so may our relationships reflect your compassion. We pray for guidelines, for goals, for disciplines and directions. We pray that we may be Your children and the instruments of Your purpose. We pray for those of our number who are ill or defeated, those who can't grasp the goodness of life in the Spirit, those hounded by frustration, those in deep need, those who are overwhelmed, those stepping out on new adventures. Hear and heal, help and lead, O Father.

As we approach our nation's birthday, we pray for our land. Make us worthy of our heritage and equal to our opportunities. May Your Church reflect the power of Your Spirit, and may Your church in all lands and among all peoples proclaim the saving and reconciling love of Christ.

Our prayers reach out to the people of Lebanon, whether they be Americans or Lebanese, or of any other land. In these days, when Christians, Moslems, Jews, Protestants and Catholics are used as a ploy by political powers, enable the forces of righteousness to break through such manipulations, that people may live together and work out their differences in peace.

Unite us as one body with all Your people in heaven and throughout the earth, O Father of us all. And now, as our Saviour Christ has taught us, we humbly pray together, saying (The Lord's Prayer)

October 24, 1976

From far-off fields, we come back home, O Father, so much needing to know that You are looking for us, waiting for us, welcoming us back.

With inexpressible joy we thank You for life; for being at home in Your presence and feeling the embrace of Your forgiveness, Your understanding and Your infinite patience.

With awe and wonder, we put ourselves in the hands of Christ, thankful that He has borne our griefs and carried our sorrows, and that in Him we find the help and strength which we alone do not possess.

Hear our prayers of thanks, O God, and now that we are back home in Your house, enter into our lives and tear down all those partitions we have built which block out Your Spirit and separate us from the free-flowing breath of Your Spirit. You know how much hostility resides in us—towards loved ones, towards associates, towards those who crowd us out, towards Democrats, towards Republicans, towards minorities and majorities, towards change. Great God, our hostilities have no end, but mostly are they subtly directed to the dissatisfactions within our lives. Come into these situations so that new room can be made for fresh beginnings, where Your Spirit may prevail.

May Your blessings be with those who have deep troubles, more obvious than our own. May Your Spirit guide those who quake in the midst of their physical, emotional and spiritual inadequacies and are unable to come to terms with problems that face them. May Your healing touch be upon those who suffer, who sorrow, who mourn; and may the grace of our Lord Jesus Christ, which loosens the burden and lightens the load, come to those for whom we pray who need so much to let go and let God take hold.

Bless our nation in this final week before another election. Unite us as a people with purpose and vision. Give Your Spirit to all who minister in Your name in all parts of the earth, and hasten that time, O God, when our openness toward one another will allow Your springs of new life to flow among us all. These prayers we pray through Christ who taught us to pray (The Lord's Prayer)

January 30, 1977

Indeed, this is the day which the Lord has made; we will rejoice and be glad in it. Indeed, this is the life the Lord has given us; we will rejoice and be glad in it. And this is the grace, love and peace which the Lord has provided; we will accept it, live in it, rejoice in it.

Great God our Father: accept our gratitude for being alive, for being able to struggle, sacrifice and serve; for having concerns greater than ourselves to increase the scope of our lives and for having resources in Jesus Christ, which are more than we are, to enable us to contend, to overcome, to embrace this day, this life, this situation.

With our thanks, we also lift our prayers for help, O Father. As the natural forces of this universe proclaim their power, may the human forces in our lives assert their compassion. In this time of statewide and regional emergency, bring out of all of us those good graces of sensitive concern and active compassion, so that we may be able to help one another. We pray for those whose jobs have been displaced by the fuel shortage; those whose anxieties have multiplied; those whose hardships are bearing down. In all these situations, may Your peace, which passes understanding, guard their lives; and may our care and concern for one another alleviate the hardship and provide the help. You have given us minds to know You, hearts to love You, and hands to serve You: in these times, may our minds, hearts and hands express Your Spirit.

Grant also Your blessing to our president, our leaders and our congress. Give to our nation high and hopeful goals. Be with Your church everywhere, Your missionaries and ambassadors who declare Your love in Christ. And may the sorrowing, the sick and suffering turn to You and find the powers of Your Spirit turning to them to uphold them, that they may know that underneath are the everlasting arms, and in those arms, find their stability and strength. This we pray (The Lord's Prayer)

February 25, 1977

Eternal God, You have set the planets in orbit and devised the laws by which we explore the stars and chart our paths; You speak mightily in the marvels of this world which we have just begun to discover; You speak eloquently in the beauty of nature and the changing seasons; You speak plaintively in the quiet desperations and agonies, the frustrations and satisfactions, of the human heart; You speak tenderly and conclusively in Jesus Christ, Yourself in our condition, our place, our world; You pronounce judgment as we behold the cross, and pour out unspeakable love in the risen Christ who calls us to follow.

For all these ways in which You have opened our eyes and melted the cold logic of our hearts, we give thanks. For our brotherhood in Christ, making us feel at home as Your family who share a common discipleship; for the yoke of Christ who Himself served and suffered and sacrificed, and who enters into our world as we live in Him—for so many blessings, we give thanks.

Grant, O God of mercy and might, that we may lose our vague relation to You, and see You with clearer vision. Like a people who have just come upon the solution to problems they have been trying to solve, come upon us in such a way that we see you in focus. Cast us down that we may cast down all false gods whom we worship; and raise us in Christ that we may be new people, looking at life through new eyes.

Bless those of our number who are ill; those who come to You with special problems; those whose responsibilities and decisions are bearing down on them. May they know that "the eternal God is Thy refuge, and underneath are the everlasting arms." Bless our nation, that we may declare and demonstrate what it is to be Christian. Grant Your blessing upon the Church wherever it manifests itself under the sway of Your Spirit. Overrule our mistakes, O God, and rule over us in judgment and mercy.

In this Your house we are mindful of the communion of saints who surround us. With them, may we abide in Your fellowship; and linked to them in spirit, enable us to run with joy and patience the race that is set before us, looking to Christ our Lord who taught us to pray saying (The Lord's Prayer)

March 20, 1977

Dear Lord and Father of mankind, forgive our foolish ways,
reclothe us in our rightful mind, in purer love Thy service find,
in deeper reverence, praise.

For we do come before You in reverence and filled with praise for Your goodness, O God. We do come, aware that Your blessings abound all around us and that we avail ourselves of so few. We do come, conscious of our own jittery nervousness, our own indecision, our own needs—and very aware that You can

Drop Your still dew of quietness, till all our strivings cease;
Take from our souls the strain and stress,
and let our ordered lives confess
The beauty of Thy peace.

May this be an hour where we direct our spirits to You and praise and wonder, O God! May it be an hour when we open ourselves to Your power and allow Your Spirit to cleanse, correct and direct our spirits. May this be a time of openness before You, where every Thought and action is prayer beamed to You.

Not only for ourselves do we pray, O Lord. We bring before You those of our number who have special trials or opportunities. Those feeling the impermanence of this life through sickness of the body; those glimpsing the uncertainty of life through unexpected difficulty or decision; those who have shared with You in the miracle of life itself through the birth of new life. Those who find life dreary and drab and are discontented because they know You did not mean it to be that way.

For all of us, in our many needs, we pray, O Lord. So too do we pray for our loved ones close in spirit, far away in body. Unite us at the throne of prayer. We pray for our congress, our president, and all those in authority, that we may ever judge ourselves by Your standards and heed Your authority over all men and matters. We pray for the church everywhere, that it may be a true witness. In particular, we pray for the seething continent of Africa and for all people there, especially Your servants. In the midst of our inhumanity to man, may Your Spirit shine.

Direct us, O Lord, in all our doings, with Your most gracious favor; and further us with Your continued help, that in all of our works begun, continued, and ended in You, we may glorify Your holy name, and finally, by Your mercy, obtain everlasting life, through Jesus Christ our Lord, who taught us to pray (The Lord's Prayer)

May 4, 1977

Everlasting Father, whose love is gentle in its firmness and tender in its strength, we approach Your presence with awe and joy: for Your sure counsel amid the babel of voices around us; for Your companionship in the loneliness of our thoughts; for your breath within us. How can we convey our thanks for all the expressions of Your love and the buoyancy of life in Your hands; the boldness of new adventure; the promise of Your power that is ready to match our problem; the beauty of friendship with its demands; the spiritual disciplines which harness our confusion; the Christian opportunities which challenge our unused talents—yes, even the patience which tries our souls and tempers our spirits.

O God, whose infinite majesty looks on us from the heavens, but whose grace and truth shine in the face of Jesus Christ, enable us to trust You with His trust, to love You with His love, to feel Your power as He felt it. Cause us to hold fast that which is good and spare us from getting stuck in the ruts of pride, petulance and prejudice. Make our faith big enough to take in the whole world, and to envelop our whole personality as well.

O God of peace, who has taught us that in returning and rest, we shall be saved; in quietness and confidence shall be our strength, We extend our prayers to those not with us: the sick of our number in the hospitals and homes; the lonely and the afraid; the old that they may reach to the future, and the young that they may build on the past; the missionaries of our church in the trouble spots of the world, both in our city and the uttermost parts of the earth; the despairing and homeless—the victims of our modern, advanced civilization.

With reverence and affection, we remember all friends and kindred who have passed within the veil which now separates us. Keep us in union with them here, through faith and love, that hereafter we may enter into Your blessed presence, and be numbered with those who behold your face in light everlasting, through Jesus Christ our Lord, who taught us to pray (The Lord's Prayer)

May 29, 1977

O God, our concerns seem so big to us, but they must be small to You. Our needs seem so overwhelming to us, but to You they must appear trivial as You survey the whole scheme of things.

Yet, O God of the eternities and Lord of life, you have made our concerns and needs to be Your own. You came among us as a man of sorrow and acquainted with grief. You took on Yourself all the assaults of this earthly life and overcame it all.

This is really too much for us to grasp, O God, except for the overarching fact that You care and You love and You give and guide. For such love, for such concern, for such assurance, we give thanks. Accept our thanks!

Accept also, O Lord, our hesitation and confusion. We know we should let go and let God; we know we should affirm the fact that the Lord is our Shepherd and we shall not want. Yet we do want and we do negate Your shepherding guidance. Forgive us, but more than that, enable us to put this business of living and dying, of hopes and fears, of plan and purpose in Your hands.

In this spirit, we pray for those of our number who are in need, who go through the valley of the shadow of death. With this spirit we pray for our families and our youth, our persons with individual needs and our elderly who feel the pangs of this mortal life's limitations. With this spirit we pray for Your church everywhere, at home and abroad, as Your people bear witness to Your transforming and redeeming power, and as people who walk in darkness begin to see a great light.

Be with our nation, O God, that we may not settle for the easy way out, that we may reach out in compassion, identifying with those at home and abroad who seek their own freedom and opportunity. On this Memorial weekend, we give thanks for our heritage and for those who gave their lives. May we as persons and as a people become worthy of the ideals for which they died.

O Lord of all worlds, before whom stand the spirits of the living and the dead: We bless Your holy name for all Your servants who have witnessed in their lives a good confession, for all those who faithfully lived and peacefully died. Take now the veil from every heart and unite us in one communion with all Your servants on earth and Your saints in heaven. To Christ may we ascribe all glory, honor and praise. Now, as He taught us, we humbly pray (The Lord's Prayer)

138 | Paul Watermulder

Almighty God, from whose riches we have all received grace upon grace: in this Your house with Your people we turn to You to offer our thanks. How wisely You have led us, even when those forces which cancel out the Spirit have impeded Your love. How greatly You have shown us what is good and true and right, even when our culture has blotted it out like a dark cloud covers the sun. In Your majesty, we bow before You in humility, recognizing that to You a day is as a thousand years or a thousand years is as a day, and yet You care for us, yearn for us and love us as Your children. Accept our thanks, O God, and enable us to live by the grace of our Lord Jesus Christ.

Eternal God, You know us better than we know ourselves. Therefore, we come to You seeking perspective and purpose. Sort out those things that have mixed us up, and show us the path of patience, understanding, forgiveness and faith.

Especially do we pray, O Father, for those who are burdened with anxiety. May they know the truth of the words, "Cast your burden on the Lord and he will sustain you." Our prayers reach out to the sick, the suffering, the dying: may they know that "the Eternal God is their refuge and underneath are the everlasting arms." Our prayers encompass all humanity, of which we are a part. May we identify with the struggles and longings, the hopes and dreams of those whose time and place in this world has brought their difficulty, until we know the satisfaction of our Lord's words that "unto whom much is given, much is expected." Bless Your Church as it proclaims Your truth. May it be an agent of reconciliation and new hope. Bless our nation as we seek to recapture our purpose. Bind us together as children of God who seek to serve, even as our Lord who taught us to pray (The Lord's Prayer)

November 12, 1977

O Lord God Almighty, who has freed our lives from their entanglements so that our spirits may flow fresh and free once more: while we give thanks for our creation, we especially give thanks for our recreation into children of God, receiving Your power, accepting Your grace, and made to be ambassadors of reconciliation toward one another. For life which has its renewal, for friends who can forgive, for opportunities to relate ourselves to You in prayer and purpose, we thank Thee, O God.

Eternal and everlasting Father: your love still startles us when we are caught short and see how cheaply we bottle it up and package it under our own trademark. Forgive us our self-righteousness, and make us human once more. And in touching base with all humanity, may we discover something of the divine, even as You, in Christ, stepped into the depths of our lives and showed us the glory of being human because Your presence is with us.

So badly we need discipline and direction! In these Sunday hours of worship, come to us so clearly that we can level with ourselves and with You, and then give ourselves in meditation, worship, and specific witness. Open our eyes that we may replace self-serving with service to those in need, and enable us to seize the blessings which surround us.

In the midst of our blessings, we seek the blessing of Your mercy, O God. Where life has been self-directed, and therefore self-defeating, turn it around. Where we have resented the problems of our day as intrusions on our privacy, enlarge our world until we may embrace those who have not had our blessings. Where we have become tight and tense, loosen us until Your Spirit can reshape our spirits. Where we have had the impression that we must carry all the problems of our life and world, remind us that not we, but You are God. Help us to do our best and leave You the rest. Chide our sophistications until we are simple enough to be real. Make us like children—receptive, eager, ready to trust Thee as our Father. Make us Your disciples.

For those in need, we pray. For the sick and the suffering, we ask for Your healing and Your help. For the distressed and the bereaving, we ask for Your comfort. For those separated from us, especially where they need guidance, be their refuge and strength. For those with hard decisions before them, we ask for Your presence to give clarity and direction. Be with our nation, our president, the leaders of our land, that they may rule with deeds of compassion and mercy, until all people may partake of Your goodness.

And now, as our Saviour Christ has taught us (The Lord's Prayer)

November 20, 1977

O God, great God who is both the Source and the Force for our life: we come to You because You have promised to give us what we ask in Your name.

Make our askings, then, in accordance with Your will. Test them by the suffering, supportive love of Christ our Lord. Verify our prayers because we ask them in Jesus's name, and He is our Advocate who pleads our cause and cares for us.

Since this is the case, how can we be anything but thankful, O God? Our hearts spill over with joy, that we may assemble in Your house and await Your Spirit to fall upon us. Our lives shout forth praise that You take us out of our humdrum existence and assure us that You care for us and give our lives shape and substance.

As we give thanks for Christ our Lord and Saviour, we also give You our prayers, asking for Your help. You know where we need it—sometimes when we don't even know. Open our eyes that we may see, our ears that we may hear the many ways You can come to us in our searching or hurting, our groping and our growing. Be with our loved ones who suffer and need You, with those who mourn and sorrow.

We pray for Your people everywhere, particularly for the servants of Your church among all people in all places. Especially today, we pray for the peace of the world. In particular, we center our gaze once more on that holy land which bears our spiritual heritage, that there, even in the Holy City, once more Your voice may penetrate and Your Spirit may heal. Even as we are bound to that land through our past, how much our present and future hopes depend upon it, O God! Strengthen the hands of Your people; may Your blessings be with such leaders as Anwar Sadat[7] and Menachim Begin, and all that they represent—that initiatives for trust and peace, for understanding and goodwill may burst forth again to brighten all the earth.[8]

And now, as Christ has taught us, we pray together (The Lord's Prayer)

---

[7] The first Arab leader to ever visit the Jewish state

[8] Dr. Watermulder references the Egyptian president's trip to Israel on November 19.

January 22, 1978

Lord God of all creation, how good it is to come unto Your house on Your day! How great it is to affirm that You are Lord of the seasons, of the winter's icy blast, the springtime's gentle hope, the summer's bounteous bloom and the autumn's wondrous harvest. How good it is to reclaim our identity as we gather here to affirm life and to affirm our time together as Your children. Accept our thanks, O God, and accept our special gratitude for the grace of our Lord Jesus Christ that reaches out to us in forgiveness, newness of life, and hope for life eternal.

With our thanks, we offer our supplications, O God, and especially for those of our number who are ill, that Your healing power and peace may prevail in their lives; for those who struggle with hardship or great decision, that Your Spirit may guide their spirits; for those whose success has turned into idols and whose ambitions have twisted them into demons, that the perspective of Your purpose may prevail once more; for those who have great goals, high ideals, lofty dreams, that the facts of this world may not turn them into cynics but may increase their reliance on You from whom comes faith, hope and love.

We pray for all families and all peoples, O God, and especially for Prime Minister Begin and President Sadat as they reach out for peace and reconciliation. Be with our congress as it reconvenes and our nation as it contends with the deceptions and allurements of this age which finds its norms in public relations, that we may seek for that which is true and honorable and right and enduring. Give us integrity as persons and integrity as a nation, O God who knows us better than we know ourselves.

O Lord God, before whose face stand the living and the dead, we give thanks for all who have faithfully lived and nobly died, particularly our former Associate Pastor, Harold Smith. Grant that all of us may be united in the bonds of the Spirit with all of Your children on earth and in heaven, and, at the last, be gathered together in Your eternal kingdom.

Now as our Saviour Christ has taught us, we humbly pray together (The Lord's Prayer)

February 9, 1978

Great God, You are ready to baptize us with Your Holy Spirit, and we won't give You a chance. You are ready to open life to new beginnings, new joys, new happenings; and we won't let You get in edgewise. You want to give us so much and to get us to open ourselves to You, but we are so preoccupied with ourselves and so dependent upon ourselves that we don't give You a chance. Sometimes we think You are a foolish notion of odd people, and so we put ourselves on our little thrones, bowing to ourselves, and wondering why everyone else doesn't see God in us.

And here today we gather with the rest of Your children, realizing that we are actually as human as they are, and recognizing that a Christian community is where people care and share, offering love and support to each other. Here we are praising You with hymns which simply pour ourselves out to You; here we are listening to the word You have for us in Your word, the inspiration and moment that might break through these heavy, protective shells which surround us.

God, we thank You that we are here! We thank You that we are made aware of Spiritual reality. We thank You for worship—for hymns and prayers, for Your word and Your way. We simply thank You for life right now and right here. Thank You, God.

Now open our eyes and ears to spiritual reality. Bless us in those situations we face with family and friends, with work and responsibility. When we've done our best, give us the sense to leave with You the rest. Help us attempt great things for God only after we expect great things from God.

May such blessings come to others: those in need, those in grief. Those suffering, those sick, those in trouble. Those wrapped up in themselves, those who know no god besides themselves. Good God, give us all a taste of grace, where we get from You what we need.

We pray for our nation and our world. Rally us as a people of peace, unite us with other nations large and small in every deliberate effort to bring joy and fulfillment and opportunity to all. Make this land once more an inspiration to all lands—of that place where freedom and hope and opportunity abound among peace—loving people; and cause us to be a people who ever turn to You and mold our justice and mercy by Christ our Lord who taught us to pray (The Lord's Prayer)

February 26, 1978

Eternal God who speaks through the earthquake, wind and fire, but who is nearest to us in the still, small voice of calm: in the hush of this hour, we pause to praise the Lord of our life and to contemplate who we are and to whom we belong. As we hold the heavens, the moon and the stars, what is man that Thou art mindful of him? As we realize how complicated even the simple things of life have become, we wonder if we can ever reach the realms of Spirit and essence.

And so, O Father, in this hour we heave a mighty sigh of relief, coupled with an immense expression of thanks, for here we know once more that You hear and heed and help. And because You hear us, we can see once more who we are and what it is we should be about.

For this we give thanks, O Lord: for the light streaming from the face of Jesus Christ. For the new life in us because we are captured by him. For our membership in one another as parts of His body, the church. For this sense of identity, this reconciliation with yesterday, this capacity for today and this hope for tomorrow—for all this which comes from these boundless spiritual sources, we give thanks.

Accept our thanks as an acknowledgment of our need also, O God. May our ways not be so set or inflexible as to make it impossible for the newness of Your Spirit to break through. The cynicism that prevents Your Spirit from going to work. In Your presence, make us glad and free, excited to have our perception replaced with Your insight.

Bless those who mourn; support the weak; watch over those in need in body, mind or spirit; and grant to our nation a new sense of purpose, a new eagerness to seek the common good, that our government may share with all the people a commitment to do justly, to love mercy and to walk humbly with our God. These prayers we offer through Christ who taught us (The Lord's Prayer)

April 9, 1978

Great God and Father of us all: the heavens declare Your glory, and the firmament shows Your handiwork! As we gather in worship, we are mindful of these many ways You speak to us, but chiefly we thank You for the gift of Your Spirit which comes through Christ our Lord. How great and good You are, O God! Accept our praise and thanks, and forgive our grumbling and despair. Put us back in Your hands—there to be refreshed, renewed, restored.

Today we pray for Your Church. May we be aware of our fellowship with Your people everywhere around the world, and may we be caught up in the communion of saints, eternal in the heavens. May we draw from Your Spirit and be tempered by Your power, that we may be found faithful as Your disciples, in spite of all our shortcomings which You know so well.

We pray for our world, O God. May we have clear visions of our purpose and place in life. May our land unite around common goals of respect and concern for one another, and may our world find those ways which make for peace. May your Church in this land and around the world truly be the instrument of Your Spirit.

To those who bear loads too heavy, be the helper; to those who mourn their loss, be the companion; to those who face decisions, be the guide; to those who are weak, be their strength; and to all of us bring the grace which picks us up and puts us in Your hands.

O God, who has ordered this wondrous world and who knows all things on earth and in heaven: so fill our hearts with trust, that by night and by day, at all times and in all seasons, we may without fear commit ourselves and those who are dear to us to Your never-failing love for this life and the life to come, through Jesus Christ:

(The Lord's Prayer)

April 23, 1978

O God, Your Spirit breathes into our spirits
Your life enters into ours
You give Yourself to us in Christ
That we might give ourselves back to You.

You crown the earth with goodness and bring freshness of life out of drab dullness. Accept our praise for the greatness and goodness of Your presence which is everywhere around us. As we behold season follow season, we give thanks for constancy and certainty, for the warmth of your love which brings new hope and life; for our pilgrimage from winter's bleakness into spring's new hope, and for our conviction that "God is our refuge <u>and</u> strength, a very present help."

God, I need Thee—
When morning crowds the night away
And tasks of waking seize my mind;
I need Thy poise.

God, I need Thee—
When love is hard to see
Amid the ugliness and slime;
I need Thy eyes.

God, I need Thee—
When the path to take
before me lies
I see it…courage flees…
I need Thy Faith.

God, I need Thee—
When clashes come with those
Who walk the way with me
I need Thy smile.

God, I need Thee—
When the day's work is
done
Tired, discouraged,
wasted;
I need Thy rest.

(Howard Thurman, *Meditations of the Heart* [1953])

We pray today for those of our family who are sick and suffering, those for whom this earthly life remains but a thin thread; those whose physical bodies have proved inadequate for their spirits; those who are in hospitals, nursing homes. And those, O Lord, who minister unto them—not only doctors, nurses, helpers, but also their loved ones. O Lord, be merciful and gracious unto them.

(The Lord's Prayer)

April 30, 1978

Almighty and everlasting Father, "our hearts are restless until they rest in Thee." We give thanks for the many evidences of Your loving kindness and constant concern. For the certainty we have that underneath are the everlasting arms to uphold us; for the hope and trust which penetrate the confusion of our lives and the chaos of our world; for the way, the truth and the life which we find in Christ; for the forgiveness and acceptance which surround our lives so that we may live with ourselves because You live with us; for the assurance of things hoped for and evidence of things not seen—for so many mercies, we give thanks.

Merciful Father, You have made us to learn, and love, and laugh, and live together. Open our eyes, that we may see where selfish concentration on ourselves, or blind obedience to outmoded prejudice, have hampered Your work within us. Enable us to face each day in the knowledge that You do not expect the impossible but You are ready to give faith, which may bring joy and conviction and purpose to life. Spare us from mere existence, lest we become the pawn of opinions and possessions. Enable us to experience the reality of the kingdom of God, doing our best and leaving to God the rest.

We commend unto Your care and keeping those who are sick, especially those near and dear to us and to this church, those who are despondent; those who are in hospitals and those who suffer; those who are facing difficulties which even they do not like to admit; those for whom life has appeared nigh impossible. May they be able to see beyond the present plight and hold fast to Your Spirit, thus receiving the patience, strength and calm until the day breaks and the shadows flee away.

O God of peace, we pray for peace and ask for ways we may help to bring it about. Give us the determination to build up rather than tear down; to offer hope at home and abroad rather than despair. Make us conscious of Your concern for all, that we may love mercy, do justly and walk humbly with our God. May we be aware of that multitude which no one can number who serve in light eternal, and in their fellowship make us glad for memories of the past and duties to fulfill in the present. These mercies we ask not of our worthiness, but through the grace of Our Lord Jesus Christ who taught us to pray together, saying (The Lord's Prayer)

June 18, 1978

Great God our Father: in awesome wonder and humility we come into Your presence, somewhat overwhelmed by the magnitude of this world and of our lives. We give thanks for planting Your Spirit in us; for caring for us and seeking us out; for coming among us in Christ; for the way, even now, He pleads our cause and becomes our companion on the way. Accept our thanks—these simple thanks—for being alive, being here, being able to pray.

We are thankful, also, O God, that you are the Heavenly Father whose love knows no bounds, for many of us need a lot of that love and a lot of Your grace today. We stand before the terrible things that can happen to us in our mortal existence; for the ever-present frailty of our mortal bodies; for the terrible pain and loss which overwhelms us when our mortal bodies are not sufficient to hold our immortal spirits. With all these combinations of feelings you give us, O God, we give back to you our heartbreak, our anxiety, our perplexity.

But most of all, O God of all life, we give You praise that the lives of our loved ones and our lives are in Your hands. Spare us from self-centered self-pity. Strengthen us with Your Spirit. Equip us with Your grace. Unite us with those loved ones who have gone on before us. Give us a firm grip on life, a healthy hold of ourselves, an abiding commitment to our loved ones, a genuine empathy with all our larger family in the church and a compassion for all people who struggle, suffer and overcome. We yield ourselves to you, O God, and in You we find our strength. In this spirit we pray for our church, for our nation, for our world. Lord God of hosts, be with us, forgive us and bless us.

And so, O Lord, support us all the day long, until the shadows lengthen and the evening comes, and the busy world is hushed, and the fever of life is over, and our work is done. Then in Thy mercy grant us a safe lodging, and a holy rest, and peace at the last, through Jesus Christ our Lord.

(The Lord's Prayer)

September 10, 1978

Great God, as we begin a new season, we begin it with praise and thanks to You. As we look out on our old world, we discover it is a new world because we live it with You and You make all things new. So the first thing we want to do in our prayer today is to thank You—thank You for Yourself, Your awesomeness and mystery, Your nearness and intimacy. Thank You for this house of prayer and these people with whom we may pray. Thank You for Your church here and Your church around the world, among all the different kinds of people. Thank You for the cloud of witnesses who surround us in eternity. Thank You for life. Thank You that the story of our lives is the story of living by Your Spirit.

O Lord, You have searched us and known us and understand our clever ways even where we deceive ourselves. So the second thing we want to do in our prayer this morning is put ourselves before You. You have heard our confession and granted us pardon. Now search us out; prod us until we see ourselves as you see us. You know how we hurt; let Your Spirit heal us. You know how we fuss; let Your presence calm us. You know how we grope; let your light illumine us. You know how we fail; let Your love reclaim us. You know how haunted and hounded we sometimes feel; let Your Spirit make us whole once more.

And now, O God of the nations, we pray for the nations. Especially right now, we pray for Carter, Begin and Sadat who meet at Camp David.[9] Meet there with them. Make the impossible possible. Use them as Your instruments. May they be open to receive the peace and wisdom of God in this meeting.

Hear our prayers, also, for all students, all teachers, all persons for whom the fall season marks a new adventure and hope. Unite us all as one with all Your children in light eternal, that we on earth and they in heaven may fill our lives with praise for Your goodness. Now, as our Saviour Christ has taught us (The Lord's Prayer)

---

[9]   Dr. Watermulder references the Peace Talks between Egypt and Israel attended by President Carter, President Sadat and Prime Minister Begin.

September 17, 1978

Great God Almighty, our Source and our Supply, the One from whom all things come: we gather together today in Your church to thank You for this company of people called apart from the rest of the world; these people who are called Your Church. In the special meaning of this holy hour, we thank You for Your church here in Bryn Mawr; your church everywhere in Montgomery County, Philadelphia, Pennsylvania; the United States; and the whole world. Especially, we thank You that, in spite of all our particular preoccupations, we are a part of that church, that company of believers. We thank You that such a fellowship forces us to think in terms larger than ourselves, our kind of people, our particular race or ethnic group, and puts us into a universal mold. Even more than this, we thank You, O God, that we are a part of the Church which is eternal, transcending time and place, and uniting us with the great cloud of witnesses who surround us. Accept our gratitude, O God, and even as You came to Your disciples at that first Pentecost, come to us now, cleanse us, forgive us, restore us, infuse us with Your Holy Spirit.

With our thanks go our prayers for our special needs, O Father. You know how we fail, how we falter, how we collapse before our frustrations. Be the good shepherd who leads us. Place us on the rock that cannot be shaken. May we know that underneath are the everlasting arms.

We also pray for others. For Christians worshipping in all lands, all climates, all places, all countries. Guide, correct and direct them. We pray for President Carter, for the Camp David meetings with Sadat and Begin, and for the peace of the world.[10] Put us at Your disposal. Use us in Your service. Direct us by Your will. Fill us with Your Spirit. Unite us with Your children in light eternal. And now, as Christ has taught us, we humbly pray (The Lord's Prayer)

---

[10] Dr. Watermulder references the Peace Talks.

November 12, 1978

Eternal God our Father, who moves across the face of the earth and who knows no limit of space or time: You are beyond our broadest thoughts and stretch the very limits of our minds. Yet You come to each one of us as a parent comes to their child, and You minister to our need as one who knows our plight.

Thank You, God, for being so great that we can be at ease in Your presence. Thank You for caring about us, one by one, while at the same time You care about us all together. Thank You for taking on Yourself the burden of our failure and frustration, and for giving us new life in the risen Christ. Thank You for Your church—the living, throbbing mystical body of Christ, moving across the face of the earth. Thank you for shattering our small worlds and smug provincialisms, and for casting our lives on the broader stage where we are part of the tug and pull of all humanity and all history. Thank You for our eternal home and for our loved ones who are at peace in Your presence.

In this context, minister to each of us where there is a special need, O Lord. Bring Your healing strength to those who hurt. Bring Your stabilizing grace to those who fall and fail. Bring Your hope and vision to those who dwell in darkness and despair. Bring the light of eternity to those who are caught in time. Bring Your peace, and power, and purpose to all who put their trust in Your eternal presence.

So, O Lord, bless our nation that we may do justly, love mercy and walk humbly with our God. Bless the Church in each land, that it may hear Your voice and proclaim Your truth. And bless all who struggle and suffer and seek to serve, that they may ever know that the eternal God is their refuge and underneath are the everlasting arms.

Now, as our Saviour Christ has taught us, we humbly pray together (The Lord's Prayer)

January 14, 1979

Almighty God, with whom is glory and majesty, dominion and power: You are the God of the living and the dead. In the storms of the winter and the everlasting constancy of the seasons, we behold Your majesty. In our restless craving, we acknowledge Your still, small voice. In gratitude for Your greatness and for the gift of life and work, we turn to You, glad that we may share in the glories of Your universe and appreciate and enjoy the things which are eternal: the struggles, ideals, loyalty to causes, devotion to friends, disciplines. For life, for work, for change, for Thy nearness, we thank You.

O God, You are closer than breathing, nearer than hands or feet. Teach us to put our trust in You. Break down the foolish pride which not only makes us think we must face our troubles alone, but which deceives us into thinking You do not care. As a child forgets fear when with a loving parent, so may we place ourselves wholeheartedly in Your hands. If there is any physical or emotional pain, give us strength to face it. If there is anxiety and doubt, give us the warmth of Your understanding and the full assurance of Your Spirit.

Eternal God, You have ordained Your church to be the agent of Your glory, and have built it upon the foundation of the prophets, Jesus Christ Himself the chief cornerstone: we pray Your blessings upon our endeavors here. Grant to the Youth courage and conviction, a cause in which they may pour their energies, and follow them with Your blessing. Grant to us all a high sense of calling as the people of God, and as such, give us the grace to speak in Your name and be Your reconciling agent.

May Your blessing be upon all who worship here and seek You here. With comfort, give courage, that in losing ourselves in Your cause, we may truly find ourselves and receive Your blessing. Bless those who are ill. You have called us to pray for one another. We pray for the sick, sad, lonely, perplexed. We do not ask for easy days which mock their troubles, but for an awareness of Your presence, a sense of Your Spirit, an assurance that You are their refuge and underneath are the everlasting arms.

O God, our help in ages past, our hope for years to come: be pleased to bless our president, our congress, the cabinet and the leaders of this land. May our Christian heritage be real, and may our awareness of Your will be strong, that You may use us, and cause us to be a blessing. Surround us with the host of witnesses in light eternal, and evermore use us to the glory of Your Kingdom, through Jesus Christ our Lord who taught us (The Lord's Prayer)

January 21, 1979

Great God of the seasons and Lord of the soul: we come into Your presence today to thank You for many things:

for this time together as Your children in Your house;
for this early tie with heaven, linking us in Spirit with those who
    have gone before us;
for this storehouse of Your gifts which we find in Your world and
    in our worship;
for this awareness of something holy, sacred and special in our lives
    which plumbs our depths and lifts us to new levels;
and above all, for the forgiving love which comes in Christ and the
    strengthening grace which helps us to go on.

Now, O God, we come to You with our particular needs. You know what ruts we get into: command us to try Your way of looking at things and doing them.

You know how fear or despair gets hold of us: make us aware of Your Presence, that we may have peace and calm.

You know how we long for that meaning which gives some point to all our effort: supply us with the living water so we thirst no more but find fulfilment in Your presence.

Today we pray for others. In particular, we remember those who grieve and sorrow over the loss of loved ones. Lead them through the valley of the shadow of death as the good Shepherd who restores their souls.

We remember those who face discouragement, and even despair, because things have not turned out right. Come to them with Your steadying strength and enable them to cast their burdens on You and live in Your Spirit.

We pray for all missionaries, all leaders of Your church, in all lands, that Your Word may be proclaimed and You may be worshiped and praised, and goodness may be restored to the living.

We pray for all leaders of government, for our own president and congress, for the people of Iran, for governments everywhere, that hatred may subside and the love of the common good may become supreme.

Hear our prayers, O Lord, and follow them with Your mercy:

(The Lord's Prayer)

January 28, 1979

O Lord God Almighty, who has freed our lives from their entanglements so that our spirits may flow fresh and free once more: while we thank You for our creation, we especially thank You for our recreation into sons of God, receiving Your power, accepting Your grace, and made to be ambassadors of reconciliation toward one another. For life which has its renewal, for friends, for opportunities to relate ourselves to You in prayer, for the sacrificial love poured out for us in Jesus Christ, we thank You, O God.

In the midst of our blessings, we seek the blessings of Your mercy, O God. Where life has been self-directed, and therefore self-defeating, turn it around. Where we have resented the problems of our day as intrusions on our privacy, enlarge our world until we may confront our culture with the compassion of Christ. Where we have become tight and tense, loosen us until Your Spirit reshapes our spirits. Where we have had the impression that we must carry all the problems of our life and world, remind us that not we but You art God.

Today, especially, we pray for Your church everywhere, O Lord. As it takes on new and bold forms, may it become the fresh channel of Your Spirit once more. As it provides us with new vistas, new visions, new creative possibilities, may it be the place Your Holy Spirit may seize us with new life. Particularly, we pray for our church here, where we may give tangible expression to what we believe. As it seeks to extend Your word and will, and as we seek to give expression to the faith through our outreach into the city, we pray for Your blessings that Your church may exalt You; and upon all who (labor) in difficult places in our city, that Your power and presence may be the light and life that illumines and inspires.

For those in need, we pray. For the sick and the suffering, we ask for Your healing and Your help. For the distressed and the bereaving, we ask Your comfort. For those separated from us, especially where they need guidance, be their refuge and strength. For those with hard decisions before them, we ask for Your presence to give clarity and direction. Be with our nation, our president, the leaders of our land, that they may rule with deeds of compassion and mercy, until all people may partake of Your goodness.

And now, as our Saviour Christ hath taught us (The Lord's Prayer)

February 4, 1979

O Lord, our good shepherd who leads us through the difficulties and decisions of life until we dwell in the calm and strength of Your presence: you are lavish with Your gifts of life and love, and You continue to surround us with the possibility of new beginnings and deeper meanings. We are at a loss to know how to thank You for the inexhaustible potentials in life. We thank You that You are in the midst of our troubles and tensions, waiting to give us perspective and direction. We thank You that You have come among us in Christ, who was acquainted with grief, with alienation, rejection. Most of all, we thank You that Christ experienced death for all of us, and that in Christ we have an advocate and friend who brings us victory.

May it not be a shallow, selfish victory, O God; but may it relate to all areas of life where death and decay, disease and destruction add their toll to the angers and hatreds of our times. Redeem these times, O God, and lead us through our valleys and shadows into the broad vistas of a useful, outgoing, giving life.

Enable us to forgive as You forgive; to care as You care; to lose ourselves in You and Your cause and thus to find ourselves. We pray for our nation—our president and congress, that they may lead us, and also for all others who would make this nation an instrument of compassion and justice and help for all. We pray for the larger family of nations, that the fears and suspicions which divide us may break down as we find what it means to be Your children in Your world. We pray for those who bear special pain or suffering or sorrow, that they may find a response as they call on You, and we pray for those separated from us and those needing help, that they may be led by You. Unite us in Your church around the world and eternal in the heavens, and make us somewhat worthy of the trust You have given us in our lifetime.

O Lord, support us all the day long, until the shadows lengthen, the busy world is hushed, the fever of life is over and our work is done. Then in Thy mercy, grant us a safe lodging, a holy rest and peace at the last.

And now, as our Saviour Christ has taught us, we humbly pray (The Lord's Prayer)

February 25, 1979
9:30 AM service

Great God of life: our hearts burst with praise and gratitude as we gather to worship. We give thanks for life larger than our experiences, for strength greater than our resources, for dreams higher than our desires, and for love deeper than our moods. Accept these words of thanks, O God, as we cherish these great gifts You have given us. Mindful of all Your children in light eternal who have gone on before us, and all Your children who dwell with us in the light and shadow of these times, we give thanks for this blessed fellowship of believers, and for Jesus Christ, the light of the world who came that we might have life, and have it abundantly.

In this moment, O God, we want to drop our excuses, leave our defenses, forget our alibis, and simply stand before You as Your children desperately needing Your presence, yet not quite sure of how to approach You or avail ourselves of Your healing, strengthening Spirit.

With such prayers we think of the anguish of others—particularly those whose search for identity has led them into so many strange paths. You know us better than we know ourselves, and we pray Your Spirit to be with those who wander, those who falter, those who fail, those who rebel, those who cry. Help them all. Surround with Your Spirit all Your children—the ill, the troubled, the grieving. May the good shepherd who restores their souls be near to them. Give to our leaders a sense of Your purposes overruling our ways, and make us a nation of compassion and peace.

Release the healing forces that bind us together as a people, that we may put down the poisons that tear us apart. Especially today, we pray for the Jewish community of Philadelphia, assaulted by the haunts and horrors of Nazism once more. Bind us all together as a people who care for each other and who look to You, our Father, as the author and perfecter of our lives.

May Your Spirit be among the nations of this troubled world, and in particular with the Chinese and Vietnamese, and the nations of the Middle East, that war may cease and respect for human life may grow.

Today we pray for that portion of Your holy catholic church known as the United Presbyterian Church. Bless its leaders, both nationally and locally. Purge it from its pride and preoccupation and make it an instrument of Your Spirit, that we may affirm what is good and true and all that prepares the way for Your Kingdom of righteousness and peace.

All these prayers we ask in the name of Jesus Christ, the great head of the Church, who taught us to pray altogether as His family, saying (The Lord's Prayer)

February 25, 1979
11:00 AM service

Eternal God, You have set the planets in orbit and devised the laws by which we explore the stars and chart our paths; You speak mightily in the marvels of this world which we have just begun to discover; You speak eloquently in the beauty of nature and the changing seasons; You speak plaintively in the quiet desperations and agonies, the frustrations and satisfactions of the human heart; You speak tenderly and conclusively in Jesus Christ, Yourself in our condition, our place, our world; You pronounce judgment as we behold the cross, and pour out unspeakable love in the risen Christ who calls us to follow.

For all these ways in which You have opened our eyes and melted the cold logic of our hearts, we give thanks. For our unity in Christ, making us feel at home as Your family who share a common discipleship; for the yoke of Christ who himself served and suffered and sacrificed, and who enters into our world as we live in Christ—for so many blessings, we give thanks.

As we give thanks for Your blessings, ever new, we also offer prayers for those of this church who are ill and need the presence of the great physician; for those who mourn and need the company of the good shepherd; for those facing decisions or confronting problems, who need the Counselor who will teach us all things. We pray for Your larger family throughout this city, this nation and this world. Unite us with the servants of Your word in all places and among all races, that Your Spirit, moving through us, may unite us one to the other. We pray for our president, our leaders and our nation, that we may turn to the Judge of all nations for the wisdom and guidance, justice and mercy which alone can make us strong.

Especially today, we pray for the Jewish community of Philadelphia,[11] assaulted by the haunts and horrors of Nazism once more. Bind us all together as a people who care for each other and who look to You, our Father, as the author and perfecter of our lives.

May Your Spirit be among the nations of this troubled world, and in particular with the Chinese and Vietnamese, and the nations of the Middle East, that war may cease and respect for human life may grow.

Today we pray for that portion of Your holy catholic church known as the United Presbyterian Church. Bless its leaders, both nationally and locally. Purge it from its pride and preoccupation and make it an

---

[11] Dr. Watermulder references the Philadelphia Nazi scandal of February 16, 1979.

instrument of Your Spirit, that we may affirm what is good and true and all that prepares the way for Your Kingdom of righteousness and peace.

All these prayers we ask in the name of Jesus Christ, the great head of the Church, who taught us to pray altogether as His family, saying (The Lord's Prayer)

February 25, 1979
Afternoon service

Great God of life: our hearts burst with praise and gratitude as we gather to worship. We give thanks for life larger than our experiences, for strength greater than our resources, for dreams higher than our desires, and for love deeper than our moods. Accept these words of thanks, O God, as we cherish these great gifts You have given us. Mindful of all Your children in light eternal who have gone on before us, and all Your children who dwell with us in the light and shadow of these times, we give thanks for this blessed fellowship of believers, and for Jesus Christ, the light of the world who came that we might have life, and have it abundantly.

Our sense of need is mingled with our prayers of thanks, O God. Truly You have searched us and known us and You understand our thoughts afar off. In this moment, O God, we want to drop our excuses, leave our defenses, forget our alibis, and simply stand before You as Your children desperately needing Your presence, yet not quite sure of how to approach You or avail ourselves of Your healing, strengthening Spirit.

With such prayers we think of the anguish of others—particularly those whose search for identity has led them into so many strange paths. You know us better than we know ourselves, and we pray Your Spirit to be with those who wander, those who falter, those who fail, those who rebel, those who cry. Help them all. Surround with Your Spirit all Your children—the ill, the troubled, the grieving. May the good shepherd who restores their souls be near to them. Give to our leaders a sense of Your purposes overruling our ways, and make us a nation of compassion and peace.

Our God, our help in ages past, our hope for years to come: we bring before You our nation. Release the healing forces that bind us together as a people, that we may put down the poisons that tear us apart. Especially today, we pray for the Jewish community of Philadelphia, assaulted by the fear and horror of Nazism once more.[12] Bind us all together as a people who care for each other and who look to You, our Father, as the author and perfecter of our lives. Guide the leaders of the nations as efforts toward peace continue, that hope and joy and life may return to all everywhere.

---

[12]   Dr. Watermulder references the Philadelphia Nazi scandal of February 16, 1979.

May Your Spirit be among the nations of this troubled world, and in particular with the Chinese and Vietnamese, that war may cease and respect for human life may grow.

(The Lord's Prayer)

March 25, 1979

Like the disciples of old, we walk our road, wondering what has happened to us. And as with the disciples of old, You join our company and open our eyes to the spiritual truths which are all around us. We thank You, O God, for taking away our spiritual blindness. We thank You for putting us in touch with Christ so we may know Your will. We thank You for the way You stretch our small, limited world into something with so much more possibility and hope. We thank You for Christ, our Lord and Saviour, our Companion and Guide.

As springtime bursts out of winter's grip, so cause our lives to respond to Your presence, O Father. As we seek Your help in our individual needs, we pray Your help to others: to those who are upset or perplexed, those who have failed and need help; those who have succeeded and need to remember their frailty; those who are sick, discouraged, depressed. Come among them all.

Today we pray for our land: for President Carter and President Sadat and Prime Minister Begin and all they represent as their nations seek peace.[13] We pray for the possibilities of peace and hope throughout the world that nations may seek to live with each other rather than fight each other. Encourage us, O God, to know that justice, mercy and love are at the heart of Your universe, and enable us to connect with those forces so that Your will may be done.

As we give thanks for the communion of saints and the hosts of witnesses of all ages who surround us in Spirit, we offer to You the prayer our Saviour taught us.

(The Lord's Prayer)

---

[13] Dr. Watermulder references the Egypt-Israel Peace Treaty meetings. The treaty was signed on March 26, 1979.

April 22, 1979

We gather on this Sunday after Easter, O Lord, mindful of all You have done for us and all You continue to do. With those first disciples, we become aware of Your presence among us and of the new power You put in our lives. With the saints of the ages, we join ourselves as Your seeking children who want to serve You with our love and our lives.

As spring bursts all around us, may new faith burst in our hearts, dispelling the winter of disappointment or little hope, and bringing to us the budding life of possibility and encouragement. We give thanks that with You these are new beginnings, and that in Your company, the old can be made fresh and new.

We pray today for our church family here: for those who joined Your church on Maundy Thursday and whom we greet at the reception this noon: may this be a new adventure in life in the Spirit, in the company of fellow seekers. We pray for the young ministers of our church who are now serving in their own parishes, and for those preparing for the ministry. We pray for all children, youth, parents and leaders who have given their time to the enactment of the ancient story of Your love and care. We pray for new officers to lead this congregation to Your Glory. We pray for the entire church family—those bereaved over the loss of loved ones, those struggling with sickness and disease; those facing troubles or confronting decisions. In each situation may Your presence become real and Your help sustain and support them through Your Holy Spirit.

Hear our prayers for our nation and our leaders, that we as a people may learn to do justly, love mercy and walk humbly with You, our God. Enlarge the circle of our lives as we join in prayer for all your missionaries and servants who hold high the faith in this land around the globe. Hear these prayers as we offer them through Christ our Lord:

(The Lord's Prayer)

September 9, 1979

O God, in the silence and beauty of this holy place, our hearts blend with the beauty and glory of all nature around us. Your world is full of Your glory and Your beauty. The seasons proclaim Your constancy. Your love surrounds us in so many ways. The persons we meet offer us opportunity to proclaim Your love once more. The new beginnings we feel in the fall of the year offer us added ways of giving thanks to You for this goodness of life.

Therefore, in the beauty of holiness and the beauty of nature, in the beauty of people and opportunities and new beginnings, we give thanks, O God—thanks for this gift of life, thanks for this wonderful opportunity which we have, and praying that our lives may spell out our gratitude for all that You have given us. With our gratitude, O God, we seek Your grace.

Enable us to know that our efforts are multiplied many times over when our efforts are placed in Your hands. May we know, O God, that when we seek to do Your will and seek Your Spirit, You come among us and give us strength sufficient for the task and strength sufficient for the need. Therefore, O God, enable us not to try so hard, not to be so eager, so anxious, so expectant, but to place things in Your hands and, having done our best, to leave You with the rest, in sure confidence that Your help is there and Your strength comes to each one of us.

Therefore, O God, may we do what we can do in each situation and then let it happen and let Your Spirit come into our lives. Give us, O God, this ease of being, this peace of mind, this sureness of spirit, which comes when we are conscious of Your grace.

Thus, O Father, equipped with gratitude for all we have and grace for all we do, we ask that we may have the affirmation for all we meet. May we be able to affirm every situation we encounter, knowing that someplace within the situation, You are present. May we be able to affirm each person we see, finding within that person the glimmer of greatness which You have placed there. May we be able to affirm every circumstance which confronts us, knowing that even in the darkest and most dreary situation, Your presence can be found and Your redemptive help may take hold.

Give us, O God, this goodness, this blessing of Your presence. We ask for these blessings not only for ourselves but for all others—those who are making new beginnings at this time of the year, especially students in school and those who teach them and lead them and inspire them—all of us, O God, as we begin the fall season and as the climate quickens our spirits, so may Your Spirit quicken our spirit that we may go forth in strength, in hope, in love, living by Your grace.

Hear our prayers for those with every kind of need—those who are in sorrow, those who are suffering, and unite us with that host of witnesses which no one can number of all Your saints in light eternal, evermore praising You. These prayers we offer through Christ, who taught us to pray (The Lord's Prayer)

November 11, 1979

Eternal God, Your mercies never fail, and Your love constantly picks us up so we may begin again. You have heard us say thank You as we praised Your name. You have examined our hearts as we confessed our inadequacy to be in Your presence. We have felt the release and renewal of Your grace as You have pardoned us so we may claim our heritage as Your children.

Now, O God, hear our prayers for our particular needs. Indecision, loss of will, lack of vision come across our lives like clouds cover the sky. Take away the gloominess as we experience Your grace, so that the sunshine of Your Spirit may brighten our path and lighten our load.

Today we pray for our land, mindful of the sacrifices of so many through all the years of our history. In these strange and changing times, give us vision and direction, that we may be instruments of peace, and bring encouragement to all. Enable us to embrace the long view, and give us a sense of duty and discipline that our government, in our time, may advance the common good of all.

In particular, we pray for the hostages in Iran, and for all people—President Carter, President Sadat and all others—who seek to bring calmness and justice into a world gone mad. Restore to us the Christian virtues of integrity and fair dealing, and enable the hostages to return safely and the relations of peace and goodwill to be restored among the nations.[14]

As our land heats up over such crises as these and over the prospects of an election yet a year away, fix our minds on the long view and the enduring truths that we may require of our land and its leaders a sense of integrity and a willingness to lead us down paths of sacrifice for our mutual good.

We pray for our number who are sick in hospitals and homes, and for those who grieve the loss of loved ones today. Restore us all by the grace of our Lord Jesus Christ and the power of Your Spirit, and bring us at last into Your heavenly kingdom. These prayers we ask (The Lord's Prayer)

[14] Dr. Watermulder references the Peace Talks between Egypt and Israel attended by President Carter, President Sadat and Prime Minister Begin.

November 18, 1979

Lord God of Abraham, Isaac and Jacob, God of our Lord Jesus Christ, God of our fathers and our father's God, our God: in the silence of this moment, in the mystery of the communion of saints, in the holiness of Thy house, we lift our hearts in thanks to You for a clearer vision of life's significance; for the sifting and shaking that comes as we put our misspent and unspent lives before You for scrutiny and adjustment, for forgiveness and direction. Make us happy and strong in the fact that You understand us, hear us, accept us and forgive us. Give us the companionship of Christ our Lord, that our days on earth may be filled with the qualities of heaven, and our desires may be steeped in Your Spirit.

O God of the daring and bold, the average and ordinary, the corrupt who are converted: you have made us for Yourself. You know who and what we are. Therefore we are unafraid to open our lives to You, seeking Your help. Make sense out of these accumulations we gather, O God. Put purpose into these hectic hours and fast-paced days. As the family of Christ, bring refreshment in common purpose and satisfaction as we seek Your presence. We also bring to You the needs of all others—those who are sick and in trouble, those who face decisions or difficulties, those who must make adjustments and face up to themselves. Be mindful of them and us, and bless us, O Lord.

Bless this church, that it may be an instrument of Your comfort and courage. Direct the teachers of our church school and make the minds of all people receptive to Your truth until they meet the Master. Bless the efforts of all who serve in Your name in the city and the world, that their labor may not be in vain. Bless our land in its abundance, that it may be a blessing to so many who are without. Direct our president and his advisors, and all who deal in the power plays as men and nations vie with one another. Especially, we pray for the hostages in Iran and for their families, praying also that love and mercy and deliverance may emerge in the midst of this awful hatred and anger.[15] As we pray for our nation in its dealings with Iran, we also pray for our nation in its effort to meet the hunger in Cambodia, that Your bounty may be shared with all Your children. Make all conscious of a power greater than natural might and an authority higher than that of temporal government. Give us calm hearts and clear heads. And grant us leadership equal to the day, conviction equal to the task, and faith to work Your power which awaits us. Through Christ we pray, even as He taught us, saying (The Lord's Prayer)

---

[15]   Dr. Watermulder references the Iran Hostage Crisis.

January 13, 1980

O Lord our God, how much we think we know about grace, but how much more You know about us!

How often we cloak our feelings in sophisticated jargon, but how well You know what is going on inside us.

How impatient we become with the progress of the human race, yet how patiently You bear with us.

How difficult it becomes to include You in our plans, but how graciously You put up with us and welcome us back home.

How readily we reduce prayer to meaningless phrase, yet how totally You are ready to respond to our deepest need.

For being this kind of a father to us, for understanding us and suffering for us, for coming among us in Christ and sending Your Spirit to overcome our fear, failure and frustration, we give thanks. Accept our thanks, O God, even when we don't always know how to act as grateful children (and even when we fret and fume in our insecurity) when all the time You really are both our refuge and strength.

Along with our thanksgiving, we ask for Your help, O God. Teach us to pray; teach us to be patient; teach us the meaning of faith. Give us that balance of personal and social concern which blends into private and public well-being because we are channels of Your Spirit. Make us simple once more, O God—simple enough to know that we are complex creatures who are made to be in communion with You, our Source.

As we grow in faith, may we grow in the compassion and concern which Christ showed and shared with all kinds of people. May Christ's Spirit surround and uphold the sick, the sorrowing, those in need, so they may know that even in their depths, Thou are the shepherd who leads them. May Your power pervade our land and our leaders. In these very uncertain times, we pray for peace: give guidance to our leaders and bring calm and direction to the nations. We pray for the hostages and their families, and for all who are captives of the kind of anger and hatred that make things worse rather than better. Open our lives to Him who is the way and the truth, even Jesus Christ the Prince of Peace, who taught us when we pray to say (The Lord's Prayer)

April 27, 1980

Almighty God our Creator, whose morning stars sang together at the dawn of creation and whose grace flows into our lives through Jesus Christ: in the midst of troubled, trying times, we place ourselves before You, acknowledging that life is in Your hands and beseeching You to give us the grace to put our lives in Your care.

With gratitude we recall all You have done for us in the past and the ways You have led us, not only over the rocky terrain but also through the valley of the shadow of death. Accept our thanks, O God, for Your merciful goodness and grace that surround us, and open our spirits to Your Spirit, that our lives may take on purpose and substance because they are the instruments of Your Spirit.

"O God our help in ages past, our hope for years to come": our prayers today for our world, our country and ourselves. Bestow Your Spirit upon us that we may think clearly and act wisely. Hear our prayers for all the peoples of the world, everywhere, that in this hour of crisis we may not be overcome by evil, but overcome evil with good.[16] We pray for our president, his advisers and our leaders, that they may be given the strength to withstand these times and to govern wisely. We pray for our country that we may not stoop to partisan politics in the hours of world crisis, and that we may keep cool and look to Your Spirit for guidance. May our prayers and our love be felt by the bereaved whose loved ones sacrificed their lives this past week in Iran, and may the hostages and their families know that the Eternal God is their refuge and underneath are the everlasting arms. Adjust our priorities and our sensitivities, O Father, so that we may seek the good and welfare of all people, and in doing so, may realize our own good and welfare. Lord God of hosts, be with us yet, lest we forget, lest we forget!

We also bring You our personal needs, O God. Where there is sickness or despair, sorrow or suffering, difficulty or decision, come to us as the good shepherd whose goodness and mercy shall follow us all our days.

So, O Lord, support us all the day long, until the shadows lengthen and the evening comes, and the busy world is hushed, and the fever of life is over, and our work is done. Then in Thy mercy grant us a safe lodging, and a holy rest, and peace at the last, through Jesus Christ our Lord. Amen.

(The Lord's Prayer)

---

[16]   Dr. Watermulder references the Iran Hostage Crisis.

May 11, 1980

Great God, it is always good to come into Your presence and breathe the spirit of Your peace and power, but especially on a spring day like this, when our minds are flooded with memories of the past and our world is bursting with new life, we are especially gratified.

O God, accept these simple words of thanks for all You mean to us and do for us, especially for coming among us in Christ Jesus, stepping into our place, and taking on our struggles and our sins. Thanks be to You, O God, for this wonderful, liberating grace of our Lord Jesus Christ! Thanks be to You, O God, for breaking through the barrier that separates us from the world of the Spirit. Thanks be to You, O God, for bringing pardon, release and peace. Thanks be to You!

Hear our prayers as they reach out to our larger family, O Lord. We pray for our president in these days of world crisis. We pray for the hostages and their families. We pray for our country—that we may rediscover who and what we are; that we may become one united people rather than many separate people; that old and young, rich and poor of all races, classes and places may unite in a common brotherhood under Your guidance and care. We are aware of how easily we can destroy ourselves, O God. Make us just as aware of how available is Your compassion and grace which enables us to reach out to one another. To our prayers for our world we add our prayers for the sick and suffering and those who need Your support.

And now, O Lord, unite us as one holy family with all Your children in light eternal—all those who have stepped through the door of death and begun the great adventure that yet awaits the rest of us. We think of children and parents and grandparents, of loved ones and of friends who no longer live in these mortal, physical bodies. Unite us with them in Spirit. As they serve You in light celestial, may we also serve You in Earth's reflected light, and as they have found Your peace and power, may we yield to Your ever-present power and know that goodness and mercy shall follow us all the days of our life and we too shall dwell in the house of the Lord forever.

And now as Christ has taught us (The Lord's Prayer)

May 18, 1980

Almighty God before whom the generations rise and pass away: we gather in Your house on Your day with Your children of our generation, mindful that we are surrounded by Your children of all generations. In this moment, as we are caught up in the Spirit, we give ourselves over to You and praise You for this gift of life. Most of all, we praise You for Jesus Christ, by whose grace we live and in whose presence we find the confidence and the courage we need.

At this springtime of the year, we pray Your blessings upon all those graduating from schools and colleges. May they understand that life is a constant adventure when it is placed in Your hands. Open their lives to the immense possibilities as they affirm Your universe and accept Your Spirit.

On this day, we pray for our members who have belonged to this church 50 years or more. May they know that You are their Shepherd, and may they know that they serve as a vital link in the chain that transmits the Christian faith from one generation to another to another.

Today we pray for our members who are sick, who are in hospitals, and who are feeling the limitations of their earthly bodies. May they be assured of Your presence, and may they draw on Your strength, and may all of us rejoice with Your children in light everlasting.

Hear our prayers for our president and our nation, that we, with other nations, may pave the way for peace, and that we may be worthy of the heritage which is ours. Cool our racial tensions and warm our spirits with the fire of Your love.

And now, as our Saviour has taught us (The Lord's Prayer)

June 29, 1980

Almighty Father, You have painted nature with vivid hues and filled it with the breath of Your peace. You provide us with the freshness of rain, the brightness of sunshine and the calm stillness of the night. We trace the rainbow through the rain and know your promise is not vain. As the seasons come and go and the earth moves in its orbit, so do You move among Your children and minister to their needs. For the love and goodness, faith and hope, for blessed memories and aching aspirations, for life's possibilities made understandable in Jesus Christ, we give thanks.

Eternal Spirit, nearer than breathing, closer than hands or feet: hear us as we pour out our individual and private needs. Make us sensible and realistic, O Lord, so that we recognize Your presence in our situations. In our fondest joys and success, may our happiness be complete because it is in tune with the promptings of Christ's Spirit. In our lowest depths and our deepest problems, may our confidence be strong because we have learned where to find help. In our sadness lift our eyes to the eternal realm where there is no death or sorrow. In our righteous dealings, may we rejoice in your holiness; in our inhumanities, may we behold the justice of Your wrath and the immensity of Your mercy.

O Creator and Father, whose morning stars sang together at the joy of creation, and who freely gave us a good world: stab us with the responsibility we have to care for and use such sacred gifts. You have blessed us with freedom of choice. Show us the consequences of our choices and cause us to choose Your will. You have given us friends and neighbors and a world full of relatives. Show us how to express our gratitude by helping us to live together as we ought.

Make us see how much we have and how little we have done with it; how much You can do for us and how little we let You do; how great and wonderful is our world and how small and miserable we sometimes make it. Get our gaze off ourselves and onto Christ! Lift us out of our despair and into His resurrections! As we breathe Your Spirit, dispel our lack of faith until in everything we can affirm Your presence. You can get along without us, but we can't get along without You, O God. Use us, then, as the tools of Your power.

Grant to our president and our country the blessings of Your presence, the light of Your truth, the judgment of Your justice; and give us the strength to be Your servants who show mercy and compassion.

"So, O Lord, support us all the day long, until the shadows lengthen and the evening comes, and the busy world is hushed, and the fever of life is over, and our work is done. Then in Thy mercy grant us a safe lodging, and a holy rest, and peace at the last, through Jesus Christ our Lord." Amen.

November 9, 1980

O Lord, You have searched us and known us. You understand us from afar, and tenderly call us home to You. For Your goodness and love; for the adventure of life and the joy of give-and-take; for being able to live with ourselves because You live with us; for the guidelines You give us and the grace which comes from Christ our Lord, we give thanks.

In this season of the year, we marvel at the beauty of Your handiwork, O Lord. The world You have given us stands in such contrast to the world we make. Just as we celebrate the beauty You have painted into nature, may we affirm the beauty of human nature.

> We've seen Thy glory like a mantle spread
> O'er hill and dale in saffron flame and red;
> But in the eyes of men redeemed and free,
> A splendor greater yet while serving Thee.

It is that inner splendor we celebrate today, O God, as we discover how much more exciting life becomes as we give ourselves to one another in care and compassion.

And so we offer special prayers for people and places around us:

For those who have no strong, sustaining faith, that they may find Your peace and power through Christ our Lord;

For all students in school, and in particular our high school students, including those who are returning from their retreat, that in Christ they may find the purpose and direction they need;

For all who mourn the loss of loved ones, that they may celebrate the life everlasting which includes both us and our loved ones who are in God's nearer presence;

For all who are lonely, all who grope and seek; all who need understanding and help, that Your wise understanding may embrace them;

For our nation—President Carter and President Elect Reagan, and all their advisers—that we may be a people who do justly, love mercy and walk humbly with our God.

For our world, caught in anger, hatred and warring madness, that we may come to recognize each other as fellow citizens of the planet Earth, led by the Lord of the Universe.

And now as our Saviour taught us (The Lord's Prayer)

November 16, 1980

O God who never fails us even though we fail You, and who continues to be our Father even when we Your children reject You: Your greatness and goodness is beyond expression, and Your love exceeds all our dimensions. Therefore, we gather together in Your house to offer the only gift we can give: our worship and adoration, our praise and our thanks. Accept these efforts on our part, O Lord, and accept us too—with all our faults and fancies as well as all our dreams and intentions.

We need you, God. We need to know that "the eternal God is our refuge and underneath are the everlasting arms." In our daily round and in the midst of our uncertainties and insecurities, we need to rest in Your embrace and rely on Your support.

As we go through these days, we implore Your blessing upon those in need. Grant to the suffering Your solace and to the troubled Your peace. Particularly, we bring to you those whom we know are struggling, fighting, hurting, needing. O God our Father, be with them.

Be with Your church, O Lord, that it may be a light and offer a life that brings wholeness. Around the world, may Your will and way be made known, but especially, may the grace of our Lord Jesus Christ become active and real. In these uncertain times we put our nation, with all its searching, into Your hands. So attune us to Your compassion, mercy and justice that we may be a people worthy of Your blessing, capable of fulfilling Your intentions.

Hear our prayers for our nation, O God. In particular, we pray for the hostages and their families, and for all leaders of government who seek to resolve the crisis, that our people may be free. We pray for our president and our president-elect, that they and their advisers may direct us in the ways of peace and hope. As ours has been a land of hope and promise in the past, may it bring assurance to people today, and may we, with our multitude of blessings, share with those who are deprived of so much.

(The Lord's Prayer)

February 8, 1981

O God, Your glory fills the earth, and we gather here in Your house to give You our praise.

Your love knows no bounds, and we come before You to marvel that You love us and come to us as we are, and taking us to Yourself.

Your Spirit touches our Spirits, and we are renewed and transformed.

Your mercy reaches down and covers us with forgiveness, and we can begin again.

For all Your goodness, we are grateful, O God. With the apostle we exclaim, "If God be for us, who can be against us!" And we lay before You our lives in both their confusion and their confidence, their self-centeredness and their self-surrender.

We give praise for the cloud of witnesses who surround us: those who bravely lived and nobly died, whose Spiritual presence envelops us now as we are caught up in Your Spirit. We pray for all who mourn that they may rejoice in the goodness of life and death and life everlasting. We pray for all who are ill or troubled that they may know they are not alone, and may know what it is to have the calm confidence of Your Spirit. We pray for our nation—our president, his cabinet, our congress, our leaders. Give us a zeal to use the gifts You have given us until this nation finds its greatest hour, not in looking back but in looking forward, not in condemning the times but in matching the need. In all our dealings, O Father, make us mindful of what You have done for us and of what we, in turn, can do for each other.

And now, as our Saviour Christ hath taught us, we humbly pray (The Lord's Prayer)

April 5, 1981

O Lord God, who moved among people in the person of Jesus Christ and brought healing and hope, meaning and understanding: move among us now as we lift our hearts in praise. Touch us with Your Spirit as we offer thanks for the ever-newness of life and the meaning that lies hidden in each encounter and experience. Fill us with Your Spirit that we may end our groping and find our completion.

O God, our refuge and strength, who is a very present help in time of trouble: today we pray especially for our nation. You have blessed us with so many opportunities and directed us with so many spiritual concerns. You have inspired us to build a nation which has offered promise and hope to people of all lands.

Now, O Lord, be with us, lest those spiritual blessings slip from our grasp. We pray especially for the health, safety and well-being of our president, Ronald Reagan, and for his wife and family. Our hearts reach out in prayer and supplication for James Brady, and for his family as they go through the torment of physical pain, suffering and loss. We pray for Timothy McCarthy and Thomas Delahanty and their families, that recovery may come speedily and totally. We pray for all who serve our land and who protect those who lead it. Hear our prayers also for John Hinkley, Jr., whose mind and will projected his wishes upon a whole nation, and for his parents who must grieve in bewildered heartache at this time.[17]

Whatever our political opinions may be, unite us as a nation that respects those who are in authority and that honors those who follow the ways of reason. In this violent age, may we see our worst sins to be in our willfulness and our self-assertiveness, and may we seek justice, mercy and peace through those channels which alone can bring it.

With our prayers for our land go our prayers for our own number: those who are sick in the hospital; those who mourn; those who face problems; those whose doubt has outweighed their faith; and those who need to know the good Shepherd who leads them beside the still waters to restore their souls, in His name we pray (The Lord's Prayer)

---

[17] Dr. Watermulder references the assassination attempt on Reagan on March 30, 1981.

May 17, 1981

Dear Lord Jesus, we come to You with a sense of intimacy mingled with awe and majesty. You have met us where we are and know who we are. You have attached us to something more than ourselves and embraced us with Your forgiveness and understanding. You care about us and call on us to care about each other. For all of this—and for these reminders of how much better life can be than we make it—we give thanks, O Lord Jesus Christ.

Great God, Father of our Lord Jesus Christ and our God and Father: we implore Your guidance and presence. Where we panic and become frantic, bring Your calm. Show us what grace is. Put Your everlasting arms underneath us so that we may prevail. O God, who neither slumbers nor sleeps, watch over us in our areas of need, of hurt and hope. Bless those who suffer the assaults on this physical body—may Your presence lead them beside still waters. Bless those who mourn—may You be their comfort and their hope. Bless those who face hardship, a decision, or those who are perplexed and who wonder where You are as they go through their valley—may they hear You say, "Lo, I am with you always."

Our prayers join those of Your many children for Pope John Paul, that strength and full health may return. Show us, O Lord, how to live in a world where life can be snuffed out so easily, and lead us to that place where we become members of a family who cares for each other.

We pray for our nation, that harmony and helpfulness, peace and purpose may become our consuming aim. We pray for our nation among other nations, that peace and goodwill may come among us. We pray for the leaders in Syria, Lebanon, Israel, that hatreds may give way to understanding and peace may return. We pray for Your church and the servants of Your church in all lands and places, that Your Kingdom may come, Your will be done.

O Lord support us all the day long,
Till the shadows lengthen
And the evening comes
And the busy world is hushed,
And the fever of life is over,
And our work is done.
Then in thy great mercy,
Grant us a safe lodging,
and a holy rest and peace at the last.
Amen.

June 21, 1981

Great God, King of the universe and Lord of our lives: You have placed us in this global village where we rub elbows with people of all races and places, all nations and stations. On this Your day, we lift our hearts in praise to You for Your goodness, for the blessings that abound, for the larger family of which we are a part, and for your church around the world which lifts holy hands in praise. May we, in our act of worship, be joined in spirit with all Your children everywhere on earth and all Your children eternal in the heavens, evermore offering You our praise, and constantly falling at the feet of Christ our Redeemer, who is the way, the truth and the life.

Accept our thanks for all Your goodness to us, O Father, and hear our prayers for our special needs. Hear us as we call out in anguish and concern for friends and loved ones. Lead beside the still waters those who are anxious and disturbed. Surround with Your Spirit those who are ill, or perplexed, or in need. Bless those embarking on new adventures. Great God, you know us far better than we know ourselves. In this moment meet us, each one, in that place of need. Hear our prayer and answer our call.

We pray for all people everywhere, O Lord, that peace and justice may overrule our ways and rule our lives. Unite us in one body and spirit with Your children in all other nations, that together we may seek Your ways. Make us in America sensitive to the crying needs of the peoples of the undeveloped nations, that Your compassion may show forth in our concern. Be with Your church everywhere, and with all who minister in Your name, whatever their race or place on earth may be. Today, especially, we offer our prayers for Ray and Ruth Dollenmayer upon their retirement. We thank You for the blessings they bring and pray that their lives may forever be blessed. We pray for our nation, our president, our secretary of state, our congress, that they may be responsive to Your Spirit as they fulfill their responsibilities. Bless those who seek to bring peace in those ancient biblical lands of Israel, Lebanon and Syria.

So, O Lord, support us all the day long, until the shadows lengthen and the evening comes, and the busy world is hushed, and the fever of life is over, and our work is done. Then in Thy mercy, grant us a safe lodging, and a holy rest, and peace at the last, through Jesus Christ our Lord. Amen.

(The Lord's Prayer)

October 11, 1981

O God, our refuge and strength, a very present help in time of trouble: we look to You for both comfort and courage for strengths and stability in a time of uncertainty. We turn to You in thanks for Your many gifts: the way You have led us in the past; the way You uphold us with Your grace; the way You give strength to help in the time of need; the way our Lord Jesus Christ takes our sin and releases us for new life.

Today, as we think of the teachers and pupils of our church school, we ask for Your blessing on all who teach, all who lead, and upon the new and growing generation—that they may know You, learn from You, and receive from You the blessings of Your Spirit.

Hear the prayers we have offered in this service for the children and teachers.

And today, O God of the nations and Lord of life, we pray for our nation as it takes its place among the nations of the world. We give thanks for the inspiration and courage bequeathed to us by Anwar Sadat.[18] We pray for the peace of Egypt, for stability in the Arab lands, for all efforts in Israel and all the Middle East that make for peace instead of war, for cooperation instead of condemnation. In the midst of the hatred and tensions of our world, bring a consuming desire for understanding. May we in our might inspire the ways of peace and brotherhood, and may all of us in this late-20th-century work as hard at building up as we work at tearing down. In a world that kills its prophets and destroys its peacemakers, raise up a new breed of people whose lives and whose lands are dedicated to that which unites us and affirms us rather than that which divides us and destroys us.

As we pray for the world, we pray for those of our number in hospitals; those whose physical and emotional lives are undergoing stress and strain. Support them; visit them with Your Spirit, heal them, and grant to us all Your peace and power, through Jesus Christ:

(The Lord's Prayer)

---

[18] Dr. Watermulder references the assassination of the Egyptian president Sadat on October 6, 1981.

November 8, 1981

[19]O Love of God most full, O Love of God most free,
Come warm our hearts, come fill our souls
Come lead us unto Thee!

In the quiet of this moment in Your house, we feel Your Spirit surround us; and we give ourselves over to You. In this moment where Spirit with spirit can meet, we are aware of the larger family of which we are a part—friends on earth and friends above. In this moment of spiritual awareness, we let go of everything we have been clutching so tightly—our fears, our anxieties, our ambitions, our obsessions, our unforgiveness, our pride—and in giving them all to You, we make room for You to give us what we need: strength, calm, peace, perspective, assurance that the Eternal God is our refuge and underneath are the everlasting arms.

O God, we pour out our thanks for so many gifts and so much love. As You gave Yourself to us in Christ, so we give ourselves back to You, O Lord, confident that You will cleanse us of our sins and certain that You will give us Your strength.

Hear our prayers, O Lord, for those of our number who undergo the trials and troubles of the mortal body, with all the physical limitations that can assault us. Surround them and their loved ones with Your presence, so that the healing streams may flow, and give them all the assurance that You are with them. Bless those who mourn, those who anguish, those who seek, that their lives may open wide and welcome the power of Your presence.

Hear our prayers for our nation and our world as we go on our maddening pace, O God. Stop us from becoming so frantic, so drunk with power that we end up destroying ourselves as well as others. Show us ways of security—both for ourselves and for our nation—that are grounded in something more substantial than mere physical power, and bring us back to those sources of spiritual power which once made our nation great. "O love of God most full, O love of God most free, come warm our hearts, come fill our souls, come lead us unto Thee."[20]

(The Lord's Prayer)

---

[19]   Oscar Clute, 1888

[20]   ibid

January 31, 1982

Great God our Lord, what a difference it makes when You come into our lives! How frantic we become until we sense once more that "the eternal God is Thy refuge and underneath are the everlasting arms." What calm in the midst of storm, clarity in the midst of perplexity, power in the midst of weakness comes to us when we turn to You.

Great God our Father, accept our gratitude for this dimension to life! Cut us loose, free us up to be Your sons and daughters, that we may drink in all of Your creation—youth and age, life and death, winter and spring— and know that all this belongs to You and we belong to You, and with You all things come together. So with You, O God, we embrace our days and anticipate our adventures. O Lord our God, how great Thou art!

Give us simplicity in Your presence, O God. Not simple-mindedness, but the purity of simplicity—being open, honest, at ease, knowing that Christ is our advocate before Your throne.

May Your blessings come to this weary world! Show us how to make peace. Give us concern for the least, for the oppressed. Open our eyes to the wonders of the world when it is Your world. Be with our president, our congress, our nation, that we may recapture the dream and clasp the ideal once more, and bring in our dealings with other nations a love of justice, mingled with mercy. Hear our prayers for the sick and sorrowing, and bring us all into Your holy presence, through Jesus Christ our Lord who taught us to pray together saying (The Lord's Prayer)

May 2, 1982

O Lord our God, with the psalmist we exclaim, "The heavens declare the glory of God, and the firmament showeth His handiwork." All around us, in the bursting beauty of spring, You speak to us. And now, as we enter Your house and give ourselves to You in praise and prayer, You speak again more clearly, more explicitly, until we become aware of Your grace and find the support of Your everlasting arms.

For such blessings, for such intrusions into our life, for the risen Christ who celebrates life with us and takes us in His care, we give thanks and praise.

Hear our prayers as we place ourselves before You. Bring the frazzled ends of our lives together; turn us in Your direction, walk beside us; where we have fallen, lift us up; where we have sorrow, bring us the joy of life beginning afresh with You; where we have special needs, clear our minds and direct our thoughts; where there is sickness, bring us Your healing and Your help.

On this Sunday, as we install our new officers, we pray for Your Church everywhere, as it proclaims Christ as Lord and as it becomes His living, active body in this world. Hear our prayers for this church—for children, youths and families; for each of us as we sort out our days; for the elderly as they celebrate the goodness of life in Your presence; for our missionary coworkers here at home and around the globe.

Hear our prayers for our nation—our president and our leaders, that all the peoples gathered here may find a common cause. As we seek for peace and strive for the common good, we pray for peace in the midst of the thunders of war. May Your Spirit prevail over our spirits, and may a new burst of hope bring light.

(The Lord's Prayer)

May 23, 1982

Eternal God our Father, who provides us with living water so that we need thirst no more, we give thanks for the many ways You enter into our lives. We give thanks that we, like Jacob, may have to wrestle and struggle in our prayers in order to learn how to let You take hold, for only through such encounters do we come to terms with ourselves.

Your patience has borne with us; Your love has held on to us; Your goodness has come to us; Your mercy and forgiveness have brought us Your grace so we may begin again. For all Your countless mercies and blessings, summed up in Jesus Christ our Lord, we give thanks and praise.

Today, as we honor those who have been members of our church for 50 years or more, we give thanks for the seasons of life—for the innocence of childhood, the exuberance of youth, the determination of adulthood and the mellowness of age. We pray that each may appreciate the other, and that together we may weave the fabric that gives beauty and design to all of life. We give thanks also for the cloud of witness who surround us who are part of the Church eternal in the heavens. May we, with them, draw from your unfailing fountains.

Lord of creation and God of the nations, who has come among us to bring peace and joy, we pray for our world today. Especially we pray for the people of Argentina and Great Britain, that their disputes may be settled in peace rather than in war.[21] May Your Spirit be upon them and upon the United Nations, as well as on our own land, that we may find those ways that make for peace and freedom, for justice and mercy. Clarify our goals and objectives, O Lord, until we develop mutual respect for each other and learn how to live on this earth You have given us.

Be with those who mourn; those who suffer; those who struggle against great odds. At all times and in all things, may they know that You are with them.

So, O Lord support us all the day long,

Till the shadows lengthen and the evening comes

And the busy world is hushed, and the fever of life is over, and our work is done.

Then in thy great mercy, grant us a safe lodging, and a holy rest and peace at the last. Amen.

---

[21]   Dr. Watermulder references the Falkland Islands sovereignty dispute which escalated in 1982 when Argentina invaded the islands, precipitating the Falkland War.

June 20, 1982

Almighty God who has filled the earth with beauty and who brings life out of death, joy out of sadness: we come into Your presence and give thanks even when our spirits are not fully thankful. We know that You are giving and forgiving, and when we do not sense these gifts, it is because of our dullness of mind and slowness of heart. Accept our thanksgiving for the constant privilege of turning back to You and finding life put back together again.

Accept our thanks for Jesus Christ our Lord and Saviour whose understanding of us baffles us, because it is so much greater than our understanding of ourselves. Accept our thanks for the time for reflection and renewal that the changing seasons bring, and for friends who reach out to us in understanding and supportive encouragement in every season of our living.

Show us how to be a redemptive, healing force in this world rather than a dividing, defensive bastion, O God. Enable us to affirm the age we live in, to bring to it our present best, not our past nostalgia, and to know that its future is in Your hands. Give us clarity of vision and singleness of purpose.

Give us the faith to place our loved ones in Your hands, for whom we pray now:

> those who are ill and need health;
> those who are despondent and discouraged and need hope;
> those who face decisions and need guidance;
> those who mourn and need healing;
> to all, give grace, strength and peace, O loving Father of
> us all.

Bless our land that we may be worthy of the new opportunities. Bless our leaders that their judgments may be shaped by Your judgment. Give to the church the power of the living Christ that it may be bold and courageous in those things that make for life. In particular, we pray for the United Presbyterian branch of the church as it meets in General Assembly this week. Renew in it the gifts of the Spirit, that the church may be an instrument of your will and way. Unite us with all Your people here and everywhere that Christian power may pervade our life. Now as Christ taught us to pray (The Lord's Prayer)

September 12, 1982

O Lord our Lord, how excellent is Your name in all the earth! In the beauty of this day, in the beauty of this hour, in the beauty of life, we give thanks for all of those blessings so often unnoticed, but so very real. For the many ways You minister to us constantly and give to us of Your strength. For the grace which is sufficient for every need and for that love which encompasses us, envelops us, and helps us.

We have already confessed how readily we worship ourselves rather than You, O God, and we have received Your pardon. Our hearts overflow as we gather here in spiritual company with Your children on earth, and Your children in light eternal in heaven. We rejoice in the adventure of life as it leads us from one phase to another, one place to the next. We give thanks for Your great understanding and forgiveness, for Your Spirit that makes all things new.

You, O Lord, ever lead Your children into new paths; lead us now as we enter another fall season. Take from us the drab dreariness of going through motions and the self-defeating preoccupation with ourselves. Set our minds on lofty vistas and move our wills with great visions.

Be with all students—children, youth, adults—as they begin school. May they worship You with the minds You have given them. Be with all teachers and leaders in school and church and home. May you be their greatest resource. Be with all persons who face uncertainty or difficulty or decision or who simply have more days to live here on earth and don't know what to do with them. Fill their lives with joy and zest as they join with others in praise. Be with those who mourn—may they place themselves and their loved ones in Your hands, with Thanksgiving. And be with our nation and world, O God, that we may show compassion for each other and find the ways of peace and brotherhood.

Our prayers include this beloved church as we make a fresh start and all missionaries to whom we are related around the world. May this church ever be the instrument of Your Spirit. Bless all who lead and teach, all who sing, and all who labor. Here may the faithful find salvation and the careless be awakened; may the doubting find faith and the anxious be encouraged; may the tempted find help and the sorrowful comfort; may the weary find rest and the strong be renewed; may the aged find consolation and the young be inspired through Jesus Christ our Lord.

So, O Lord, support us all the day long, until the shadows lengthen and the evening comes, and the busy world is hushed, and the fever of life is over, and our work is done. Then in Your mercy grant us a safe lodging, and a holy rest, and peace at the last, through Jesus Christ our Lord, who taught us to pray together saying (The Lord's Prayer)

September 19, 1982

O God eternal, the Lord and the creator of the ends of the earth, who renews the strength of those who wait for You; O God, the power and force behind all life who enables those who wait for You to mount up with wings as eagles, run and not be weary and walk life's daily round and not faint; O God who out of great love for us made us alive together with Christ:

We praise You! We adore You! We magnify Your name!

With all Your children on earth and all the hosts of heaven, we gather in Your holy presence and marvel at Your goodness to us. Accept our thanks for the many ways You meet our needs—directing our thoughts, correcting our ways, strengthening our resolve, pulling us up when we fall and giving us abundantly of Your grace.

Hear our prayers for all humanity as we stand bewildered in this world of progress and invention, of management skills and public relations know-how. Hear us as we pray for all those persons who can't live with themselves; or with their husbands or wives; or with their friends or associates. Make us wise enough to see how foolish we can be, and make us humble enough to receive Your wisdom.

In the midst of the ways we tear each other up and produce the destructive forces that can turn our Earth into a technological nightmare, we give thanks for the splash of joy that has come in the life of a storybook. Princess like Grace Kelly. Enable us all to allow life to have some of the carefree joy You intended. In the midst of the hatreds, factions and divisions, and the strange alliances that our nation makes with other nations, we pray for the people of the Middle East, and in particular the people of Lebanon, who have been the immediate victims of our late-20th-century way of life. We also pray for Israel, occupying that land we once called the Holy Land. Even as that land now symbolizes destruction, may it once more be the place where the angels speak of "peace on earth, goodwill to men." Lord of the nations, enter into our nation and world, and give us the grace that makes for peace.

Hear our prayers for the ill and those in need, O Father, that all of us may drink at the unfailing fountain of Your grace.

These mercies we pray for through Christ our Lord and Saviour who taught us (The Lord's Prayer)

September 26, 1982

God of our life, through all the circling years,
    We trust in Thee;

In all the past, through all our hopes and fears,
    Thy hand we see.

With each new day, when morning lifts the veil,
    We own thy mercies, Lord, which never fail . . .

And so, O Lord, we gather in Your house on Your day with Your people to praise You; to adore You; to bless Your holy name. We give thanks for this gift of life, but supremely we thank You for the gift of Yourself in Jesus Christ—for all He does to bring us back home so we may begin again; for all He means in showing us the Father and pointing us on the way.

O Lord, in this chaotic year we confess that we have not handled Your gifts very well, and we need Your help. We have used Your gifts of knowledge and technology, of psychology and sociology, only to find ourselves more firmly trapped in our ingenious ways. So we pray for help that gives us the same compassion and concern that Christ had; that enables us to forgive as He forgave; that forces us to reach out to those in need as He did.

We pray for our world this day: For the kind of image that the United States projects upon the rest of the world, that we may stand for that which ennobles and upbuilds life. For the people of the Middle East, particularly those in Lebanon, who suffer the atrocities of our inhumanity toward one another; and those in Israel who foment war and bloodshed. We know that all things are possible with you, O God, and that you call us to a kingdom of righteousness and peace. Give us the hope that makes us work for that peace. Give our missionaries and all who bear the good news of the gospel with its healing, helping power the assurance of Your presence and the power of Your Spirit.

Hear our prayers for Your people in this church, O Lord: those who are bewildered, those who are suffering, those whose earthly life is about to give way so the wonder of Your heavenly world may become real. Bless them all, and bless this church—her officers and leaders, her seeking, sinning, serving souls, for we all need to be touched by Your grace and strengthened by Your spirit.

God of the coming years, through paths unknown we follow Thee,
When we are strong, Lord leave us not alone, our refuge be.
Be Thou for us in life our daily bread
Our hearts true Home when all our years have sped.

October 17, 1982

Eternal God whose Spirit calls to our spirits, and whose love ever seeks to teach us to pray so that Your power may renew our lives: hear us in all humility as we express our profound gratitude for life.

For the beauty of the earth, for the beauty of the skies,

For the love which from our birth, over and around us lies,

Lord of all, to Thee we raise, this our prayer of grateful praise.

For friends and loved ones who share life's agonies and expectancies, we give thanks. For friends and loved ones who have gone before us and whose memories brighten our days, we give thanks. For griefs which cause us to grow and circumstances which call forth Your presence; for divine discontent with life as it is and divine drives within us to make life better; for the challenges which confront each age, and the wisdom of the past given us for guidelines; for the Christ who understands what our yearnings mean and the Christ who puts our lives back in order; for this sense of Presence, this knowledge that we are not alone, we give thanks.

Today we pray for the perplexed, whether they be young or old, that they may gain insight. We pray for all who are eager, all who seek, all who wait for an awareness of Your Spirit. We also pray for those who aren't eager and who don't seek because they think they know, and those who don't wait because they think they can live apart from their spiritual source—that the limits of their lives, too, may be enlarged, until the new dimensions, the new possibilities, the awareness of the matchless compassion of Jesus Christ overtakes them.

In such days as these, we especially pray for our president and our leaders, that they may be humble before Thee, and for our nation that we may measure greatness in human sensitivity and concern for all who suffer. May peace and reconciliation overrule our ways and rule our lives. Hear our prayers for the sick, the sorrowing, and those who have special need, and enable us to receive the peace which the world can neither give nor take away. May the Church reflect the beauty and presence of Her Lord Jesus Christ; and may we, the members of the church, be instruments of peace, love and concern, because all these things have been poured into our lives through Jesus Christ our Lord, who taught us (The Lord's Prayer)

October 10, 1982

Great God, who speaks in the beauty of the world around us; in the crying needs of people in trouble; in the experiences we go through each day:

Speak to us now, here in Your house on Your day with Your people, as we lift our hearts in praise to You, let loose the pent-up sense of gratitude we have for this world with Your presence each day. Sometimes we grumble and mutter, and at other times we make life unpleasant for everyone else; In gratitude, O God, we would heed the word of the hymn:

> Count your many blessings, name them one by one and
> it will
> Surprise you what the Lord has done.

Speak to parents, babies baptized, teachers commissioned, and pupils involved.

Filled with this thankfulness, give us a new affirmation for life, even a new willingness to face what is before us because You are there with us. And when we have done our best—however good or poor that may be—give us the good sense and the strong faith to leave with You the rest. Your grace floods over our lives and enables us to do and to be. Come now, O Lord, and fill us with Your Spirit.

Enfold us in Your family of faith, O Lord. As we pray for our larger family, the Church, we pray for our own families. Bless all young people and their families, their parents, their loved ones that they may find the reality of Your presence as the days go by. Comfort those who mourn; strengthen the weak; support the sorrowing. And to our nation be the conscience and the vision, the hope and the dream, that we among the nations of the earth may learn the ways of peace and mercy, strength and compassion.

(The Lord's Prayer)

February 6, 1983

O Lord, our Lord, how excellent is Thy name in all the earth! As we gather in this Your house, we become sensitive to the many ways You show Yourself to us; and in the midst of the worries and problems that beset us, we offer our profound thanks for all Your mercies and blessings, but especially, we give thanks for Christ our Lord in whom we place our trust and confidence, and who leads us back to the realms of Your grace and the powers of Your Spirit.

May Your grace become abundant in our lives, O God. Give to the young the sturdy, steady strength of the old who have learned how to take it and to keep going without making a fuss about it.

Give to the old the anticipation and eagerness of the Young who know there is something new around the next corner.

And give to the middle-aged the capacity to life without drumming up a whole bunch of midlife crises, as though no one else had ever been through middle age before.

In brief, O God, may we let You take hold to direct and correct, and may we know always that underneath are the everlasting arms which uphold us when we would fall.

May Your church be worthy of Her Lord and equal to her task because She is equipped with Your grace and given Your vision.

May the sick know the solace of Your company and draw on the healing voices of Your Spirit as they open themselves to Your power. May all who struggle—with themselves, their jobs, their associates, their world—know that You enter the struggle with them so that they may overcome.

Bless our land in these days, that we may earnestly seek the ways of peace at home and peace with nations. Give us the will to turn swords into plowshares and spears into pruning hooks, so that the lion and the lamb may be able to sit down together and acclaim their creator. We are mindful of the strike among the truckers, of the battles in congress, of the vast numbers who seek work but cannot find it. May Your Spirit settle upon all of us that we may do those things that bring Your kingdom and glory. And now as our Lord taught us, we humbly pray (The Lord's Prayer)

February 13, 1983

Great God of life, Lord of the peaceful moments as well as the stormy days, a thousand years can be as a day, or as a day is a thousand years to You.

On this wintry day, with snow all around us, we praise You for life, for variety, for the seasons. We thank You for the good that seems to emerge when we are in trouble, for the way difficulties can call out the best in us.

Most of all, we give thanks for what You do for us, so that even though our sins may be as scarlet, they shall be white as snow. Even as we have confidence in the seasons—each bringing its own unique climate—may we also have confidence in Your grace, O God, knowing that even as You came among us in Christ, You come to each of us, understanding us, identifying with our need, directing us and then taking on Yourself our trouble and sin and bringing us back to You. O Lord, we give thanks that we have "an Advocate with God the Father, Jesus Christ the righteous," and we give thanks that in Him we may find the pardon, purpose and peace which our lives so desperately crave.

On this day, we pray for the cold, the hungry, the homeless. Through the many agencies You put before us, may we channel our compassion so that people are fed, sheltered, and clothed. We pray for all with special needs, that we may rise to meet those needs and to see to it that our kind of a world makes it possible for everyone to work and to find a fulfilling life.

We pray for those whose lives are surrounded by loss and sorrow today. May they affirm their grief and give thanks for all the good things behind them and all the blessings You bring them for this day and the years to come. May they, and all who are ill, all who suffer, all who have need find that underneath are Your everlasting arms to uphold them.

Bless our congress and our leaders, O Lord, that we may not be governed by petty privileges but by great dreams, lofty goals and a burning concern for people everywhere. May Your church at home and around the world ever put before us the prophetic vision until Your Spirit possesses our spirits and we become the children of Your new creation.

(The Lord's Prayer)

May 1, 1983

[22]Great God, we sing that mighty hand
By which supported still we stand
In scenes exalted or depressed,
Thou art our Joy, and Thou our Rest;
Thy goodness all our hopes shall raise,
Adored through all our changing days.

As we gather with Your people on Your day, just as Your people have gathered down through the centuries, we are mindful of the framework You put around our lives so they can hold together, and of the power You pour into our lives so that we may endure.

Accept our thanks, O God, for all the ways You minister to us: for coming to earth in Christ our Lord and perpetuating His living body in the Church; for sending the Holy Spirit so that we can be renewed; for bringing forgiveness and understanding where we might settle for rancor and revenge.

Direct us, O Lord, in all our doings, with Thy most gracious favor, and further us with Thy continued help, that in all our works begun, continued and ended in Thee, we may glorify Thy holy name, and finally, by Thy mercy, obtain everlasting life through Jesus Christ our Lord.

O Heavenly Father, who hast filled the world with beauty: open our eyes to behold Thy gracious hand in all Thy works; that rejoicing in Thy whole creation, we may learn to serve Thee with gladness, for the sake of Him by whom all things were made, Thy Son Jesus Christ our Lord.

O gracious Father, we humbly beseech thee for Thy Church, that it may be filled with truth and peace. Where it is corrupt, purify it; where it is in error, direct it; where in any thing it is amiss, reform it; where it is right, establish it; where it is in want, provide for it; where it is divided, reunite it; for the sake of Him who died and rose again and ever liveth to make intercession for us, Jesus Christ Thy Son our Lord.

Bring peace to our hearts and peace to our land. Send comfort to those who hurt and hope to those who despair. And in all things and at all times, may we have the confidence that You are our shepherd and we shall not want.

Now as our Saviour Christ hath taught us, we humbly pray together saying (The Lord's Prayer)

[22]   Philip Doddridge, 1755

May 22, 1983

O loving Father, whose invisible forces cause the drops of rain to nourish the earth and the rays of sun to unfold new life out of apparent death; whose unseen hand speeds this earth in its orbit so that winter melts into spring and stars continue their course, where are the earthbound words to express our heaven-felt gratitude for all the simple unnoticed miracles of life? For our spiritual creation and the challenge to give its expression in this physical world, we give thanks; but most of all, we give praise for Jesus Christ, the perfect combination of physical and spiritual, through whom Your Spirit enters our life and carries our load.

Mindful of the cloud of witnesses and the world of the spirit, we ask for Your blessings upon all who struggle today against mortal and physical hardships. On those families of our congregation that have met with suffering, bereavement and sorrow, look down in tender comfort and compassion, O great Physician of body and soul. Upon our president and leaders who must make decisions, we implore your spirit of love and mercy, O God and Father of all mankind.

Send Your Spirit upon us, O Lord, and equip us for life. Send Your Spirit upon those who labor in Your name in distant and faraway places. Send Your Spirit upon the church, that it may respond to Your vision. Send Your Spirit upon the Middle East, that out of that strife-torn world there may come a common concern. Send Your Spirit upon us, that we may know how to handle the increased powers at our disposal. Send Your Spirit upon us, each one, that we may hear your voice and heed its word.

O Creator and Father, whose morning stars sang together at the joy of creation, and Who has given us such a good world: stab us with the responsibility to care for and use such sacred gifts. We are blessed with freedom of choice; enable us to dignify our personalities by offering them in service and concern. We have friends and neighbors and a worldful of relatives: show us how to express our gratitude and live together as we ought.

Bless this congregation; bless us as we seek to be a people who are attentive to Your word.

And now, as our Saviour Christ taught us, we humbly pray (The Lord's Prayer)

September 4, 1983

O Lord our Lord, how excellent is Thy name in all the earth. As the seasons roll around and summer ease gives way to autumn duties, we come before You mindful of Your constant presence and Your purpose which directs our days. As our youth return from Camp Susquehannock, we join them as persons wanting a different dimension in their lives, where Christ becomes our Lord who gives us strength and where Christ becomes our Saviour who brings us into Your presence. Mindful of all Your children in heaven and all our sisters and brothers on planet Earth, we lift our hearts in praise for this gift of life and for all it can become.

Hear our prayers, O Lord, as we put before you our own anxieties and concerns. Give us confidence in Your nearness. When we have done our best, give us grace to leave with You the rest. Bless those who walk this day through the valley of the shadow of death, that they may know that You are with them and they shall not want. Bless those who seek Your help, that they may discover that underneath are the everlasting arms. Bless those who have special needs, that they may find in You both their refuge and their strength.

O Lord, who came among us as Prince of Peace, hear our prayers for our world this day. May Your comfort be with those who have lost loved ones through the inhumanity we heap on one another. Lead us through this present crisis with Russia with cool heads and clear objectives, and show us the ways that make for peace and concord among all people. We pray for the peoples in the Middle East and in Africa, those in Central America and Ireland; we pray for people everywhere who seek to settle differences through war and bloodshed, that all of us may find a better way. Make us to know the measure of our days and who we are, that we may submit ourselves to the gracious workings of Your spirit, and somehow step into the tangled web we have made of our world and give us the guidance to put it together as You intended it to be.

Hear our prayers, O Lord, for we ask them in the name of our Lord Jesus Christ who taught us to pray, saying (The Lord's Prayer)

September 11, 1983

Great God of glory and Lord of love: all nature sings and round us rings the music of the spheres. As a new fall season begins, we begin again too, O Father. In gratitude we come into Your house and blend our spirits with Your Spirit. In expectancy we turn to those roots of our faith as found in the Scriptures, the Christ, the Church, and await Your word for today. In appreciation we thank You for the past, anticipate the future, and place the present in Your hands. In exultation we blend our spirits with all the heavenly hosts.

Great Lord and Father of us all, be with us in the fall of 1983. Personally, give our lives a center around which they pivot. Socially, bind us one to another in compassion and understanding. Politically, give us goals that go beyond partisanship, and loyalties that make us seek to fulfil the lofty aims of our heritage. Spiritually, put us in tune with the reality at the center of the universe which is You, O God, and open up to us the mysteries of Your presence and the meanings of our existence in Christ. Grant comfort to the sorrowing, strength to the sick and clarity to the perplexed. Be with those who mourn, that both they and their departed loved ones may drink of Your Spirit.

On this national day of mourning, we pray for family and friends of those passengers whose lives were snatched away on the jetliner.[23] Give us all a clearer perception of the evil that lurks in ourselves as well as our enemies, and of the need to transcend hot anger until we can find reconciliation. We pray for the people in Lebanon, and everywhere where our stay is one of anger, revenge, bloodshed. We pray for our missionaries and leaders in the Middle East and Africa and Central America, that the power of Your Spirit may become the true power in our world.

So may Your blessings be upon us, O Lord, that we may become the instrument of Your blessing to others. We pray through Christ who taught us (The Lord's Prayer)

---

[23] Dr. Watermulder references the incident of September 1, 1983, when Soviet jetfighters intercepted and shot down a Korean Airlines passenger flight, taking the lives of 269 people.

October 9, 1983

O God, were we to try to record all that Jesus has done for us and for our world, we would not have sufficient space or adequate words to express His goodness. Therefore, we gather in Your house on Your day with Your people

to stand in awe before the mystery and majesty of life;
to listen to the spiritual forces that beat upon us;
to give thanks for the adventure and anticipation of life;
to affirm the fact that you accept us, understand us, love us, remake us, strengthen us;
to praise you for your matchless grace which becomes so real in Jesus Christ our Lord and Saviour, and
to place ourselves back in his hands so that he may forgive and heal and direct us.

O God, You are ageless—the Lord of the young and the old and of every age. Be with children as they grow; with youth as they question; with adults as they seek; with the aged as they wonder what is to come.

We put before you, loving Father, our own members:

those who are sad
those who need strength and reinforcement
those who face troubles
those who must make decisions
those who are sick and need health
those who feel cut off, alone, even forsaken

Be to all—young and old—our God, our help in ages past, our hope for years to come.

Be to our country both judge and guide, that we may do justly, love mercy and walk humbly with You.

Grant Your grace to every person here, that having done their best, they may leave with You the rest. Now as Christ taught us (The Lord's Prayer)

October 30, 1983

O God our help in ages past, our hope for years to come:
Our shelter from the stormy blast and our eternal home . . .

At all times we turn to You as our source and supply, but especially in tragic times of turmoil and trouble we instinctively seek You as our refuge from the storm and as the One who equips us for the battle.

So today we gather in Your home with Your people on Your day to mingle our voices with those of Christians around the world and those who have gone before us to heaven, to praise Your holy name, to thank You for Your grace, to lean on Your everlasting arms and to place ourselves—our souls and bodies—in the hands of Christ our Lord and Saviour who knows us, understands us, forgives and save us.

O God of compassion, hear our prayers for the bereaved loved ones of marines who gave up their earthly lives in Granada and Lebanon.[24] Surround them with Your support. Supply them with Your grace.

O God who binds up the broken heart, hear our prayers for all others who have lost loved ones and who feel the pangs of heartache. You have blessed our lives with friends and families who are clearer than life itself. In our grief, may we affirm our grief knowing it is another way we express our love; and in our grief, unite us to them that they and we may receive the blessings of Your spirit.

O God who knows how frail we are, hear our prayers for the sick and all whose physical body is not sufficient for their spirit. Breathe Your Spirit of healing upon them; strengthen them with the knowledge of Your presence; bless those who minister to them; restore them in body, mind and spirit.

O God of the nations and Lord of life, hear our prayers for the United States as it relates to all other nations and peoples of the world. In these changing times, may we discover and define our goals, draw on our values and establish a sense of unity and solidarity among our people. Enlighten our minds as to our role in this world; enhance our understanding of others; increase the means by which we make peace and maintain it among friend and foe alike. Spare us from making the deaths of our people, and the defense of our land, a partisan issue, so that all of us of all persuasions may together find what is good and true and right for us as a nation.

---

[24]   Dr. Watermulder references the 1983 events of the US-led invasion of Grenada, and the Beirut barracks bombings during the Lebanese Civil War.

We pray for all nations and all people. We pray for our enemies, as you have told us to, that all of us together may find how to use the remarkable resources of Your universe for good, so that Your glory may be reflected in our daily lives.

(The Lord's Prayer)

November 6, 1983

God of the eternities and Lord of all time, Lord of our time: to You a thousand years can be as a day or a day as a thousand years. Yet You step into our time, so right here, in the world of November 6, 1983, we implore Your direction and correction upon us, even as we give thanks for our many blessings.

We thank You for putting us in this time toward the end of the 20th century. In each age You have given Your people hard decisions to make, and we realize that our age is no exception. Therefore, we give thanks for the sense of purpose and perspective You bring to our lives, so we may separate the trivial from the significant, the abiding from the passing.

As we think of the time we live in, we think of former times—for friends and family who fought a good fight, kept the faith and are at rest in Your presence; and we give thanks for the inspiration and memory, and for the ties that bind us together around Your throne of grace, where both they and we draw from Your Spirit.

As we think of the time we live in, we pray for those who know their time is about to come when they leave us, and for those who mourn the dying of loved ones. Support them with Your presence. Strengthen them with Your Spirit.

As we think of the time we live in, we pray for the nations and the peoples of our world, especially for all the warring factions in the Middle East so bathed in hatred, revenge and bloodshed. We pray for the peoples of the Caribbean and Central America, so caught in the grip of competing politics. We pray for our nation, our leaders and decision makers who have the power to wage both peace and war. May they be given insight and boldness, and may Christ, the Prince of Peace, rule their hearts and minds. We pray for peace in this angry, frantic world, O Father. Before we destroy each other, enable us to make peace wherever we are, in whatever we do.

O Divine Redeemer, in this time in which we live, be near to the sick and the troubled, that the Good Shepherd may restore them in body, mind and soul, and life may blossom with the blessings of Your grace.

These mercies we pray for through Christ who taught us to pray together, saying (The Lord's Prayer)

November 13, 1983

God of our life, through all the circling years, We trust in Thee
In all the past, thru all our hopes and fears, Thy hand we see
With each new day, When morning lifts the veil
We own Thy mercies, Lord, which never fail.

We give thanks for this overarching sense of Your presence, O God. We give thanks that in good days and bad days You do not forsake us. We give thanks for all our days, mindful that they are in Your hands. We give thanks for special days which stand out like beacons directing our lives. We give thanks for the day when Christ entered our lives, and the many days He steps into our lives to lift them up.

With our thanks, we also seek Your help, O loving Father. You know where we despair and feel defeat; You know where we do not give ourselves over to You and experience the weakness of life without Your power. In the midst of grief over the loss of loved ones, or difficulties with our work or our relationships, or loss of physical health and strength—in all these situations, O God, we ask for Your healing hand, Your empowering Spirit.

We pray for Your church here and around the world—Your church so beset with human fault, Your church so unequal to the task, Your church in need. As in times past, breathe Your Holy Spirit upon it, raise up men and women who seek to do justly, love mercy and walk humbly with You, their God.

We pray for our nation amid the nations of the world. In the midst of bloodshed and hatred, may we bring peace and light. Give to us those qualities of compassion for all people which once brought inspiration to so many, everywhere. Give to our leaders—in all walks of government—insight, understanding, courage, that we may bring hope to all peoples everywhere.

So,

O Lord support us all the day long,
Till the shadows lengthen
And the evening comes
And the busy world is hushed,
And the fever of life is over,
And our work is done.
Then in thy great mercy,
Grant us a safe lodging,
and a holy rest and peace at the last.
Amen.

February 5, 1984

[25]God of our life, Through all the circling years, We trust in Thee.
In all the past, through all of our hopes and fears, Thy hand we see.
With Thee to bless, the darkness shines as light,
And faith's fair vision changes into sight.

With joy in our hearts we come before You, O God, praising You for our creation and our re-creation. With thanksgiving we sign Your praise, mindful of our salvation. With eagerness we face each day and each situation, whether good or bad, knowing that You are with us.

Hear us, then, O God, as we lay our needs before You. Sometimes the confusions and perplexities overwhelm us. Sometimes our own strength fails us. Sometimes the road ahead seems blocked with barricades. Make us to know that all the times You are with us, and enable us to put ourselves in Your hands.

Hear our prayers for those of our number who mourn the loss of loved ones. Comfort them with fresh courage. Draw near to those who are both physically weak and Spiritually weak. Breathe Your Spirit upon them and bring healing to body and soul. Go with those who face uncertainties and troubles. May they sense Your presence and Your power.

Hear our prayer for our world, so unsettled, so seething with religious and political extremist factions. Through the great changes that are taking place, bring Your Spirit to bear. In humanity's hunger for God, bring us all to temperate, strengthening faith so we do not fall into fanatic intolerance. In the reconciling power of Christ, may we see what is the way, the truth and the life. Especially, we pray for the people of Lebanon and the Middle East, where zealous factions destroy one another. We pray for our land and our leaders, that we may not be swayed by slogans and easy answers, but may apply ourselves to justice mingled with mercy, strength borne of peacemaking concern. In the name of Christ, we pray (The Lord's Prayer)

---

[25]   Hugh T. Kerr, 1916

April 8, 1984

Eternal Father, you have called us to love You with all our heart and mind and strength, and to work out our salvation with fear and trembling, for You have endowed us with minds to know You, hearts to love You, and wills to serve You. So on this Your day, we gather in Your house to thank You for the gifts You have given us and to seek Your help that we may use these gifts wisely. But especially, we gather to praise You for the delight in being in Your presence. With all our heart, and mind and strength, we praise You for Jesus Christ who became like us that we might become like Him. With hearts overflowing, we give thanks for Your mercy that forgives, Your grace that understands, and Your Holy Spirit that brings Your power into our lives. Beyond our efforts and arguments, we simply stand back and receive Your precious gifts, knowing that the Eternal God is our refuge and underneath are the everlasting arms. May we feel those arms upholding us when we would fall, and in the midst of our efforts and endeavors, may we get ourselves out of the way, be still, and know that You are God.

In so many ways, You work among us, O Lord; and as winter's bleakness gives way to spring's brightness, we too would shed our despair and disappointments, our grudges and our grief, and allow Your springtime of the soul to come into our lives. Give us the capacity to begin again. Enable us to do the work that is set before us and, in doing it, to find satisfaction. Direct us in concern for those in trouble, those who are lost, those who are lonely. Make us citizens whose love for our land finds its roots in our love for your way. Show us the ways of peace and brotherhood in the midst of the fever of war and hatred. Use us to bring Your peace to all. Bless our president and congress, and all our leaders, that we may truly seek to do justly, love mercy and walk humbly with our God.

We commend to Your care those who mourn, those who need help, those who fight immense battles, those who face difficult times. May they find in You the good shepherd who leads them beside the still waters to restore their souls; and may they also be united in spirit with those who already dwell in the house of the Lord forever. These mercies and blessings we pray for through Christ who taught us to pray together saying (The Lord's Prayer)

April 29, 1984

Eternal Father, in the silence of this house and the hush of this holy place, we feel ourselves surrounded by the host of witnesses of all ages, places and races. With awesome adoration we join them in offering You our praise and thanking You for this gift of life, for its adventure and for the assurance of Your love as it comes to us in the life, death and rising again of our Lord Jesus Christ.

Today, especially, we give thanks for Your church, eternal in the heavens and active on earth. Accept our thanks for our officers and leaders—both those who have completed their work and those who continue and those who are newly installed today. Make this church a channel of Your Spirit and a source of power to all who come here.

Today we also pray for our new members who joined our fellowship on Maundy Thursday. Bless them individually as they enter into this company of the faithful, and bless us all together as Your Spirit unites us together in our worship, work and witness.

And as we express the joy of living and the meaning of Your ongoing creation, may all of us become sensitive to the myriad ways You speak and the countless blessings You bestow. So enable us to affirm the blessing of variety, both in the ways we declare our faith and in the ways we express it in life.

Hear our prayers for this family of faith, O Lord. Be near to those who are ill, those in hospitals, those who mourn, those who face decisions and difficulties. May they be able to exclaim, "The Lord's my Shepherd, I'll not want." And as they walk through the valley of the shadow of death, may they rely on Your companionship.

And as we behold the wonder of new life bursting in old forms all around us, we pray that Your Spirit may bring new life to our land: a sense of purpose and unity, of high goals and strong resolve. May this spirit touch our president and his leaders, our legislators and all those who lead, that we may do justly, love mercy and walk humbly with You, our God. These prayers we offer through the sacrificial love of Christ our Lord, who taught us (The Lord's Prayer)

September 9, 1984

The heavens declare the glory of God
And the firmament showeth his handiwork.
Day unto day uttereth speech
And night unto night showeth knowledge.

Even as You speak to us in the beauty of the fall season, You also speak in the way we look at life and the way we handle our problems. We hear Your voice as we listen to one another and when we reach out to the people in need we hear You say, "In as much as you did it unto one of the least of these, You did it unto me."

So we come into Your house on Your day with Your people to offer our thanks for these many ways You speak and for the many new beginnings You bring. For the forgiveness which lets us let go of the past and the Christ who gives us strength to rise to newness of life, we thank You. For this Sunday habit of placing ourselves in Your hands and letting Your spirit touch and heal, we praise You. For the host of witnesses who surround us—those who have gone on before us and those yet to follow after us—we give thanks. For distant goals and hopes beyond our reach, for the vigor which comes with great visions and tasks of service, we praise Your name.

As schools begin, we pray Your blessings upon children and youth—all the way from those little ones just beginning and on to those in colleges and universities. Indeed, make all of us young, O Lord, so that we may learn something beyond our pat answers, our easy prejudices, our unbending opinions. May Your Spirit rest upon all who teach—not only here in our church school, but also in the schools and colleges of the land, that all may find truth to be another of the languages by which You speak. Indeed, O Lord, may our jobs and our associations be the greatest school of all, where You teach us Your ways. Whether we live alone or in family groupings, may Your blessing attend our days.

We pray for those who mourn; those who have met with unexpected, unwanted shock or sorrow; those for whom the pressures and schedules are too much; those for whom the future, as well as the present, looms too large; and those others who seize both present and future as arenas in which to play the game of life. To all of us—in joy and sadness, sickness and health, plenty and want—be the Good Shepherd who restores our souls and leads us in the way everlasting.

We offer these prayers, O Lord, in a world beset with hatred, mistrust and deception. We offer these prayers in a day of remarkable advancement in so many ways, only to find our blessings becoming our curse. Show us how to use our gifts, relate us to all the peoples of the earth, use us to bring hope to those who have not had our opportunity, and lead us all into Your heavenly kingdom, through Jesus Christ who taught us to pray together saying (The Lord's Prayer)

March 24, 1985

O Lord of this universe, far above our small islands in time; O light of lights, so dazzling that our eyes cannot absorb Your brightness; O life behind all life, breathing movement and meaning into everything around us; O Father, whose mercies are beyond calculation and whose brand of love is seldom, if ever, understood: what can we do but express our praise and appreciation? Your goodness and love surround us even when we disregard it. With all the hosts of heaven, we join in offering our praise and thanksgiving for life and spirit.

O Lord our God: we behold the majesty of the universe and the constancy of the seasons, and we wonder what it is to be human. We marvel at the limitless possibilities within us and the incredible opportunities which our skills develop, and we wonder, *What is life?* We feel the tug to be something more, the wistfulness that disturbs us, the drives—hopes and fears, antagonisms and anticipations—that spur us on, and we confess how incomplete we are without true faith.

Everlasting Father, You have breathed your spirit into us so that we are restless until we rest in You: hear us as we stumble and blunder with our heartaches and needs, our resentments and our rationalizations. We know there are immense choices before us. We know we can get away with timid half-life existence. We know, also, that You have come among us in Christ; that Your Spirit is a match for every problem; that You honor our anguish and hear us as we seek. Come among us, O Lord, with Your Spirit. Make us to feel ourselves a part of something more than ourselves.

Eternal Spirit, God of all: bless with Your presence those who struggle with illness of body as well as those suffering from starved spirits. Comfort those who mourn; those who must begin again but are afraid to take the leap; those separated from us who need Your strength and presence. Bless our president and our leaders, both in Washington and Geneva, and stir our nation with a sincere seeking after the human dignity and integrity that brings the justice, mercy, and peace of God. Unite us in one holy family with all your children on earth and all your family in heaven, as together we offer the prayer Christ taught us (The Lord's Prayer)

May 12, 1985

Great and eternal God our Father: even as the skies and trees blend together to offer You the praise of new life, so all of us—singly and together in families—gather together as your holy family, to worship You and greet each other as fellow persons, to feel Your embrace as members of the household of God.

Accept our praise and our thanks.

Forgive our shortsightedness and petulance.

Open to us wider vistas so that we may see life whole rather than in little pieces.

Open our minds and hearts that we may let Your life, Your way, Your grace overshadow all the forces that are clawing at us and crushing us.

May we be aware that we are members of a very big family, O God. Enable us to see each other as brother and sister, as parent and child, and to live together in the kind of outgoing love that Christ brought.

Above all, enable us to rest in Your grace. When we have done our best, may we leave with You the rest. Give us a faith that is big enough to do that, so that we are not cramped in the stuffy little cubbyholes which we have called life.

This is the prayer we offer for all members of this great family of faith, O Father. Be with those who mourn; who suffer, who struggle, those who are ill and need your healing touch. Give patience to us all and bring a special blessing where there is a special need. Bless our president, our leaders and our nation, that we may do justly, love mercy and walk humbly with you. Bless Your Church in all places, that Your peace and power and purpose may penetrate our lives, through Jesus Christ who taught us to pray (The Lord's Prayer)

June 16, 1985

Almighty God who has filled the earth with beauty and who brings life out of death, joy out of sadness: we come into Your presence and give thanks even when our spirits are not fully thankful. We know that You are giving and forgiving, and when we do not sense these gifts, it is because of our fullness of mind and slowness of heart.

Accept our thanks for Jesus Christ our Lord and Saviour whose understanding of us baffles us, because it is so much greater than our understanding of ourselves. Accept our thanks for the time for reflection and renewal that the changing seasons bring, and for friends who reach out in understanding and supportive encouragement.

In your presence we seek the power of Your Spirit, that we may be a redemptive, healing force in this world, rather than a dividing, defensive bastion. Enable us to affirm the age we live in, to bring to it our present best, not our past nostalgia, and to know that its future is in Your hands. Give us clarity of vision and singleness of purpose, and the faith to place our loved ones in Your hands, for whom we pray now:

> those who are ill and need health;
> those who are discouraged and need hope;
> those who face decisions and need guidance;
> those who mourn and need comfort.

To all, give grace, strength and peace, O loving Father of us all.

We pray for all who are held hostage in this world, so full of bitterness and barbarism. Our prayers continue daily for our friend and colleague in ministry, the Reverend Benjamin Weir, and for all others held hostage, both on land and in the air.[26] May Your grace go with them, and may the ways of peace supplant the threats of war. In this day so filled with many types of blatant religious extremists, bring us all back to the great and sturdy faith and the calm courage of those who possess the fruit of the spirit: love, joy, peace, patience, kindness, goodness, faithfulness, self-control.

So, O Lord support us all the day long, till the shadows lengthen

And the evening comes and the busy world is hushed, and the fever of life is over, and our work is done.

Then in thy great mercy, grant us a safe lodging, and a holy rest and peace at the last.

Amen.

---

[26] Dr. Watermulder references Reverend Weir, a graduate of Princeton Theological Seminary, who was one of the American hostages abducted in Lebanon.

June 23, 1985

Great and eternal God, who breathed Your Spirit on all creation and brought life, breath and meaning to all things: we pause this day to acknowledge Your greatness, and the goodness of life lived in Your all-encompassing Spirit.

Therefore, with all creation, we give praise for this good gift of life; for its wonder and mystery; for its joy and possibility; for its adventure and hope; yes, even for the grief and poignancy whose shadows reflect the brightness of our hopes and dreams. Now we know in part, as seeing in a mirror, dimly, but our trust and perception come from Your Spirit in our life. Help us affirm it, celebrate it, seize it and rejoice in it, O God, until that new day dawns when we shall know even as we are known.

Great Father of us all, forgive us for our self-preoccupation and for confining ourselves to the little worlds of our present experience when You are ready to initiate us into such a larger, more vibrant and vital world. Give us the mind of Christ, that our minds may be corrected and directed, and give us His compassion, that we may sense our kinship with and concern for all Your children who are our brothers and sisters.

You have placed us in families, O Father, so we pray for the larger family of your church and world. Show us the way to peace and give us the will and wisdom to achieve it. Bless those who mourn; strengthen the afflicted; comfort those in need; and guide the perplexed. For all who are ill and need guidance, grant Your Spirit. We commend to you our high school students and their leaders as they embark on their work trip.

In the midst of the confusions of these days, we pray for those who are held hostage and for their families. Give them the strength of Your Spirit to endure. We pray for the president, all those who seek to negotiate with the terrorists that life may be spared. We pray for the kind of understanding that will bring peace, and not war, in the Middle East, that land which has been such a center of controversy through the ages and make us all, O God, a part of the answer rather than a part of the problem.

(The Lord's Prayer)

June 30, 1985

As the deer pants for the water brooks, so our thirsty souls quench their yearnings in Your Presence, O Lord. Your greatness overwhelms us, and in our smallness, our souls cry out for the completeness which comes in Your Presence. Where even our desolations and difficulties take on new meaning. Accept our gratitude for this life and the transforming fascination of living it as servants of Christ. We offer our thanks for our homes and loved ones, for memories that brighten our days and dreams which drive us on, for days of work and hours of leisure. Most of all, we give thanks for Christ our Lord, our Saviour, and our Guide.

Eternal Power who taught us to say Father, we come before You as little children. We need Your comfort: enfold us in Your mighty arms. We need Your guidance: point to us the way. We need Your strength: breathe on us a breath of God. Give us a robust thankfulness for being alive, a courageous daring to tackle the problems we have been toying with, and a consuming faith that will sustain us. Take us as we are, O God, and enable us to be what you meant us to be.

O Good Shepherd who leads us beside the still waters to restore our troubled souls: we pray for the sick, the discouraged, those with special needs, that Your presence may bring them peace. Our prayers arise for our nation and our world. We give thanks for the release of the hostages and pray for them a safe and speedy return home. And now, O Lord, help us in all lands not to be hostage to those powers which only make things worse and prevent us from finding the ways of peace. May Your Spirit surround us all—enemies, friends, the hostages from the place and the other hostages, like the Reverend Ben Weir, who have been held captive for so many months.[27] May we allow Your Spirit to make us into a family of nations who seek peace and purpose for all. Bless our president and our leaders and all in our land as we celebrate our nation's independence this week with the awareness of the spiritual heritage which shaped us all.

Lord of all worlds, before whom stand the spirits of the living and the dead: we bless Your name for all Your servants who have finished their course and kept the faith. Take now the veil from every heart, and unite us in one communion with all the faithful on earth and in heaven, through Jesus Christ our Lord who taught us to pray together saying (The Lord's Prayer)

---

[27] Dr. Watermulder references Reverend Weir, a graduate of Princeton Theological Seminary, who was one of the American hostages abducted in Lebanon.

September 1, 1985

Almighty God from whom we come, to whom we return, and in whom we live and move and have our being: we give thanks for new beginnings and fresh starts; for the renewal that comes with September and the new possibilities that come as we leave the past behind and plunge into the future. In Christ You have made all things new, O God. The old is finished and gone; the new has come. In Christ You are always renewing us, forgiving our past and opening our future. Today we affirm that faith, and today we begin again.

On this special Sunday, we give thanks for youthful vigor, energy and enthusiasm. We give thanks for leaders of youth—those from our staff, from our church, from our families. May Your blessings be with all parents and children and youth as they make new beginnings this fall. Be with all teachers and leaders in the schools around us and in this church. Whatever our age, enable us to accept it and affirm it because in Christ You accept and affirm us, and thus enable the young to give inspiration to the old, and the old to give direction to the young. May this church be first and always Your church, O God, the body of Christ at work in our lives and in our world. May Your pardon, peace and purpose rest on all who worship here, all who seek Your presence in the midst of the beguiling and indifferent world around us. May Your Spirit be upon Your missionaries and workers as they bear witness to the power of the risen Christ in places near and far, and may all of us be caught up in Your one great family.

We pray for our world—as we know it here in Philadelphia, as we relate to it throughout our land of promise, as we share it with peoples in lands where the opportunities are so limited. We lift special prayers for those who are ravaged by storm and tragedy. Sustain them, O Lord, that their spirits may surmount those natural forces which forever remind us that we are pilgrims on this earth. Our prayers go with all the peoples of South Africa as they struggle with the age-old dilemmas which we humans inflect upon one another. May a new day be aborning where Your Spirit will open eyes and warm hearts and clear heads, that life may be abundant and joyful. We put before You all our needs, O Lord, and look to You for the grace and guidance we seek. All these mercies we ask.

Be with the leaders of our land that they may seek the ways of peace for peoples everywhere. Make us instruments of that peace, first with each other, then with other lands. May our conquests of outer space not outrun our concern for inner values, motives and directions, and may the Christ who makes all things new rule our minds and hearts so that every situation may be the very place where we may sing unto the Lord a new song.

These mercies we ask not of our worthiness, but through Your great, forgiving love in Christ Jesus, who taught us when we pray to say (The Lord's Prayer)

September 8, 1985

Great God our Father: You fill our lives with great possibilities and surround our days with new opportunities. In Your majestic splendor and might, You stoop down to us in love and care.

For the blessings of this life; the ministries of Your grace; this faith we hold and these friends we share; for Your church around the world and this worshiping congregation here in Bryn Mawr; for the larger life to which You call us, the small and petty ways from which You spare us; the expansive sense of being part of a world far bigger than our small confines—for so much we give thanks, but especially we give thanks for Christ our Lord, His grace that surrounds us; His guidance that directs us; His perception that enlarges us; His life and death and rising again that saves us and brings us into Your holy presence.

May Your Spirit be with us as we begin this fall season. May those who have special problems get a new grip on themselves and new guidance to direct them. May those beginning school—teachers, pupils, parents—be instructed in the ways that open both mind and heart, that enhance both body and soul. May those of our members who are sick or in special need feel your breath upon them, and may all who have lost loved ones find themselves drawn closer to our heavenly home and give thanks for the days they have shared in this life.

Bless our land in these troubled times, O Lord. As our legislators gather, give them direction that transcends political advantage. Our prayers reach out to all Your children in South Africa, that peace and purpose may return to that troubled land and all people may find a new freedom as they glorify You by serving one another. We pray for Jews, Muslims, and Christians in the Middle East, that leaders may bring reconciliation and hope. Especially for our prayers to continue for those Americans yet held hostage, among them the Reverend Ben Weir[28]. Stand with them, O God, and stand with all who strive for peace.

(The Lord's Prayer)

---

[28] Dr. Watermulder references Reverend Weir, a graduate of Princeton Theological Seminary, who was one of the American hostages abducted in Lebanon.

September 15, 1985

Eternal Creator and Father of all, whose morning stars sang together at the dawn of life and to whom we sing praises for our life: we give thanks for the rhythmic balance of our days and the restoring contrasts of our years:

For summer's pensive joy and autumn's anticipation; for tasks which tax our strength and rest which refreshes our spirits; for quiet summer days and eager autumn plans; for friends whose understanding puts us at ease and friends whose needs require deep understanding from us; for the interior life of faith as it renews us in solitude and meditation, and the communal life of the Spirit we find in church as it separates our whims from your will; for this blessed community gathered in prayer and praise today and then scattered in witness and work throughout the week; for the immense varieties that you bring to the so-easily settled and somber patterns we yield to, we give thanks, Lord of the years and lover of our lives.

O God, our help in ages past, our hope for years to come: bless this church, that it may be a blessing. Bless these people, that their cares and concerns, their troubles and difficulties may be transformed into experiences of growth and victory. Bless our leaders, our workers and all who lead us on our staff. Not only do we pray for our number, but we pray for this world. Bless the peoples of South Africa as they struggle for a freedom that can bring a sense of dignity to everyone there, and make us be sensitive to those ways we can bring reconciliation and peace. May Your presence sustain our loved ones who are separated from us. Show us how to make wars to cease, how to ease the plight of the oppressed, how to bring Your joy and goodness to earth. Then give us the faith to seek Your guidance and the strength to do Your will, through Jesus Christ our Lord, who taught us to pray (The Lord's Prayer)

October 27, 1985

Almighty God, the light of the minds that seek You, the strength of the wills that serve you, and the life of the souls that love You: today we join in spiritual fellowship with all the hosts of heaven in praise of your steadfast love and continuing concern for us. When the morning stars sang together, Your creation proclaimed Your glory; still today as science unveils the precision of this universe, we behold the wonder of Your constancy and the marvel of the mind. When you sent persons in faith and gave them strength to criticize the idolatries of their time, Your guidance came to humanity; still today, speak through those whom we reject in one age and venerate in the next. When You came among us in Christ, we beheld a love which goes all the way in compassion; and renewal in submission to Him who unveils life's meaning. When Your church has grown proud, You have chastened it; still today Your judgment makes us weary with our easy answers. Amid this host of witnesses and among all Your children on earth and in heaven, we come before You as individuals with our particular needs, but also as the people of Your church, in which we find our identity and claim our destiny.

Lord, You know us better than we know ourselves. Forgive our pride and vindictiveness; forgive the many ways we play God, the many hypocrisies which exploit our faith, the many prejudices which become our idols and shrines. Forgive, also, O Lord, our smallness of faith, and enable us to trust in You when we have done what we can. Assured that nothing can separate us from Your understanding love, make us aware of the stream of history in which we move, that we may be recipients of Your peace and power, as well as instruments of Your purpose.

May Your blessing be upon our nation as we meet with the nations of the world, and may Your Spirit guide our president and our leaders as we seek to develop the ways of peace with Russia and all their nations.

We pray for Your church everywhere in all lands and for the church in this place. Here may the faithful find salvation and the careless be awakened; may the doubting find faith and the anxious be encouraged; may the tempted find help and the sorrowful comfort; may the weary find rest and the strong be renewed; may the aged find consolation and the young be inspired, that we may yet be instruments of your compassion and concern.

We give thanks, O Lord, for all Your children who have kept the faith, finished the course and now have found wholeness in Your presence. With them we ascribe to You all honor and glory, that we, with them, may receive the blessings of Your Spirit. And now as our Saviour Christ has taught us, we humbly pray (The Lord's Prayer)

November 17, 1985

God of our life, through all the circling years, we trust in Thee;
In all the past, through all our hopes and fears, Thy hand we see.
With each new day, when morning lifts the veil,
We own Thy mercies, Lord, which never fail.

Never let us lose sight of the grandeur of living because it becomes so self-possessing, O Father. Never let the sorrows which love has brought, nor the decisions which opportunity has handed us, plunge us into despair. Always give us hearts of thankfulness for this gift of life, this richness of friends, this variety of experience. Always enable us to the grace to live the adventure of life's present chapter with its new demands, and with those duties which beckon us beyond the prison of pity and self-preoccupation. In all things, may we be thankful that Your grace is sufficient for every need.

Make us a part of the stream of life which finds its meaning through trust and concern, through love of Your creation and commitment to Christ Your Son our Lord.

May this depth of trust support those who grieve and those who sorrow; may it strengthen those who are ill; may it fortify those who are weak; may it direct those who are weighted with decisions; and may it humble those who think they know it all.

Bless the Church. May the Church proclaim the truth of God's saving power in Christ, and may that power overcome and overwhelm our lives, so that all else falls before its impact. Bless the missionaries of Your Word here at home and in distant places, that they may know the power of Your promise. "Lo, I am with you always."

Our prayers reach out to our world and to the role our nation plays in our world. May Your blessings be with President Reagan and the Soviet leader Gorbachev, that they may seek the peace and security of all people everywhere and explore the paths that lead to mutual understanding.[29] You have called on us to do justly, love mercy and walk humbly with You, our God. May Your grace touch our lives and make those words a reality, through (The Lord's Prayer)

---

[29] Dr. Watermulder references the Summit Meeting in Geneva.

August 14, 1987

Great God of all creation and Lord of our lives: ow good it is to be here, spiritually surrounded by the saints of the ages and physically back home as Your family, receiving Your Spirit which restores and renews. As the rain gently falls to nourish the ground, so may Your Spirit fall upon us to refresh us by renewal. Accept our gratitude for all the sacrifices of life these good gifts we so readily take for granted: for homes and friends; for church and faith; for love and loyalty; for the joy of receiving these good blessings and the greater joy of being a blessing; for the power, the presence, the purpose we find in Jesus Christ—so great a companion, so faithful a friend, so understanding a counsellor, so demanding a guide, so totally our redeemer—Your son, our Lord.

Mindful of the blessings of quiet summer days, our prayers reach out to those whose struggles and troubles have engulfed them. Give them light beyond their light and purpose great enough to consume their difficulty. Show them the way and give them the will to follow it. Bless those who suffer and endure the hardships of this mortal life. Give them the knowledge of the Good Shepherd who leads, loves and directs. Unite us in spirit with those who have moved from this life to the next, and comfort us with Your assurance. And out of these days, O Lord, make us a people who find our identity here in Your house, and with Your Word, so that we may be in but not of the world, drinking deeply from the springs of faith, sharing gladly the gifts of Your grace, and expressing Your kingdom's power. In the midst of today's confusions, renew our sense of integrity and purpose, strengthen our loyalty to Your way and to one another and bind us together as a people—repentant, hopeful, useful. Bless our land. Bless our leaders. Baptize our politics from Your cleansing streams. Endure Your Spirit here and everywhere in every place and race. Bless us with Your Spirit which unites, reconciles and renews. So carry us from the quiet of summer into the quickening of the fall, equipped, sustained and directed by our Lord who taught us to pray (The Lord's Prayer)

February 26, 1989

Almighty God our Father, You have come to us in ways we never dreamed, caring for us with a love we have never understood, gently calling us home with a love that will not let us go. We gather in Your house on Your day with Your people to respond to that love with praise and thanksgiving, joy and gratitude.

We behold the wonders of our world—the stars in their orbit, the seasons in their cycle, the immutable laws that govern this created world, the opportunities You give us and the challenges You put before us in our time—and we bow in awe and expectation. Enter into our lives and direct them beyond ourselves. Enter into our situations and touch them with the light and life of Your Spirit. Enter into our plans and infuse them with Your purpose.

As we think of all You can do with people who seek Your will and way, we pray for our nations. Aware of the heritage we have, we pray for Your guidance in the destiny that we choose. May we do justly, love mercy and walk humbly with You, O God, looking to Christ the Prince of Peace. Even as we were an inspiration to the world in days gone by, may we take initiative for peace so that we may be used for the healing and helping of all peoples once more. Give compassion to our leaders—our president, our congress and all in authority—and give us a sense of responsibility that dispels indifference.

We pray for those who mourn and those who are ill. O God, walk beside them. Come to those who are disturbed, upset and in need, that they may drink from Your Spirit. And now, as our Saviour taught us (The Lord's Prayer)

SECTION 4

Special Occasions

Fifth Anniversary with Bryn Mawr Presbyterian Church
September 10, 1967

Everlasting God, who in Thy patience hast borne with and led Thy children through the ages, we thank Thee for Thy guiding hand today. [30]"We've felt Thy touch in sorrow's darkened way" and found ourselves anew while serving Thee. In the midst of the change and upheaval of this age, we turn to Thee, our refuge and strength, the one who knows us better than we know ourselves; and in Thy presence, we are made whole again.

Today we pray for Thy Church everywhere and for this church here in Bryn Mawr, that it may ever by Thy church, not subject to the whim of men. Grant to all of us—staff, officers and congregation—a willingness to seek Thy will, a wisdom to walk in Thy way. Make this church a great channel of compassion and concern, flowing through us into the world. Today, also, we pray for all pupils and teachers, that true learning may take place and enlightenment may disburse the heat of emotion and the darkness of ignorance, and with knowledge may there come an appreciation of Thee, the Lord and Giver of the laws of life, and of Jesus Christ, Thy truth incarnate.

May Thy Spirit be with our president and leaders, and enable us to resolve the horrible tensions and troubles of this day, particularly our war in Vietnam. Bless and guide those who must make decisions, and spare us who do not bear the weight of decision from too easy answers and too facile judgment. Bless our men who must do battle and surround them and us with Thy love.

O Lord of all worlds, before whom stand the spirits of the living and the dead: we thank thee for this holy place and this communion of saints, uniting us in spirit with those who behold Thee in light eternal. By Thy Grace keep us ever in this holy communion and finally unite us in that kingdom which has no end. And now as our Saviour Christ hath taught us, we humbly pray (The Lord's Prayer)

---

[30]   Calvin Weiss Laufer, 1919

June 13, 1971

Great and everlasting God who hast put us on earth as Thy children and called us unto Thee as our Father: we thank Thee

for the beauty of the earth
for the glory of the skies
for the love which from our birth
over and around us lies.[31]

For the blessings which may attend us in Thy church, which is the family of God, and for the sensitive awareness to our need which comes in Christ who understands and forgives us, we thank Thee, God.

Today, especially, we beseech Thy blessing upon the children of this church and church school who participated in their special services; upon all children and parents, both here and abroad, that goodness in life and its growth may be restored. Grant Thy love to all college students as they seek and strive to find the answer to their restlessness. Give the breadth of Thy understanding and patience to all parents. To all who venture forth for truth, give Thy love and leading.

Bless us as a national family, O God, that we may care for each other. Bless us as a global family, that we may blend our efforts for peace and for everyone's welfare, with such prayers we add our prayers for those in need, those who are ill, those in trouble, those we mourn.

(The Lord's Prayer)

---

[31] Folliott S. Pierpoint, 1864

May 14, 1972

The heavens declare the glory of God, and the firmament shows His handiwork! For this good world; for new life springing all about us; for sun and rain and night and day; for a world brim-full of joys we pass by or forget; for our senses and feelings, our friends and our hopes; for so much more than we can mention, we give thanks, O God of creation, redemption, recreation.

O God, You have so richly given us all good things to enjoy, we give thanks for all these gifts, and on this family day we give thanks for the memories welling up out of the past, the guidance surging through the present, and the hope beckoning us to the future. We offer praise for the simple things of life which can be shared by all regardless of circumstance. For fathers and mothers, brothers and sisters and friends, who care; for homes which are knit together in love because their center is in more than themselves; for children growing older and learning and loving; for adults growing younger and sharing and laughing; for the larger family of the Church, where in the give-and-take, we may find the priceless quality in every person; for ways too numerous to mention but so often gathered all together in the Christian home, we give thanks today.

Bless the homes of this land; bless the children as they grow in body, mind, and spirit. Bless the homes of this congregation. Bless the church which makes us at home within Your Kingdom in this life and the life to come. And everywhere, where Your children pray, bind them together with one another in love and understanding.

Our prayers reach out to the sick, those confined to their rooms, the sorrowful, those who feel the loss of loved ones. Our prayers reach out to our nation that we may be to ourselves and to all the world, but especially before God, a people of peace who seek to do justly, love mercy and walk humbly with our God.

Eternal God of all, unite us in spirit with those who have gone before us, catch us up in the cloud of witnesses who surround us, and at the last, gather us into our eternal home, through Jesus Christ.

(The Lord's Prayer)

June 30, 1974

Almighty God, Father of our Lord Jesus Christ, creator of all life and judge of all persons, in whom is no darkness and whose light casts shadows on our path because we obstruct its beam: we offer thanks for the many good gifts You have given us, even though we have neither acknowledged nor deserved them. For the joy of work, and new problems to surmount; for the love of friends, and the simple, homey blessings we may share with them; for the memory of accomplishment and the good sense to forget it; for all Your children, and the growth in grace it takes to love them; for our own experiences and achievements, and the humility we need to endure them; but most of all, for the clear focus we have on You and Your purpose as we see Jesus Christ and the way He brings us into Your presence where sin is forgiven and life becomes fresh again.

Eternal Father, whose strength is sufficient for all who lay hold on it and who knows our weaknesses far better than we do: You have taught us to turn to You as children seek their loving father. We bring before You the doubts and disappointments that make cowards of us all, asking You to refine them in Your fire until courage and conviction return. In this clever age, save us from our own cunning, lest our life become an alibi rather than an answer. Give us drive and determination in our work, but link it with dedication, discipline and devotion, lest we become monsters we cannot control. Help us to face our faults, and then with all the divine dignity You breathe into us, make us big enough to lay them at Your feet, seeking the pardon and power that comes to us through Christ.

O sovereign ruler in whose hands are the destiny of the nations, we pray for our leaders and our life together in this blessed land. Link us, hand in hand and heart to heart, with all our fellow citizens, that together we may grow and share, work and care for one another. May Your Spirit guide our land. May our nation rise to its new challenges as it has in the past, and become the promising hope of those who despair. Bless the ill, O Father; comfort those in grief; give guidance to the perplexed; and bring health and healing to us all through Jesus Christ our Lord:

(The Lord's Prayer)

March 4, 1973 (Boy Scouts)
February 18, 1979

Bless, O Lord, these Your servants Peter and Doug, and follow them and their fellow scouts in all that is true and honorable, just and good.

We give thanks for the ways You come to all of us here in our time and place, giving us the joys of this community, the opportunities to learn, the blessings of good company. For children and homes, for people who find a larger life in service, for Jesus Christ both Lord and Saviour, for the sheer glory of life when we air it out and know it is in Your hands whether we live it here or beyond here, we give thanks.

Show us, O God, how futile is self-deception and how miserable becomes self-worship. Teach us to pray as we ought to pray. May we be trustworthy, that the honor of our word and our dependability becomes our strength, ever calling forth the integrity in others. Show us how to be loyal to the high and true and noble. Teach us to be helpful, knowing that if we want to find the joy of life, we must learn to forget ourselves. Teach us to be friendly, not putting down others or minimizing the significance of each person's dignity and worth. May we be courteous, respecting the needs of others who may be bearing far heavier burdens than our own. Make us kind, dispelling the tension and fever which arises from race and class snobbishness and spreading the peace which comes from being servants of God. May we be obedient to those to whom we owe honorable obedience, but most of all to our Lord. Make us cheerful, seeking to understand others and to be understood; teach us, O Lord, to be thrifty, with the immense resources which are investments You have entrusted to our care, and to be brave, because inward resources give us strength. In these smoggy times, make us clean in Thought, act, and association, that life may flash with the freshness of Your presence. Above all, make us reverent, handling holy things with awe and appreciation, knowing that no one is truly whole until Your Spirit is present, and that life is cheap if it loses its reverent respect.

Eternal Lord, You hear the simple prayers of earnest souls: We pray not only for ourselves but for others, particularly within the family of this church. Especially, we remember the sick and suffering, those whose life remains in this world but dimly, those who fear what the next day and hour brings. Reach forth Your strong hand and be unto them a companion and comfort. Spread forth the healing rays of Your Spirit, that peace and calm may come to souls, and physical healing may speed forth. We pray for our nation and our leaders—for the president, his cabinet and advisors and for our congress. We pray for our world—for those involved in conflict in Vietnam and China, in Iran and all the sensitive places on our globe. Lead us to the ways of brotherhood, righteousness and peace through Jesus Christ.

(The Lord's Prayer)

February 25, 1979
Presbytery service

Eternal God, who through the ages has sought out a people, led them and fed them, corrected them and directed them, and who in the fullness of Your glory came among us in our Lord Jesus Christ and made us become members of God's mystical body, the Church:

You have heard our praise and prayer, and we have heard Your word. Now we offer to You our thanksgiving for this sacred moment when we may join with all the hosts of heaven and all Your children on earth in ascribing to You all honor and glory, praise, dominion and power.

In Your presence we find our meaning, O God; in Your purpose we find the direction our lives should go; in the power of Your Spirit we gain the strength we need. Accept our thanks: that we may turn to something more than ourselves for the insight we need; that we may drink from the ever-flowing fountains of Your Spirit; that we may rest in Your grace and be caught up in the company of all Your children of all ages, places, and races.

May we see how much we have and how little we have done with it; how much You can do for us and how little we let You do; how great and wonderful is our world and how small and miserable we sometimes make it. You can get along without us, but we can't get along without You, O God. Use us then as Your servants, until our noblest achievements are but a reflection of Your skill and power.

We are mindful of the communion of saints in whose presence we worship, O God, and today we are especially mindful of our relationship to each other as members of the United Presbyterian Church and in particular of the Presbytery of Philadelphia. Where it is in error, correct it; and where it is an instrument of Your will, direct it with courage and compassion. May we, as a branch of Your holy Catholic Church, be true to the Word and submissive to the Spirit.

As we meet here this day, we offer prayers for our world: for the people of Philadelphia, that we may unite in the struggle for human rights and opportunity; for the members of our Jewish community who have felt the old suspicions and hatreds revive; for the people of China and Vietnam where warfare threatens anew; for our whole world of 1979, aching for light and love but living in darkness and hatred. May the fresh breath of Your Spirit open the possibilities for reconciliation and peace, and may the people of Your church be in the vanguard.

Restore to us the joy of our salvation, O Lord, and hear these prayers which we ask through Christ, the great head of the Church. Amen.

January 25, 1981
9:30 AM service

We Americans have just gone through a remarkable week that calls forth our joyful prayers of thanksgiving to God. For fourteen long months, a part of that which makes us America has been disrespected and ill-treated.[32] During the time that 52 individual Americans were held hostage, something of each one of us was there with them. To them and their families our hearts have reached out in anguish, and now bursts forth in joy. To the degree that they were, in effect, America held hostage, all of us felt something of the pain and the humiliation that they individually had to endure.

But now they are free and somehow we too are free— free to reassess our role in this world; free to grapple with the dynamics of the new nationalisms that occupy this different world of the late 20th century; free to discover what it means to be the foremost power in a world where the earth's resources for energy grow scarcer; where nuclear warheads grow more abundant and where the possibility of global annihilation is never far away.

> So today we pause in our Sunday-morning service to offer special prayers of thanksgiving to God; to seek God's guidance; to pray for all peoples all over the world, that all of us together may learn how to live in this global village, where each group so readily asserts itself.

First we will offer our silent prayers to God; then I will lead us in our prayers together; then we will sing of our country, praying that our fathers' God, and our God and our Father, may guide us into the future as God has led us in the past; that as God directs and corrects us in the momentous days to come, we may find ourselves becoming the instruments of God's sovereign will.

Long may our land be bright with freedom's holy light,
Protect us by Thy might, great God, our King[33].
Let us bow in silent prayer:

(The Lord's Prayer)

---

[32] Dr. Watermulder references the end of the Iran Hostage Crisis.

[33] *America the Beautiful*. Katherine Lee Bates, 1910

January 25, 1981
11:00 AM service

In the silence of this hour, we hear Your voice, O God. In the vastness of the world of the Spirit, we lift up our Spirits, O Father, giving thanks for the knowledge of Your love, the power of Your Spirit and the strength of Your presence.

With the psalmist we declare, "God is our refuge and our strength, a very present help in time of trouble. Therefore, we will not fear."[34] For You are our refuge when the storms assail us, O Lord: in You is our hiding place in time of need. And You are our strength, O God: through You we are able to face our circumstances and rise to our challenges.

So today, "we give special thanks for the release of our citizens who have been held hostage.[35]

We give thanks that the long ordeal is over, that all captives were brought forth alive and ready to begin the adjustment. We give thanks for their ability to withstand the ordeal under fire, and for their parents, loved ones and friends who were their support. We give thanks for this great land of America—that with all our faults and imperfections, our growing pains and impatience, we have come to this day in peace with honor.

Now, O Lord, use this terrible nightmare for our growth and understanding. Expose our thoughts to the realities of this late-20th-century world. Unite us as a nation, that we may feel pride in country and solidarity with each other. Lift up our ideals, that we may be strong in that which makes for peace and joy. Blend our toughness with tenderness, our sensitivity with strength, that we may seize the opportunities of this decade to exhibit the disciplines of liberty, the goodness of justice and the beauty of integrity.

Grant us wisdom and insight, O Father, that we may not yield to the baser drives of hatred and revenge, for we know that hatred turns in on itself and hurts the one who hates as well as the one who is hated. May our motives be governed by Your Spirit, that in the remaining years of

[34] Psalm 46:1-2
[35] Dr. Watermulder references the Iran Hostage Crisis.

this century we may be used to fashion peace, to extend freedom and to open the doors of understanding.

You have blessed us in the past, O Lord, and given us this great land with its constitution as our heritage. Now may we rise to the occasion that is thrust upon us to give leadership to our own land and hope to people everywhere.

So may we celebrate during this week, O God, rejoicing that we are reunited as a people and united as a nation in seeking to do justly, to love mercy and to walk humbly with our God. And when the tumult and the shouting dies, may we remember that:

"Still stands thine ancient sacrifice, a humble and contrite heart.
Lord, God of hosts be with us yet, lest we forget, lest we forget."[36]

These prayers we offer in the name of Him who showed us how to serve as he suffered and sacrificed for us all, even Jesus Christ our Lord, who taught us to pray saying (The Lord's Prayer)

---

[36] *Recessional.* Rudyard Kipling, 1897

February 1, 1981

Almighty God before whose face the generations rise and pass away: age after age the living seek Thee and find that of Thy mercy there is no end. Our fathers in their pilgrimage walked by Thy guidance, and we, their children, seek to follow in their steps.

Today, with the cloud of witnesses surrounding us, we give thanks for the life of our former Senior Pastor, Rex Stowers Clements. With joy have we partaken of the many benefits of his ministry. With affection we remember his years among us as he led this family of faith; as he proclaimed Thy word; as he established the high standards of ministry in our midst. With gratitude we recall the instances in the life of this congregation when he ministered to us in sickness and in health, in joy and in sorrow, in plenty and in want. With warmth we recall the times he made transcendent for us as he baptized our children and buried our dead; as he married us, counseled us, inspired us and directed us.

Now, O Father, we give thanks that sickness and death being passed, with all the dangers and difficulties of this mortal life, his soul is at peace in Thy presence, where he is tasting to the full the eternal life he proclaimed throughout his earthly days. With him, and with all the hosts of light eternal—the people of this church who fought a good fight, kept the faith and finished the course—we rejoice in Thy holy presence, blending our voices with all the heavenly hosts in proclaiming, "Blessing and honor and glory and wisdom and power and might be unto our God forever and ever."

As we give thanks for his life, and for those of our own church family and individual families who have gone on before us, we pray that Thy mercies and blessings may attend us. Give us a clear understanding of what is vital and true, of what matters and what endures. Enable us to drink from Thine unfailing fountains and to receive the blessings of Thy Spirit, that we may be able to declare, "Thy grace is sufficient for every need."

With these prayers of praise and thanksgiving, we blend our prayers of intercession for the sick, the needy, the despairing. May Thy Spirit rest upon our president and our government that we may be a nation deserving of Thy blessings as we relate to all peoples everywhere.

"So, O Lord, support us all the day long, until the shadows lengthen and the evening comes, and the busy world is hushed, and the fever of life is over, and our work is done. Then in Thy mercy grant us a safe lodging, and a holy rest, and peace at the last, through Jesus Christ our Lord." Amen.

(The Lord's Prayer)

November 22, 1981

Eternal God, who is the same yesterday, today and forever: age after age the living seek You and find that of Your mercy there is no end. Our fathers in their pilgrimage walked by Your guidance, and in our day we seek Your presence. For the blessings of this life: its work, its hope, its change and challenge, we give thanks. If we were to count our blessings, they would number more than the sands of the sea. Accept our gratitude and make us truly thankful, O God, that as tenants on Your property, using Your tools and drawing from Your funds, we may ever turn to Christ who is the way, the truth and the life.

O loving God who loves us with a love more tender than we have ever known, we pray for Your church, here and everywhere, that as people seek You they may find You, and find the church both as the end of their quest and the beginning of the greater adventure on the road of life. Give to us something, O Lord, that will make us worthy of our blessings. Give us a faith and purpose that will save us from ourselves.

O tender Shepherd who leads us beside the still waters to restore our souls, bless all who are perplexed and anxious, upset and insecure. May they feel Your everlasting arms around them. Minister to those of our number who are sick and to all those who need Your healing touch. Surround with Your Spirit all who sorrow, all who grieve.

In Your hands, O God, are the destinies of peoples and nations. For this land of freedom, bought so dearly and founded so strongly on an awareness of Your presence, we again offer humble thanks on this Thanksgiving weekend. Especially, we praise You for the dignity and hope of democracy, and the freedom which comes when people bow as servants before Your eternal power. Lift us above the easy path of anger and hate, to the holy ground of love and compassion. Place Your hand upon our president and our leaders, that they may be led through the turmoil of these days. Bring the Spirit of peace to this world and enable us to be your peacemakers. Hear our prayers for the suffering peoples of the earth, especially those caught in the tragedy of Cambodia. May we in our abundance reach out to them in their need.

All these cares we put before You, O God, in the name of Jesus Christ our Lord and Saviour.

(The Lord's Prayer)

May 9, 1982

Almighty God, mysterious in majesty and beyond our comprehension, but whose will and way is revealed in Jesus Christ: we have learned that in whatever situation we are, we may have composure and confidence, because You are with us. In this mortal world, we experience headache and heartache, but we have found the secret of facing hardships as well as joys, because we let go and let Christ take command.

For this knowledge of Your love and this experience of Your power, we give thanks, O God. For the memories surging out of the past, for loved ones both with us now and separated from us by the passageway of death, we praise You. For the company of Your people on earth in heaven, we laud and magnify Your holy name.

Today we ask for your blessing upon all homes and families, all children and parents. May they find direction for their lives in their dedication to Christ. We pray for our larger family, the Church, that we may claim one another as our brothers and sisters and find the peace of being a part of Your family. Give us that kind of companionship that makes us strong: that enables us to face ourselves; that draws strength from your presence. Bless those who minister in Your name in difficult places, and give to your church new strength that Your peace and Your power may enter the lives of people everywhere.

As we pray for our family within Your church universal, we also pray for our relatives around the world. May we appreciate one another's differences and learn how to learn from one another. May we identify with each other and find the ways of peace among nations and plenty among people. Guide our president and congress in these days of domestic unrest and global warfare. Bring to bear the Spirit of Christ Who came not to be served but to serve and show us the ways of peace. We pray for all those—especially of our own number—who are sick or suffering, who have lost hope or lost direction. May we all be blessed by Your presence and thereby become a blessing to one another. These prayers we offer in the name of Christ, Who taught us to pray together, saying (The Lord's Prayer)

July 4, 1982

Great God our Father, whose scriptures declare that "blessed is the nation whose God is the Lord," and who has led us through turmoil and triumph, through joy and sorrow, who constantly calls us home and tells us, this My child was dead and is alive again, was lost and is found.

With all the hosts of heaven and all the children of this land in all places and of all races, we pour out our souls in praise, adoration and thanksgiving. For such a rich heritage, for hopes so great and visions so glorious, we give thanks.

We confess, O Lord, that the dreams of our forefathers are not fulfilled. We acknowledge that we often hide behind our high-sounding words so that our low-living ways might escape notice.

And yet, O Father who understands us so well, we dare to ask for new strength, new vision, new courage. We even dare to thank You for our present world, with its factions and its troubles; for all these bespeak a people seeking to find themselves and become what they might be. Help us to seize the times and claim the hour. Give us spirit and zeal to rise to the new challenge for a new and better world.

As we celebrate the freedom we have, we also reach out to all peoples, O God, as a nation that seeks peace and opportunity and freedom for all. And as Your Spirit so richly led us in the founding of this land, may we seek anew the mind and the spirit of Christ, who came not to be served but to serve and to give His life as ransom for many.

We pray for our president and our congress, and for all who would lead us. Our prayers reach out to the Middle East, to Lebanon and Israel, that ways of peace may be established.

As we pray for our world and our nation on this Independence Day, we also pray for our own number here at home: those who are ill and need healing; those who are lost and need saving; those who are depressed and disturbed and need hope; those who are sad and need cheer. To all, be the good shepherd who leads us beside the still waters to restore our souls.

(The Lord's Prayer)

January 8, 1983

O God our help in ages past, our hope for years to come,
Our shelter from the stormy blast and our eternal home[37]:

We look to You in these first days of the new year, O God, knowing that as You have been faithful in years gone by, You will be faithful for years to come. Make us faithful to You, O God, and thankful. Thankful for the memories of the past, the hopes for the future, the strength in the present. Thankful for Jesus Christ, the eternal word of God—for all He means to us in interpreting our lives, directing our way, supporting us in our need. Thankful for life and the anticipation it brings, and for friends who bring us balance and who love us not for what we pretend to be but for what we are.

Great God our Father, our world is full of suffering, struggling, hurting people. Forgive our inhumanity toward one another and increase our compassion so the hurts may be healed. Bring fresh hope and zeal to us all, that together we may make this day count. Show us the way to peace in the Mideast and peace at home. May Your blessing be upon our president and his advisors, our legislators and leaders. May Your Spirit infuse Your church in this land and across the world with new vision, new loyalty to Christ, new strength. May our life together, as we live out the last years of the 20th century, be an experience of Your power in our midst and Your peace in our hearts.

Today we place in Your hands our loved ones and friends who are sick, and all those for whom this physical body is not sufficient for their spirits. Surround them with Your peace, and may Your presence give them new strength. We pray for those who mourn the loss of loved ones, that this new tie to their heavenly home may increase their strength and give them a new experience of Your grace. Enable us all to affirm the life You have given us so we may celebrate it each day with each other and with You, the one whose love and understanding goes beyond all expectations.

God of the coming years through paths unknown we follow Thee.
Where we are strong, Lord leave us not alone, our refuge be.
Be Thou for us in life our daily bread, our hearts true home.
When all our years have sped.[38]

(The Lord's Prayer)

---

[37]   Isaac Watts, 1719
[38]   Hugh T. Kerr, 1916

May 8, 1983

O God who set in motion the laws which move this universe and who saw that it was good, and whose Spirit is planted in our spirits and whose presence broods over all creation: we praise You for Your dramatic witness to us in the beauty and color of springtime, in the constancy of Thy seasons, in the restlessness within our souls that won't allow us to be satisfied with elemental existence alone. Everywhere and in everything You speak, O God, but particularly we praise You for the still, small voice which causes us to take stock of ourselves and bow once more before Your great act of coming among us and restoring us to Yourself through Christ Jesus our Lord.

O God our Heavenly Father who has set the solitary in families: look in favor upon the homes of Your people. Defend them against evil and supply all their needs according to the riches of Your grace. Make precious the heritage of godly parents, may we in our generation give the historic in faith a vital expression for our world, even as they did in theirs.

Unite us in Your larger family, the Church, until we reach out to one another in understanding love and compassion, and relate to the rest of the world as people whose blessings must be shared through understanding and concern.

Bless all parents and children, that they abide under the shadow of the Almighty and find Your love that knows no limits. Bless our youth as they embark on life's greater adventures, that they may happily be themselves because they are Yours and are at home in this world because they are at home with You.

Be with us as a nation, that we may find our common unity as Your children, and thus be led to new avenues of understanding. Even as You have given us vision and courage to break with past wrongs in other centuries and generations, so equip us to plunge forward toward a new day which makes our land worthy of Your blessings. Give to our land and people a leadership which is neither partisan nor prejudiced, but honest and earnest in seeking Your peace and purpose for our world.

With grateful memories we thank You for those who have gone on before us, O Lord; and with tender love we beseech Your peace upon those who mourn and sorrow, and your power upon those who are ill or in need. These prayers we offer through Christ who taught us to pray, saying (The Lord's Prayer)

June 30, 1985

Almighty God, loving and patient, knowing us better than we know ourselves, always ready to welcome home those who respond to compassionate love: we thank you for this quiet hour when we take our bearings and find our moorings. We bless You for quiet summer days which heal our spirits and refresh our bodies. Mindful of the many ways You speak to us, we thank You most for the clear revelation of Yourself in Jesus Christ, and for the new life we find as we are fed by the Holy Spirit and share in the fellowship of a redeemed and redeeming community of believers.

With our expression of thanks for your mercy, O Lord, we express our needs for ourselves and others. May our moments of summer relaxation not separate us from our world, but equip us to wage the warfare our lives were meant for. May our understanding of the faith, whether clear or cloudy, not allow us to be smug, or smother the creative forces you have given us, but may our faith reflect its force in the quality of our lives and the compassionate concern of our attitudes. Jar the well-grooved prejudices which use us as their pawns. Awaken within us the inquiring and sensitive spirit until we see what life looks like through the eyes of others. Give us goals too great to grasp and a sense of Your forgiving peace too deep to explain. Put meaning into this often-silly treadmill of existence and make us good for something, O Lord, before our day is done.

Bless all who seek to be disciples of Jesus Christ and who present a clear witness to Him before the world. May the Church of Jesus Christ reflect the compassion of the Christ who claims us all. May Your blessing and wisdom attend our president and leaders, that we may truly become a nation under God. Give us a gratitude for our freedom and responsibility for the ways we express it.

America, America, God mend Thy every flaw

Confirm thy soul in self-control

Thy liberty in law![39]

To those who are sick, those who sorrow, those who face difficult decisions and those who need assurance: grant Your peace which the world can neither give nor take away, and be to them the good shepherd who restores their souls. We give thanks, O Lord, for the faithful departed, and

---

[39]   Dr. Watermulder references "Pikes Peak," which was the original name of Katharine Lee Bate's poem first published on July 4, 1895, and later set to music known as "America the Beautiful."

for the fellowship in the spirit we have with them. Unite us in spirit with one another and grant us the awareness of Your peace and a sense of Your purpose, through Jesus Christ.

(The Lord's Prayer)

November 24, 1985

With hearts filled with thanksgiving, we come into Your house on Your day, O Lord Most High. With joy in the fact that we are not alone but that You are with us always, we praise You, O God. With a sense of release, renewal and new strength, we give thanks for Christ our Lord whose sacrificial death brings life and hope to us so we may share with Him in the joy of living.

Give us grace to give ourselves away to each other, O God. Use us as the instruments to carry His peace and understanding, Your comfort and courage to others. Consume us with something ourselves because we are at peace with You.

We pray for those who are sick and those who need help, who are battered with the infirmities of our mortal bodies and who need the touch of Your Spirit to become whole once more. Come among them as the good shepherd who restores their souls. Grant to the lonely, the friendless, and the sorrowing the peace of Your presence and the power of Your Spirit. As we approach our national holiday of thanksgiving, may we do so mindful of how much we have and how much so many others need. Out of our abundance, may we contribute to their necessities; and out of our blessings, may we become a source of blessing.

We pray for our nation, our president, our congress in these confusing times. May the meeting of the world leaders at the Summit[40] issue forth in new resolve, new commitment to find the ways of peace. Restore to us a sense of common purpose, and make of us a nation filled with compassion, ever mindful of from whence we came. In the midst of threats of nuclear war, may all peoples, here and around the world, value those instruments that give life, more than those instruments that bring death. And may we know the meaning of our Lord's words, "Blessed are the peacemakers, for they shall be called the children of God." Now hear us:

(The Lord's Prayer)

---

[40] Dr. Watermulder references the 1985 Geneva Summit held on November 19 and 20, 1985.

125th Church Anniversary Prayer,
January 11, 1998

Almighty God,   the light of the minds that know You,
the life of the souls that love You,
the strength of the wills that serve You,

Hear the prayers we have offered on this anniversary Sunday:
Prayers of gratitude for Your many blessings,
Prayers for all nations and races;
Prayers for all who minister to others.

Hear us now, O merciful God, as we offer prayers for ourselves:
We confess our personal inadequacies, our sins and
shortcomings, and the many ways we stifle Your will as
we exalt our desires.
The walls of gold that entomb us,
The swords of scorn that divide us,
Take not Your thunder from us
But take away our pride.

Lord Jesus, assure us of Pardon for our sins; give Purpose to our lives; and
grant us Power for our journey.
Through many troubles, toils and snares,
We have already come.
'Tis grace has brought us safe thus far,
And grace will lead us home.

Here we are, O God, "standing in the living present," poised between 125
years of memory and hopes for all the years to come, forging our
own link in the chain which connects the future to the past. Enable
us to do this, mindful that "the church's one foundation is Jesus
Christ her Lord,"[41] and that "unless the Lord builds the house,
those that build it labor in vain."[42]

---

[41]   Samuel J. Stone, 1866
[42]   Psalm 127:1

Mindful that "others have labored and we have entered into their labor," we pray that we may do in our times what those who have gone before have done for us. Therefore, O Lord:

Inspire us as we recall the dedication and determination of those sixteen souls who gathered with members of this presbytery to establish this church.

Broaden our perspective as we contemplate the thirty-three years of ministry with our first pastor, William Hamilton Miller.

Enlarge our horizons as we call to remembrance our past members and leaders, so many of them near and dear to our hearts whom we "have loved long since and lost awhile."

Renew our commitment as we ponder the vision and devotion of these former pastors, many of whom we vividly remember today:

– Andrew Mutch, with his deep love of people, his jolly warmth and his Scottish burr.
– Rex Clements and the associate pastor Harold Smith, whose thoughtful and judicious guidance directed our congregation and community through years of growth.
– All those women and men, both pastor and laypeople, whose commitment to Christ has brought leadership, exquisite music and increased our ability to discern Your will and speak Your word.
O God our help in ages past, our hope for years to come: grant grace and guidance to Gene Bay, to each member of the staff and to the leaders and members of this church—all moving toward the day when "nation shall not lift up sword against nation, neither shall they learn war anymore."[43]
"Seeing that we are surrounded by so great a cloud of witnesses,"[44] we pray that here in this sacred place: [45]may the faithful find salvation and the careless be awakened; may the doubting find faith and

---

[43] Isaiah 2:4
[44] Hebrews 12:1
[45] Book of Common Worship, published by Presbyterian Church in the United States of America

the anxious be encouraged; may the tempted find help and the sorrowful be comforted; may the weary find rest and the strong be renewed; May the aged find consolation and the young be inspired,

Through Jesus Christ our Lord, who long ago taught His first disciples to pray, and whose disciples continue to pray until the end of time saying (The Lord's Prayer)

A Daily Prayer[46]

O Lord support us all the day long,
Till the shadows lengthen
And the evening comes
And the busy world is hushed,
And the fever of life is over,
And our work is done.
Then in thy great mercy,
Grant us a safe lodging,
and a holy rest and peace at the last.
Amen

---

[46]   Book of Common Prayer. John Henry Cardinal Newman, 1834

Benediction

Go forth into the world in peace
Be of good courage
Hold fast to that which is good
Render to no one evil for evil
Strengthen the fainthearted
Support the weak, help the afflicted
Honor all persons
Love and serve the Lord
Rejoicing in the power of His Spirit
And may the blessings of God Almighty,
Father, Son, and Holy Spirit
Descend upon You and abide within You
Both now and forevermore.

Printed in the United States
By Bookmasters